HYPERREALITY
AND GLOBAL CULTURE

This book explores a world where the boundaries between reality and representation have become blurred, a world where fictional dramas on TV are used as teaching aids, or where a company promotes itself by advertising an imaginary product.

Drawing on examples from around the globe, Nick Perry presents a fascinating and at times highly entertaining analysis of both familiar objects and situations as well as the more unusual and absurd. Meals served in British pubs, motorcycle gangs in downtown Tokyo, Australian movies, American corporate whistle blowing and the drama series 'LA Law' are just some of the examples used by the author in his engaging survey of the many contemporary manifestations of a modern sense of the 'unreal'.

Hyperreality and Global Culture also engages with well known theorists of contemporary culture, from Baudrillard and Umberto Eco to Jameson and Said. It is essential reading for students, both those involved in media and cultural studies as well as sociology and social theory.

Nick Perry is Associate Professor of Sociology at the University of Auckland. Recent publications include *The Dominion of Signs* (1994).

SOCIAL FUTURES SERIES
Barry Smart

HYPERREALITY AND GLOBAL CULTURE

Nick Perry

London and New York

First published 1998
by Routledge
11 New Fetter Lane, London EC4P 4EE

Simultaneously published in the USA and Canada
by Routledge
29 West 35th Street, New York, NY 10001

Typeset in Galliard by Routledge

Printed and bound in Great Britain by Biddles Ltd, Guildford and King's Lynn

British Library Cataloguing in Publication Data
A catalogue record for this book is available from the British Library

Library of Congress Cataloguing in Publication Data
A catalogue record for this book has been requested

ISBN 0–415–10514–5 (hbk)
ISBN 0–415–10515–3 (pbk)

FOR JAN

CONTENTS

List of Illustrations   ix
Acknowledgements   xi

Introduction: from original/copy to original copy   1

1 Antipodean camp   4

2 Am I rite? Or am I write? Or am I right?   24
  Reading *The Singing Detective*

3 Post-pictures and Ec(h)o effects   36

4 On first buying into Munich's BMW 325iA   47

5 The emporium of signs   69

6 Indecent exposures: theorizing whistleblowing   101

7 Dead men and new shoes   124

8 Travelling theory/nomadic theorizing   150

Notes   169
Bibliography   173
Index   187

ILLUSTRATIONS

Figures

1.1	(Former) New Zealand Prime Minister David Lange and friend	7
1.2	A rock and a hard pla(i)ce – pottery by Peter Lange	9
4.1	The *Vierzylinder*, BMW's administrative building, Munich	57
4.2	Alexander Calder art car	59
4.3	Frank Stella art car	60
4.4	Roy Lichtenstein art car	61
4.5	Andy Warhol art car	62
4.6	Michael Jagamara Nelson art car	64
5.1	Pachinko parlour in Kobe	82
5.2	Advertisement in Tokyo subway	87
5.3	Sign outside fashion boutique, Tokyo	88
5.4	Manhole cover, Tokyo	89
5.5	Shop front, Tokyo	90
5.6	'Locked in Love': news item, *Mainichi Daily News*, June 1991	92
5.7	*Ema* at entrance to shrine, Kyoto	93
5.8	Suntory's 'Beer Nouveau 1991 Natsu' with design by Ken Done	96

Table

8.1	*The Economist*'s 1993 'Big Mac' currency index	155

ACKNOWLEDGEMENTS

Chapter 2 is an updated and expanded version of material which featured in a collection of my essays entitled *The Dominion of Signs* (1994). Parts of Chapter 6 are incorporated in a forthcoming paper (with the same title as here) in *Organization Studies* and Chapter 8 is a much revised version of an essay which appeared in *Organization* 2 (1) in 1995.

The photograph of David Lange and friend is reproduced by permission of *The Evening Post*, Wellington Newspapers Ltd; the photograph of Peter Lange's pottery is by courtesy of the *New Zealand Herald*. BMW AG in Munich kindly provided photographic materials on the BMW art car collection and their headquarters and granted consent to their use. The studio shot of 'Beer Nouveau 1991 Natsu' was taken by the photography section of The University of Auckland's Audio Visual Department, who were also responsible for transforming my snapshots of Japan into black and white prints. The *Mainichi Daily News* were approached for permission to reproduce a photograph of the 'Locked in Love' item from their pages but had not responded at the time of going to press.

My thanks to friends and colleagues Terry Austrin, Ian Carter, John Deeks, Geoff Fougere, John and Liz Jackson, Mike Hanne, Roger Horrocks, Roy Larke, Robert Leonard, Bob Lingard, Barney McDonald, Greg McLennan, Kazuo Mizuta, Ravi Palat, George Pavlich, Mike and Ceris Reed, Laurence Simmons, Yoshiaki Ueda, Roy and Jill Wilkie for their hospitality, comments and criticism. Thanks also to series editor Barry Smart, both for asking me to write the book and for the forbearance which both he and Routledge senior editor Mari Shullaw showed as the deadline for delivery of the manuscript came and went. To Routledge's reviewers for their sympathetic and constructive readings of the draft manuscript. To Kate and Lisa, for tolerating my variable demeanour as the book was being written. Above all my thanks to Jan – for being Jan, really – and thus routinely combining affection and intelligence in first presenting me with a copy of Umberto Eco's *Travels in Hyperreality*, in bringing to my attention the *LA Law/Sutherland's Law* observation in Chapter 2; the Lexus advert in *Wired* in Chapter 4; Bickerton's pidgin/creole distinction in Chapter 5; and Lennane's *British Medical Journal*

(*BMJ*) paper on the health hazards of 'blowing the whistle' in Chapter 6. This book is your fellow traveller's indirect way of saying – in what Eco's post-Barbara Cartland subjects have pre-emptively recognized is an age of lost innocence – that I love you madly.

INTRODUCTION
From original/copy to original copy

Umberto Eco (1987) employs the term hyperreality to invoke what he understands as those culturally specific situations in which the copy comes first, whereas
for Jean Baudrillard (1983b) it corresponds to that altogether more general
contemporary condition in which both representation and reality have been
displaced by simulacra (defined as copies without originals). Inasmuch as the
concept was developed against the background of either a settled sense of history
(Eco) or a dystopian conception of the future (Baudrillard) an effect has been to
invest it with an aura of either condescension or anxiety. The former sentiment
has, however, tended to be subverted by Eco's sub-textual fascination with the
exotic and the latter by Baudrillard's positive enthusiasm for excess. The potential
for a less axiomatic, more secular approach to the subject is nevertheless
discernible in Eco's more generous moments and is hinted at in the mellower
melancholy of Baudrillard's *America* (1988) and *Cool Memories* (1990). This is
what this book aims to build upon. It does not presume that the meaning of
hyperreality is either invariant or unavailable, but rather treats such meanings and
the responses to them as subjects for investigation. It is about hyperrealit*ies*, with
these approached through a series of probes, rather than about hyperreality, as
this might be understood in relation to such blunt (if powerful) instruments as
'late capitalism' or 'consumerism'.

The book is therefore less about the elaboration of a theory of hyperreality
than about the development of an appropriate mode for theorizing the plurality
of its determinations and the diversity of its manifestations. The essay form is
consistent with interpretations that are provisional and with interrogations that
are seriously playful. There is an emphasis on doing theoretical work that is
responsive to details and which prioritizes bricolage as a working principle. One
effect is to cut across distinctions between indigenous and imported cultures; to
probe for what is referred to in the final chapter as the parochialism of the
cosmopolitan and the globalism of the local; to offer neither yet another vindication of the international, nor yet another celebration of the marginal, but rather a
problematizing of such a contrast.

A location at the edge of the (Western) world is especially conducive to these
kinds of Delphic observations. If you routinely have your head in one location

and your feet in another, then the oracular effectively becomes the secular. For under such conditions hyperrealities seem in no way exotic. For example, the snow scenes on New Zealand Christmas cards signal the arrival of summer – just as the fertility symbols of Easter (eggs and rabbits) signal its departure. Or again, the nation has a higher proportion of overseas content on its national television than anywhere else in the Western world. There is a cavalier mixture of Australian, American, and British material plus a smattering from other locations. What results is not the experience of a radical otherness, but rather glimpses of difference. This makes for distinctive forms of peripheral vision, elliptical rather than optical, flashes of understanding that can serve as an early warning system for others.

They can do so because under the impact of globalization this kind of cultural circumstance has ceased to seem idiosyncratic. It has instead become paradigmatic in that – to rework and qualify McKenzie Wark's (1994) felicitous maxims – we have aerials as well as roots and terminals as well as origins. The confused mixture of signals that results from being poised between discrepant discourses is, however, not just where I happen to live. It is also where I find myself at home. It is (to paraphrase the New Zealand poet Allen Curnow (1962)) a small house with big windows, which is, however, neither built upon a densely-layered and generally stable notion of the past nor does it face towards an apocalyptic conception of the future. The incoming images are necessarily refracted through the glass of a culture and a history that is both stained and flawed – attributes that are both the source of pleasures and the cause of difficulties. For what can be seen from such a location is a disorderly combination of fragments; glimpses of Britain, America, Japan, Germany, France, Italy, Australia, science, literature, television, shopping and theme parks. What follows is therefore part methodological quest, part methodological guide to such a landscape – explorations that are at once exemplars for the lived experience of hyperrealism and ways of interrogating it.

Each of the eight chapters may be read as a self-contained essay but each forms part of a cumulative argument. The bulk of the book thus consists of a series of substantive cases which range across the planet, but which have been constructed with an eye both to their global familiarity and their foregrounding of forms of local distinctiveness. The opening chapter is an interpretation of the cultural conditions from which the book's methodology emerges – that pattern of stylized subversion and sardonic distancing that is shared by Australian and New Zealand cultural producers and which I have called 'antipodean camp'. Chapter 2 employs the modes of reading associated with such a location in order to investigate the representation of 'Britishness' (and its relation to the idea of 'America') in the BBC television series *The Singing Detective*. The third chapter explores what Roland Barthes (1977a: 32–51) has called 'Italianicity' as it is manifested in Benetton's advertising and in Umberto Eco's travels in America. The notion of 'Germanness' is considered in Chapter 4 by way of one of its best known icons – a BMW. Chapter 5 focuses upon Japan, or rather upon how the exoticizing uses made of Western images within modern Japan introduces instabilities into conventional Japan/West distinctions. Chapter 6 has a specifically American setting but a universally relevant subject – the fate of the truth claims of scientific 'whistleblowers' under hyperreal conditions. The two remaining chapters can either be read as attempts to weave Ariadne threads through this global eclecticism or, alternatively, as a pedagogical and theoretical soft policing of its disorderliness. Hence Chapter 7 is about the pedagogic problems posed by, and the procedural lessons that can be gleaned from, the hyperreal's expanding jurisdiction. The subject matter of Chapter 8 is the notion of a theoretical community; the objective is to probe the implications, for the practice of theorizing, of the globalization of theories.

1

ANTIPODEAN CAMP

An essay by Walter Benjamin contains the most famous allegory on the experience of modernity which the archive of critical theory has to offer. Benjamin conceived of a Paul Klee drawing entitled *Angelus Novus* as having portrayed 'the angel of history', in that:

> His face is turned towards the past. Where we perceive a chain of events, he sees one single catastrophe which keeps piling ruin upon ruin and hurls it in front of his feet. The angel would like to stay, awaken the dead and make whole what has been smashed. But a storm is blowing from Paradise; it has got caught in his wings with such violence that the angel can no longer close them. The storm irresistibly propels him into the future to which his back is turned, while the pile of debris before him grows skyward. This storm is what we call progress.
>
> (Benjamin 1968: 257–8)

Theodor Adorno (1977: 194–5) was subsequently to interpret this same drawing as 'the angel of the machine . . . whose enigmatic eyes force the onlooker to try to decide whether he is announcing the culmination of disaster or salvation hidden within it'. A further transmutation of Benjamin's inter-war image of the ruins of modernity occurs in Wim Wenders' 1988 film *Wings of Desire* in which the angel confronts the bleak cityscape of a divided post-war Berlin and its inhabitants. *Wings of Desire* was completed just before the Berlin Wall was itself reduced to ruins, and in Richard Wolin's (1994: lii) intellectual biography of Benjamin, the film is interpreted as an inordinately dispirited and characteristically post-modern borrowing, one which has the effect of excising that utopian sensibility that Wolin sees as infusing Benjamin's work (as expressed, for example, in the notion of Paradise as the source of the storm). What Wenders', Adorno's and Benjamin's permutations on this allegory have in common is a pervasive melancholy, a melancholy that reaches across the historical distance and contextual distinctions between their texts. That allegory's mythic associations are, however, now so subdued, if not lost, as to edge them all, but Wenders in particular, towards an unsought 'campiness' (this tendency is aided and abetted in *Wings of*

Desire by the presence of Peter Falk as a 'Columbo'-like figure). The result is that the foregrounding of artifice fails to function as a Brechtian-style provocation or incentive by which to forge a connection with that lived reality external to the text. Rather the effect is of a sliding in the very processes of signification which works as if to tacitly confirm the instability of that conception of meaning and representation on which such a connection is premised.

In Peter Sloterdijk's (1988) attempt to formulate what has been called a post-modernism of resistance, the allegorizing is altogether less angelic and ethereal and altogether more embodied and down-to-earth. His *Critique of Cynical Reason* derives from Diogenes and is exemplified not only by the Greek philosopher's famous injunction to the young Alexander of Macedonia to 'stop blocking his sunlight', but also by his indifference to the prevailing dress codes and by his act of public masturbation in the Athenian marketplace. This invests the traditionally derisive epithet, 'wanker', with a somewhat novel set of associations, whilst yet cryptically affirming that wry reflection from Martin Crowley's stage play *The Boys in the Band* that, 'the great thing about masturbation is that you don't have to look your best' (1970: 12).

Yet both Andreas Huyssen and Jürgen Habermas hint at continuities between Benjamin's imagery and Sloterdijk's text. Huyssen (1988: ix) prefaces his foreword to the book with a quote from Brecht, 'Reduced to his smallest dimension, the thinker survived the storm'. And the English translation of the book carries an observation from Habermas' review of the German edition which suggests that Sloterdijk, 'gleans from the pile of rubble a piece of truth. He calls this truth the cynical impulse'. Sloterdijk's search for the 'lost cheekiness' of Diogenes and the Greek cynics, prompts him to see that,

> In intellectual trash, in the cynical show, in the hysterical uprising and in the crazy parade, the suffocating armor around the well-behaved wild ego loosens up: *Rocky Horror Picture Show*, the hot–cold hissing death drive of the hunger for oneself.
>
> (Sloterdijk 1988: 128)

Although Sloterdijk is on to something here, by viewing the appeal of such practices through the filter of a high modernist lens he can find only the apocalyptic, the nihilistic and that antipathy to meaning and form which such an avant-gardist perspective valorizes. What is missing is both a recognition of, and responsiveness to, what Dana Polan identifies as 'a fundamental *weirdness* in contemporary mass culture' (1986: 182, italics in original) and, more specifically, an awareness of that playfulness (that is not quite affection) which accompanies such thoroughly stylized subversions of, and sardonic distancing from, hitherto dominant forms. This is only another way of saying that *The Rocky Horror Picture Show* was written by a New Zealander (Richard O'Brien) although it is not to say that it could *only* have been written by a New Zealander. But it is perhaps only in New Zealand, or just possibly Australia, that a conservative former Prime Minister

(Sir Robert Muldoon) would prove willing, eager even, to take time out from advertising gardening products in order to act as the master of ceremonies for a stage version of *The Rocky Horror Picture Show*. In doing so he was no doubt aware that, in Auckland as elsewhere, a suburban cinema had for several years regularly screened the film version on Saturday nights. And that the film's loyal audiences were prone to signal their thoroughly institutionalized familiarity with the screenplay by replicating the actors' modes of attire and emulating the action as it unfolded on the screen.

The Rocky Horror Picture Show, the matter of fact willingness of an ex-Prime Minister to act as its MC (Master of Ceremonies) and to subsequently appear, complete with the appropriate cloak and make-up, as Count Robula, (the host for the horror movie on late-night television) are all instances of 'antipodean camp'. Are these utterly marginal differences or central signs of the times? Politics/business as usual or institutional cross-dressing? The same familiar fetishisms or is something rather strange afoot? Another recent New Zealand Prime Minister did it somewhat differently than his conservative predecessor – and did it whilst in office. For example, as the head of a Labour Government, David Lange warmly welcomed Mickey Mouse to his prime-ministerial suite (see Figure 1.1). Faced with the cooling of official diplomatic relations with America as a result of his government's ban on nuclear ship visits, he was photographed in an anti-nuclear 'Nukebuster' tee-shirt whose design was inspired by the then topical 'Ghostbusters' motif. In an appearance on breakfast-time American television he observed that, 'I've been four times to Disneyland, but never to the White House' going on to (accurately) point out that invitations to the latter location had none the less been extended 'to all sorts of hoods'.

Although both Muldoon and Lange could thus be seen to be 'camping it up', in the sense of both consciously fabricating their performances and being concerned to convey that consciousness to the putative audience, it is none the less misleading to read their respective versions of the practice of camp as purely artifice, as empty of meaning (cf. Sontag 1966). The style *is* the meaning, so that although at one level they are presented as performances without weight, or at best as light entertainment (cf. Dyer 1992: 135–47), they were also explicable as movements in orbit around contrasting centres of gravity. As such, their self-mocking patterns of self-protection served to do more than signal their differing personal vanities. They also, albeit more or less incidentally, insinuated competing conceptions of what politics is for. And they showed how such conceptions might be represented within, but against, the forms and conventions of a journalistic realism that was understood as inadequate to the task of their dramatization. If a cartoonist might have been prompted to caricature Muldoon as Richard the Third playing Lear, then perhaps the corresponding image in Lange's case was of Hamlet playing Falstaff. Their performances were, however, not so much symptomatic of the principle that anything goes but rather that an 'anything' can be made into a 'something' through the style of presentation, in that the response which the style calls up is potentially a means of identification and a political

Figure 1.1 (Former) New Zealand Prime Minister David Lange and friend

resource. In this respect their conduct might appear somewhat analogous to those public performances by Ronald Reagan which had prompted Travers (1993: 131) to cite Weinstein's (1988: 175–6) suggestion that 'The unity of the Reagan mind is not ideational, but is constituted by the impulse to feel good about himself . . . and it is this passion that unites him to the public at large'.

What was scandalizing about Reagan, however, and what tended to reduce his critics to oscillating between condescension and bafflement, was that he not only seemed unaware of his own banality but also indifferent to its policy consequences. By contrast, Muldoon and Lange's performances were altogether more knowing – if altogether less consequential. They offered ways of making something out of marginality through representations which otherwise serve to confirm and reinforce it. Thus whereas Muldoon parodied *through* appearance that very power and conception of self which he had been so reluctant to relinquish, Lange signalled his particular understanding of the limits of the very power for which he had struggled by parodying it *as* appearance.

Is this sufficient to account for the bleak edge to the style's surface whimsy, the difficulty of determining whether its practitioners be categorized as affirmatively comic or resignedly ironic, the sense that caught up within these practices is a pathos which is so resolutely resistant to the tragic as to almost invoke it? In offering to share its open secret of triumphant failure, such antipodean camp is constitutively oxymoronic. Compromised if made explicit, yet determined to signal its affirmative hostility to the world's indifference, it shows what it must not tell. These principles might be said to have been merged and made consciously aesthetic in 'A rock and a hard pla(i)ce' (see Figure 1.2), a ceramic artifact through which the potter Peter Lange indicates that he is both his own man and New Zealand's, as well as being David's brother. The whimsy is primary – no matter whether one considers the pottery or the politicians – but there is also something that is both locally grounded and rather fishy about their explicitly authentic fakery. Not quite the brothers grim(m) meet Dracula, but a coded foray into uncharted territory none the less. Uncharted, in that they seem to waver between parodying, and participating in, received critical assumptions about New Zealand culture. For it has long been something of a critical cliché to point to a darkness and profound unease at work in New Zealand's films and novels, something as yet unnamed that is seen as linked to the cultural dominance of evasiveness and guilt about the nation's history. What isn't clear is whether the style is explicable as a populist influenced mockery of such a gloomy (high) cultural orthodoxy or whether, rather like Roland Barthes' (1973: 15–25) account of wrestling it represents its transposition and continuation within a more explicitly popular idiom.

Read one way, this would seem to return us to that which Sloterdijk detects, and responds to, in *The Rocky Horror Picture Show*. But inasmuch as the Australians offer their own permutation on antipodean camp, a version which seems no less suffused with the cynical impulse, but yet is free of any such affinities with either Gothic foreboding or Germanic melancholy, then it becomes difficult

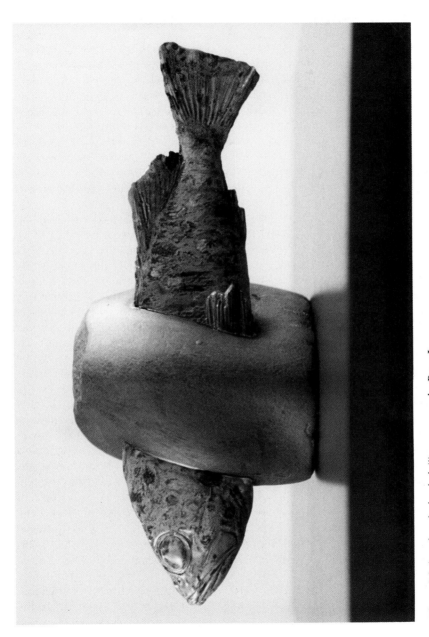

Figure 1.2 A rock and a hard pla(i)ce – pottery by Peter Lange

to determine whether such associations are fortuitous or elective. This is despite the not entirely whimsical suggestion by New Zealand's best-known historian (Keith Sinclair) that the New Zealand population consisted of the 'South Pacific's three million Prussians'.

The differences between Australia and New Zealand matter greatly on each side of the Tasman. For those north of the Equator, however, they may be more difficult to detect. For example, if in 1988 Wenders had chosen to film Brisbane's river rather than Berlin's Wall, then the imagery he might have captured would have been no less startling, but startlingly different. For at the official opening of the Brisbane Expo 1988, the Queen of England had sailed up one side of the Brisbane river in her Royal Barge, whilst a submarine of the Australian Navy, painted bright pink and complete with a perspex deck and more than thirty dancing girls, had sailed down the other. Meanwhile, the contingent of local wharfies who had earlier bared their buttocks as the Royal Barge had sailed past, returned to their more traditional watersiding pursuits.

To read the parable of Alexander and Diogenes into the Royal Barge/wharfies incident is plausible enough. It also bears comparison with the aphorism by which James Scott introduces his *Domination and the Arts of Resistance* (1990). Scott anticipates his critique of hegemony as a concept by citing an Ethiopian proverb, 'When the great lord passes by, the wise peasant bows deeply and silently farts'. The Australian wharfies share this critical impulse, but proved to be a great deal more theatrical and irreverent in its expression, not least because it can be read as not just a symbolic challenge to a traditional authority but as a symbolic confirmation of the traditional ordering of gender relations.[1]

That submarine and its female entourage shrug off any such clear-cut definition however. Even by the standards of what Guy Debord (1994) has called the society of the spectacle, there is something strangely equivocal and indeterminate about it, a kind of phallic androgyny. Whether in terms of the anthropological puzzle of how such a phenomenon was *possible*, or in terms of the metaphorical possibilities which it creates, it succeeded in making all else at Expo seem positively circumspect. The authentically fibreglass New Zealand sheep and the authentically Australian living statues were pedestrian by comparison. One wonders what the Chaplin of *The Great Dictator* would have made of such a combination of militarism and entertainment, such a blending of state power and mockery of disciplined authority, formal ceremony and happy-happy-joy-joy, cheerleader and jeerleader, Count Robula and Nukebuster, oppression and seduction, death and desire. It is the antinomies which pile skyward here, yet in each of these couplets the first terms are so ambiguously shored up by the second as to insinuate the instability of their authority. In George Orwell's (1950) classic essay on 'Shooting an Elephant', he had pointed up the effectively precarious hold of a presumptively stable system of colonial control, and, more generally, issued a reminder to the powerful of what they are up against. 'Decorating a submarine' would seem to offer an inflection on such a theme, but an inflection which wavers between the securely colonial and the eclectically postmodern, a masquerade of/on the patriarchal.

Yet one of the many ways in which the differences between Australia and New Zealand do matter is that although Brisbane might signify 'Australia' on one side of the Tasman, on the other it is more likely to mean 'Queensland'. In 1988 Queensland may not have been the only Australian state in which farmers drove station wagons bearing the bumper slogan 'Eat Beef, Ya Bastards', but in 1988 it was none the less that state in which such an exhortation seemed more menacingly redneck than assertively funny. Likewise if the 1988 Expo had been held not in Brisbane but in Melbourne or Canberra, then that submarine would have been altogether less likely to have graced either the former city's Yarra river or the latter's Lake Burley Griffin. Nevertheless the closing ceremony at the Atlanta Olympics in 1996 made it clear to a global audience that the Brisbane episode had been no flash in the pan but rather a glimpse of Australia's own precious metal, destined for authentic coin of the realm status. No elephants were shot, but some marsupials were blown up. For in anticipation of the Sydney 2000 Olympics, the officially sanctioned image of Australia which was flashed around the world from the Atlanta stadium was of over-inflated, synthetic blue kangaroos perched precariously on bicycles.

This is a second order version of kitsch, one in which the cultural cringe (i.e. the nominal repudiation, but tacit genuflection to European canons of taste) although it is still at work, shows signs of being not so much transcended as assimilated into the realm of cultural history. 'Australian' is, in part, still signified by the invocation of that once fresh pattern of mockery and condescension towards cultural pretension which are the stock in trade of a now thoroughly globalized Dame Edna Everage and a now thoroughly Anglified Clive James. This is, however, interwoven with a reflexively informed exaggeration of its own banality, and it is through such amplifications that it signals that it has already anticipated, internalized and immunized itself against any such criticism of its own practices. One begins to understand why Australian cultural critics were so quick off the mark (cf. Frankovits 1984; Gross *et al.* 1986) in the formation of an English-speaking constituency for Baudrillard's work.

A culturally ordained willingness to play with, and on, cultural codes, and an associated treading of a line between demotic affirmation and a boorish smugness was recognized and exposed in Meaghan Morris' (1988: 241–69) definitive reading of the structural complexities of the film *Crocodile Dundee* (aka 'a croc and a hard case'). In the less obviously self-satisfied, if more obviously sentimental *Strictly Ballroom*, there is an anticipation of that widening of the emotional repertoire and social range of this Australian version of camp which is evident in such films as *Muriel's Wedding* and *The Adventures of Priscilla, Queen of the Desert*. Yet because it is more clearly framed by and signalled as a response to social repression, the camp of these later films seems more nearly tactical, more obviously the object of representation rather than its guiding principle. It is none the less presented as culturally constitutive and not simply as camouflage or protective coloration. The layered, more or less ambivalent populism that is evident in some Australian cultural criticism also seems to be expressive of such a tendency, albeit refracted through the requirements of scholarly discourse and the obligatory nod towards Bakhtin and the carnivalesque. (It is 'more or less ambivalent' in that a work such as *Myths of Oz* by John Fiske and his colleagues is less obviously celebratory than, for example, John Docker's *Postmodernism and Popular Culture*.)

Inasmuch as camp is a response to cultural dominance then it displays a family resemblance to such phenomena as the 'put-on', one of the practices through which Afro-Americans trod the line between resistance to subordination and accommodation to it. But ever since Susan Sontag's classic essay on camp (1966), commentators on the topic have recognized and emphasized the congruities (although Sontag herself somewhat underplayed them) between a camp sensibility and a gay aesthetic. Sontag (1966: 280) interprets the mode of sexuality which suffuses classic camp as 'the triumph of the epicene style . . . the convertibility of "man" and "woman", "person" and "thing"'. In developing the distinction between gay and straight camp, however, Richard Dyer (1992: 145) suggests that the wit, knowingness and ambivalences of camp have facilitated its adoption by the straight world and he cites Clive James' television criticism as typical of such a move. But Dyer further argues that with its appropriation, camp tends to lose its cutting edge and permits, even encourages, the endorsement of that which it purportedly mocks. For example, says Dyer (1992:145), 'Camp allows straight audiences to reject the style of John Wayne; but . . . it also allows a certain wistful affection for him to linger on . . . (which) can only be in reality affection for that way of being a man'.

Antipodean camp is distinguished by a generically nationalist inflection of the distinction which Dyer makes. For it has emerged from within cultures for which colonization was constitutive. Thus the forms of cultural dominance to which it is a response are the master discourses of (m)other countries, and the versions of cultural identity that it prioritizes are those which amplify the accident of place. Its multiple manifestations are, of course, never *just* nationalist. But if one considers, for example, Crocodile Dundee and Priscilla, Count Robula and Nukebuster then what is striking is that after subtracting, or otherwise controlling, that signifying of manifest social differences between each of the parties in these odd couple(t)s, their signs nevertheless go on working. Working, that is, to call up nationalist sentiments through cultural images that are constructed in accordance with bricoleur tactics, placed in quotation marks by the signalling of their own fabrication and asserted through self-mockery.

The kind of cultural work which gets done through such conceptions, what Raymond Williams (1977: 128–35) would refer to as their 'structures of feeling', is suggested by the New Zealand film *Smash Palace*. The film's title is a reference to the central character's car wrecking yard, but it is also a metaphor for both his deteriorating marriage and his overall cultural situation. In charting the erosion of his dream of assembling a successful local 'vehicle' from what are leftover bits and pieces of overseas materials and machinery, the narrative mockingly exposes the limitations of that antipodean mythology which sustains such an aspiration. Yet as it moves towards a conclusion the movie nevertheless aligns itself with the central protagonist's energy and desperate resourcefulness in seeking to maintain the myth.

This is clearly revealed in its tense, concluding joke, a joke that is played with death and on the audience. The film's anti-hero has taken hostage the policeman who is his wife's lover and holds a shotgun to the policeman's head as they sit together in an antique open car. The car straddles a railway line as a train rapidly approaches in a scene which evokes both the Keystone Kops and a Don Seigel thriller. This is given a further local twist by the visible presence of a length of the iconically significant Number Eight fencing wire. The wire is looped tightly around the shotgun barrel, its trigger and the hostage's neck, thus allowing his captor the freedom to drive. 'Number Eight wire' is a vernacular metaphor which nowadays occupies a culturally ambiguous position; it stands both for antipodean ingenuity and resourceful making do, and for an outmoded tolerance of tempo-rary, makeshift, imprecise solutions to a problem. Gun, wire, driver, hostage and car all hold firm as the train barrels towards them – but at the last second the train lurches away from the car on to that different track that it was travelling on all along. Laughter from the car's driver. This closing sequence thus perfectly displays that ability to 'move freely between dark drama and banal comedy' which a film reviewer for *The Times* suggested characterizes New Zealand and Australian films, and perhaps the New Zealand and Australian temperament as well (the remark was prompted by the film *Utu*, but the examples now proliferate). The reviewer's observation is approvingly cited by the New Zealand poet Bill Manhire, who goes on to reflect that,

> The poetry I write is strongly marked by tonal drifts and lurches, and I think that these come mainly from the diversities, disjunctions, juxtapo-sitions and incongruities which constitute my experience. Much of my experience is derivative, a matter of influence and imitation. I think that's a fairly normal thing not a matter for apology.
>
> (1987: 152)

The shared, knowing matter-of-factness with which a real poet and the fictional owner of a car wrecking yard approach the materials of their trade points up a distinguishing attribute of antipodean permutations on the angel of history allegory. Thought is not seen as shaped and limited by the restraining givenness of the ruins, but as derived from the prospects that such debris opens up for future scavenging and bricolage. Antipodean *Heavenly Creatures* (as in Peter Jackson's film of that name) strive to live their lives forward by reaching out towards myth rather than facing back towards history. Those charming, murderous schoolgirls who are the film's central characters are inspired by a campish conception of the sublime, in which Mario Lanza presides over a Paradise fabricated from the detritus of the culture industry. History is none the less at work, of course, so that *Heavenly Creatures* is yet another realization of 'dark drama and banal comedy', a tragi-comic vision for which the highly accomplished schlock, splatter and bad taste of (Jackson's) *Brain Dead* was a preface and an apprenticeship.

It is, however, seriously misleading to read that history as if it were a farcical repetition of European tragedy. Misleading, most obviously, because the very tendency to turn away from colonial history, or towards a transparently mythical version of it, becomes supportive of colonizing in the present. But misleading also because the antipodes experienced modernity without modern*ism* (or more specifically, without a modernism that mattered). Those distancing and defamiliarizing procedures that were determinedly enjoined by literary high modernism did not depend upon importation of the associated discourse. Rather they were effectively inscribed by the facts of geographical position. As Simon During puts it,

> It is not merely that we have not had the population, the institutions, the money to provide an audience for high culture, nor is it just that there has not been the desire for that culture. More profoundly it's that there has not been the need. Because the distance was already there.
>
> (During 1983: 88)

Moreover, the hybrid (more or less critical) local versions of social realism, against which such a literary modernism might be defined and constructed, were themselves so precarious as to be sustained only at the cost of claiming that the locals were either in a fretful sleep (Pearson 1974), a waking dream (Stead 1971) or a backwater awash (White 1983). Under these circumstances, what price modernism's oppositional or dehistorizing procedures and the idea of an avant-garde as their custodians? Read one way, such concerns were explicable as the frustrations of intellectuals without an intelligentsia. Yet from 'cricket' to 'Christmas' the extant terms and practices were perforce subject to a pragmatic interrogation. Merely to unpack such baggage had involved rearranging the former relation between its component parts, thus tacitly making it over and investing it with novel meanings. For 'sea change' read '(practical) deconstruction'.

So read another way, those very attributes of 'silence, exile and cunning', which James Joyce had paradigmatically defined as a high *modernist* artist's best resources in an antipathetic social order were so culturally endemic as to appear foundational to those antipodean cultural nationalists concerned to establish local versions of *naturalism*. Amongst the present generation of contemporary cultural producers, one of the consequences of this paradox has been to induce a developed awareness of culture, including the very idea of a national culture, as artifice. Combine this with an explicit recognition that received and established forms that were generated in and for other contexts are at once consequential for, and circulate within, such a culture and yet are inadequate to the task of representing it. Add in the anxiously powerful incentive to fill in the local, and locally divided, discursive space. Stir furiously. This is the solution which produces the problem which antipodean camp displays but does not name.

14

So although an angel contemplating ruins *can* be seen at work in the examples cited here, it is not what invests them with their informing tone. It offers only a restricted vision of them, a gravity whose pull is altogether too compelling, and whose language is too mordant, too spatially and semiotically constrained, to hold all of these fragments in those relations-in-suspension which define their distinctiveness. For what is of interest in antipodean camp is not just its display of modernity's destructive forces, but the rules which govern its own assembly, the principles through which hitherto disparate elements are combined.

This is also the concern which underpins the adventures of Lewis Carroll's (1929) heroine. Notwithstanding Alice's generally priggish and thoroughly bourgeois demeanour, the experiences of Carroll's character might therefore shed light on precisely those instances of antipodean camp, such as the opening of Brisbane's Expo, which otherwise threaten to outstrip the imaginative resources of a traditionally conceived critical theory.

Alice's fall down the rabbit hole at the beginning of *Alice in Wonderland* had quite literally meant that for her, 'all that is solid melts into air'. As a character she was in blissful ignorance of, and privileged insulation from, the upheavals and social transformations which that then contemporaneous maxim from *The Communist Manifesto* had sought to bring to attention. But thanks to Rosa and Charlie Parkin's 'Peter Rabbit and the Grundrisse' (1974), with its path-breaking excursion through Mr McGregor's cabbage patch and its attentiveness to Beatrix Potter's silences, we now know that any reading of Alice's innocence cannot itself be innocent, but is necessarily symptomatic. To be sure, the Alice manuscripts of 1865 and 1871 predate that epistemological break whose implications are fully developed only in *The Hunting of the Snark* (1910). My swift, modest proposal is, however, that such structural forces are discernible within the immature human-istic problematic of these earlier texts. But only by reading against the grain.

At the beginning of the text, Alice, like Benjamin's angel, is unable to see what she is coming to. She does, however, have time to look around her and to ponder upon what may be going to happen next, with her capacity to reflect upon the intersection of prior experience and the present flow of images as her guide and resource. On the way down she sees that the sides of the hole are filled with cupboards and bookshelves, together with maps and pictures. As she tumbles past these repositories of learning, culture and information she takes a jar down from a shelf; the jar is labelled as 'Orange Marmalade' but it proves to be empty. Still falling, she begins to talk to herself, both reprising some of the knowledge she has acquired in school and rehearsing some words whose meaning she has not grasped. Specifically she wonders 'what Latitude or Longitude I've got to?' because she 'thought they were nice grand words to say'. She goes on to reflect on the prospect of falling right through the earth and of finding herself amongst people who walk with their heads downwards, 'The Antipathies I think . . . Pray tell me Ma'am, is this New Zealand or Australia?' (Carroll 1929: 4–5).

This latter question is never answered, nor are we told to whom Alice had intended that it be addressed. But it does anticipate the working methodology by which Alice makes her way around this new territory, namely, the attempt to establish what the rules are and who or what is the locus of authority. As a flurry of subsequent commentators have been concerned to suggest, however, the Wonderland into which Alice enters is a coded representation of the location from which she has purportedly departed. For example, that 'location' might be understood spatially as the grounds of an Oxford college and the interior of the University Museum, or theologically as the contemporaneous Oxford debate on Christianity (Taylor 1952), or historically as the Victorian 'gospel of amusement' (Blake 1974) or philosophically as the ambiguities of the English language (Sutherland 1970). Thus Sutherland (1970: 123) describes the jar label 'Orange Marmalade' as false, not only because it doesn't accurately designate the contents of the jar, but also because it purports to designate and denote something that is not present. He invokes it as an instance of what Hayakawa has called 'maps without territories', a metaphor which describes those situations in which representations have no correspondence to the world of reality. Moreover, in Alice's usage 'Latitude and Longitude' are empty labels too, not just in the sense that she does not know what these words conventionally refer to, but in the sense of terms which have no application at the centre of the Earth.

The narrative goes on to present Alice's general problem as one of how to understand the (fictional, post/modern) world(s) in which representations are powerfully constitutive of material reality, when she tacitly relies upon a theory in which representations are understood as powerfully determined by the presumptively unproblematic reality of her (material, early modern) world. Moreover, the instabilities of the (fictional, post/modern) world(s) which Alice enters into are immediately and disturbingly consequential for Alice's conception of who she is. In her words 'I know who I *was* when I got up this morning, but I think I must have been changed several times since then . . . I can't explain *myself* . . . because I'm not myself, you see' (Carroll 1929: 36–7, italics in original). On having achieved a provisionally secure conception of herself, however, she is presented as prone to prejudge everyone else. It is therefore not Alice, but the lessons which her creator sought to convey which provide guidance to the Wonderland of antipodean camp.

The allegorical Alice is no angel looking back at the ruins of modernity. She is introduced as a novitiate stranded at the post – and seemingly bereft of stable (self) representation(s). *But she looks forward to the modern*, which she is imperfectly aware of as ambiguously other, as antipode. As Alice puts it, 'Its a great game of chess that's being played – all over the world – if this *is* the world at all, you know . . . I wouldn't mind being a Pawn, if only I might join' (Carroll 1929: 123, italics in original). And join she does, although:

> Alice never could quite make out, in thinking it over afterwards, how it
> was that they began, all she remembers is that they were running . . . and
> the Queen went so fast that it was all she could do to keep up with her:
> and still the Queen kept crying 'Faster!' but Alice felt she *could not* go

faster . . . . The most curious part . . . was that . . . things around them never changed their places at all: however fast they went they never seemed to pass anything. 'I wonder if all the things move along with us?' thought poor puzzled Alice.

(Carroll 1929: 123, italics in original)

When they briefly pause to rest , everything is just as it was when they began running.

'Well, in *our* country' said Alice, still panting a little, 'you'd generally get to get somewhere else – if you ran very fast for a long time, as we've been doing.' 'A slow sort of country!' said the Queen. 'Now *here*, you see, it takes all the running *you* can do to keep in the same place. If you want to get somewhere else you must run at least twice as fast as that.'

(Carroll 1929: 124, italics in original)

This is available for a reading which sees it as a bundling together of those yearnings for the centre of things that are variously associated with the provincial dilemma, the cultural cringe, and the colonial('s) experience. Yet it was produced at the centre (of both Empire and learning). So it can also be read another way, one which continues to recognize such yearnings but in which both their origin and direction are reversed. What one can therefore also read for is a still traditional centre which, as modernity begins to gather pace, is becoming aware of its repression of its own movement towards marginality. To put it another way, a contemporary functional equivalent to Alice's fascination with Wonderland is the enthusiasm of British television viewers for the Australian soap-opera *Neighbours* during its 1980s heyday. Each offers the enchantment of the already modern. Such an allegorical Alice suggests how the global currents of modernity which surge through both the northern and southern poles of the antipodes might be understood as inducing such an alternation between positive and negative, between core and margin.

If what can be seen in the textuality of antipodean camp is the wedding of Benjamin's angel and Alice's Queen, then it is the Bellman in Lewis Carroll's *The Hunting of the Snark* (1910) who can be said to have brought them together and sanctioned their union. For their mutual attraction is founded upon that version of the nationalist impulse which is expressed by the Bellman's method of searching for the elusive Snark (Carroll 1910: 15–16):

He had brought a large map representing the sea,
Without the least vestige of land:
And the crew were much pleased when they found it to be
A map they could all understand.

'What's the good of Mercator's North Poles and Equators,

Tropics, Zones, and Meridean Lines?'
So the Bellman would cry: and the crew would reply
'They are merely conventional signs!'

'Other maps are such shapes, with their islands and capes!
But we've got our brave Captain to thank'
(So the crew would protest) 'that he's bought *us* the best –
A perfect and absolute blank!'

This is not one of Hayakawa's 'maps without territories' but an empty sign. On its own, it is inexplicable and uninterpretable. In the context of that interpretative community which Carroll constructs for it, however, its perfect emptiness is promptly filled. Filled that is, with the pleasure of proclaiming both its easy accessibility as a signifier of community and the manifest superiority of the community thus signified. This offers a quirky permutation on those processes of inventing and imagining a nation which Benedict Anderson (1983) describes. Quirky, in that what comes with it is a positive relishing of, and investment in, a crisis of representation, particularly as the technologies, processes and sustaining conventions of representation are understood as having come from somewhere else.

In antipodean camp, however, such blankness is revealed not through content but through *form*, that is, through its revelling in the promiscuous plurality, randomness and contingency of its specific manifestations. What the associated distancing from all signifieds thus signifies is a desire for liberation from their control; a longing to escape from the stage of history by entering into the play of pure textuality. But (*pace* Derrida) there is no place outside the stage and no play without it. History not only enters with the assembled fragments, it organizes the order of their assembly, and seeps through the gaps between them. Viewed historically, antipodean camp is explicable as a 'post-colonial' aesthetic for the beneficiaries of colonialism. In its classic form it signals the attempt to outflank the cultural categories and control of metropolitan powers without, however, directly confronting either the historical conditions of its own possibility or the counter narratives which the historical pattern continues to generate. Hence its appeal to those 'dominion subjects' whom Meaghan Morris (1992: 471) pithily describes as 'dubiously postcolonial, prematurely postmodern, constitutively multicultural but still predominantly white, . . . (and who) oscillate historically between identities as coloniser and colonised'.

What makes it of particular critical interest is that it is still evolving. Thus the temporal (and qualitative) distinction between *Brain Dead* and *Heavenly Creatures*, or between *Crocodile Dundee* and *Muriel's Wedding*, or *Goodbye Pork Pie* and *Utu*, is the distinction between antipodean camp as form and antipodean camp as idiom. The shift here is from an acceptance of that form's internal logic to a concern to gesture beyond it, such that the second films in these pairings walk a line between camp as constitutive (of frivolity) and camp as camouflage (for seriousness). The effect is of a doubling, of texts which move no less easily between 'banal comedy and dark tragedy', but yet also strive to determine that movement's pulse by pressing down on the very wounds which it opens up.

On the far side of this tendency, but lying beyond its bounds, are such acclaimed and accomplished Australian/New Zealand films as *The Piano* and *The Navigator*. Each has something of the mannerisms of camp, with its play of, and with, stylistic surfaces, its surprising juxtapositions, its excesses and exaggeration. Each is, however, concerned to explore, display and implicate the spectator in what is respectively, an emotionally intense, erotically charged sensibility and a spiritually heightened one. Each is thus remote from camp's sardonic distancing from its chosen subjects and its flattering complicities with its favoured audiences. Each seems particularly vulnerable to parody – but faced with the studied recklessness and carefully constructed waywardness of these films, then only a tender parody could hope to succeed. For although each film is distinguished by an obsessiveness and sustained by a premise that would seem to be made for camp, their cinematic realization is so visionary as to escape the ridicule that they might otherwise appear to court.

Vincent Ward's *The Navigator* can better serve to dramatize this claim. This is despite that tempting serendipity which sees *The Piano* featuring an eight-year-old girl from the nineteenth century who, when combining the roles of agent and witness, wears an angel's wings.[2] Yet *The Navigator* runs even more risk of being mocked than does *The Piano* – as even the barest plot summary indicates. It is about a small group of fourteenth-century Cumbrian peasants who, guided by Griffin, a nine-year-old boy, strive to save their village from the Black Death by tunnelling through to twentieth-century New Zealand. Although the strands which are characteristic of antipodean camp are discernibly woven into the film's painterly vision and affirmative bleakness, they are firmly subordinated to the imperatives of the latter.

At the beginning of his story the nine-year-old boy has 'angels in his head' (Ward *et al.* 1989: 4) in that he dreams images of the future, of a modernity that has not yet come to pass. Amongst the images which the screenplay identifies are: a rock fissure which seems bottomless; men tunnelling; a vast luminous city at night; a black shape looming out of the sea; a cathedral spire and a figure silhouetted against it; a *'face flattened and distorted by a fierce wind, a face that is anguished and clinging to something, screams . . . . We see the distorted face screaming, screaming . . . but also moving at great speed'* (Ward *et al.* 1989: 3, italics in original); the figure on the spire losing his footing; a village celebration near the tunnel entrance; and a coffin being pushed out into a lake. Flashes of these dream images occur and reoccur as the narrative of the group's night-time journey unfolds. When one of their number becomes stranded, unable to venture across a motorway in spite of repeated attempts, it *'becomes sad and comical all at the same time'* (Ward *et al.* 1989: 28, italics in original).[3] At this point the image of a wind distorted face is repeated, leading the boy to infer that it is the face of the stranded man (Ward *et al.* 1989: 33). Somewhat later in their night-time odyssey, however, the boy briefly closes his eyes and this image reappears. This time the shot is held for long enough for he, and we, to see both the speed at which the face is moving and to see that it is not the face of the man they left on the other side of the motorway. It is instead the face of a member of the group who has gone on ahead in order to rig the cathedral spire for the spike they intend to place at its apex – an act of faith by which to stop the plague.

In order to reach the cathedral, the group of medievals are obliged to cross the harbour, only to be confronted with '*the distinctive huge black shape of a nuclear submarine*' (Ward *et al.* 1989: 45, italics in original) looming out of the dark, travelling fast and threatening to smash their small dinghy. In an echo of the dream's imagery '*the sea beast submerges, the spear thrust of the cathedral soars into view*' (Ward *et al.* 1989: 47, italics in original) prompting yet another showing of the dream sequence, including yet again that distorted screaming face. Shortly thereafter the character whose face it is, is shown in an ill lit railway yard, menaced by the movement of excavators and with heavy duty trucks bearing down on him from different directions. He manages to back on to the front of a stationary train and thankfully closes his eyes as the trucks (replacements for a passenger train and a locomotive in the original screenplay) pass by. The scene thus echoes the concluding sequence of *Smash Palace*. But then the stationary train itself begins to move, rapidly picking up speed along tracks which run parallel to the harbour and which are therefore visible from the dinghy with its medieval crew. What they and we see is that he is '*spreadeagled across the front of the engine clinging for all he is worth – his face is flattened and distorted, all the sound snatched away as he screams into the on-rushing wind*' (Ward *et al.* 1989: 50, italics in original). It is just like the dream image – only now it has become clear just what is propelling him forward, just as it is only towards the end of the film that it becomes clear that it is the boy himself who falls from the spire.

It is neither the ruins nor the antinomies, but the associations which pile up here. Reaching back to the pre-modern allows Ward to use the dream of a medieval boy to gather together the imagery of Benjamin's angel of history, Adorno's angel of the machine, and Wender's angel of desire into a coherent narrative. Sloterdijk's Diogenes can be glimpsed there too, along with James Scott's proverb(ial peasant). They, however, are present not in the shape of any of the characters nor even in the particulars of their actions, but in the film's diffusely political objective of 'giving a voice to the underprivileged – a nonentity, a mere child, from a tiny isolated pocket, unimportant in world events . . . where a group of people protect something they love' (Ward *et al.* 1989: xiv).

The narrative is made this-worldly through the parallel between the Black Death and that black nuclear submarine. A conceptual link is thereby forged between the film's small isolated medieval village and modern New Zealand, a move which Eco (1987: 61–85) would recognize as congruent with his theme that there are affinities between the Middle Ages and the present. Eco would also recognize that it is the contemporary authority of the hyperreal which is being signalled when Griffin runs blindly into a shopping arcade. For the television sets in the video shop window show the image of the submarine captain saying:

This is the real world 1989. You have an alliance with America. You can't isolate one little pocket of the world and proclaim it nuclear free. Because there is no pocket, no refuge, no escape from the real world. This ban they want . . . they're spitting against the wind.

(Ward *et al.* 1989: 58, italics added)

Spitting against the wind not only offers a metaphorical link to the real 'real world's' small boat protests against nuclear submarines entering New Zealand harbours and to the film's analogous encounter between the medievals' dinghy and the submarine. It also evokes that flattened and distorted face from which all sound has been snatched by the onward rush of another, earlier icon of the real world of modernity.

Griffin, like Alice before/after him, strives to infer the logic of the social and material world he has entered on the basis of his working assumptions about the structures of representation. But whereas for Alice the ambiguities and problems of interpretation were linguistic, Griffin is concerned to probe the meaning of images, to construct a grammar of the visual and a narrative of how to see. The film's medieval sequences are shot in black and white whereas the present is shot in colour. Those colours are, however, medieval colours, so as to convey a sense of the present as if seen through medieval eyes. Thus Ward notes that:

The blues used by the Limbourg brothers in the Duc de Berry's *Book of Hours* I used in the azure of roadside telephone boxes, police car lights and the moonlight grey blue apparition of a nuclear submarine. Similar blues are found in Chartres Cathedral (a blue it is said that glaziers have lost the art of making). This blue is contrasted with the fiery hellish tones of Bosch, Breughel and Grunewald. The fires of medieval torches – the sodium from the orange lights of the motorway and the burning gold of molten metal.

(Ward *et al.* 1989: xiii)

And whereas the crew in *The Hunting of the Snark* place their trust in the blankness of the Bellman's map, the medievals in *The Navigator* have faith in Griffin's imperfectly remembered dream imagery as the guide to their redemption.

At one level Ward's film is thus a manifestation of what Eco (1987: 61–72) has documented as a contemporary interest in 'dreaming about the Middle Ages'. At another, it is an exposition of Eco's (1987: 73–85) subsequent theme that we can be said to be 'living in the new Middle Ages'. So just what is it that is added by the film's organizing principle, the emphasis which it gives to a medieval's dream of *our* time and subsequent participation in it? There is a hint in Ward's own answer that, 'Written by a sceptic, my story was about faith – about the basic need to maintain belief in something, anything, no matter what' (Ward *et al.* 1990: 87). The tension in this observation both plays against, and bears comparison with, what Sontag (1966: 281) identifies as that awareness which comes with a camp

21

sensibility of 'a double sense in which some things can be taken . . . the difference between the thing as meaning something, anything and the thing as pure artifice'. *The Navigator* shows a group journeying through a world in which everything seems to be on the move and for which they have no map other than their own imaginings and few resources other than their own ingenuity. The film is thus able to allow for both the improbability of such belief and the necessity for it. For what defines and sustains them is just such a combination of bricoleur tactics and vision as that which defines and sustains the film itself, what Nick Roddick (1989: xi) refers to as those 'elements of sharpness and strangeness, of intense practicality (see, for instance, the scene in which the spike is cast) and intense peculiarity, like the horse in the boat'.

The bricoleur and the visionary also meet in that combination of qualities evoked by the film's title. 'Navvy' is the British term for a labourer on civil engineering and construction projects; it is an abbreviation of 'navigator' and originally referred to those who, around the time of Captain Cook's Pacific voyages, began to excavate and build the canal (and subsequently the railway) systems which were integral to the development of industrialism. For New Zealanders, however, the notion of 'the navigator' has another set of associations and another kind of history. Sometime during the European Middle Ages (and hence hundreds of years before Cook or Tasman), the Polynesian navigator Kupe and others had journeyed thousands of miles across the Pacific and established Maori settlement.

There are no Maori in *The Navigator*'s group of medievals. There is therefore no presumption to speak for them, or to cast them into a role shaped by the priorities of the dominant culture rather than their own. This is no trivial piece of casuistry, a warrant for saying nothing. In the medievals' first encounter with inhabitants of the modern world, the latter can only speculate on whether they are Maori or Irish or Scots or 'from the old country . . . ' but what they are able to recognize is the care and integrity with which the medievals work on what matters to them (Ward *et al.* 1989: 34–8). *The Navigator* does not speak *for* either Maori culture or Ward's own, but it does none the less speak *to* them both. In an earlier film, a documentary called *In Spring One Plants Alone*, Ward had sought to show the day-to-day rituals of an old Maori woman's life in an isolated rural community, a community which came to occupy some three years of his own life (Ward *et al.* 1990: 1–32). The innovative form of this film was indicative of his attempt to both respect and keep faith with his subject and yet realize his own view of her. What Ward did was to spend many weeks carefully observing her routines, the details and minutiae which made up her days. Only when he was thoroughly familiar with them, did he set up the camera accordingly and let her actions come into the shots. The overall effect is oxymoronic, a highly stylized naturalism. This anticipates how, both in *The Navigator* and subsequently in his geographically remote, but historically more proximate *Map of the Human Heart*, Ward went on to construct an allegorical myth that was ambiguously positioned between the different histories of two now discrete, now intertwined, cultures; a myth through which their respective concerns might circulate. In her exploration of a very different myth, Donna Haraway (1985) has famously suggested that she would sooner be a cyborg than a goddess. Ward likewise evokes a hybrid mythological creature by giving his central character the name Griffin.[4] Which prompts me to say that I'd sooner be a navigator than an angel – when I grow up, that is.

2

AM I RITE? OR AM I WRITE?
OR AM I RIGHT?

Reading *The Singing Detective*

Despite a substantial growth in the volume of academic work on television, the most prestigious forms of textual interpretation and cultural analysis continue to express those notoriously over-literary emphases which have long been characteristic of the Anglo-American intelligentsia. Thus it is still deemed professionally legitimate, rather than seriously amusing, for a professor of communications to exhibit outright hostility towards television as such (Postman 1985) – whereas the notion of a McLuhanesque professor of English literature who hates all books would seem promising only as a subject for satire. Although antipathy towards the medium is rarely quite so explicit, such jeremiads are none the less symptomatic of a wider failure of critical practice. The dominant tendency might be characterized as one of malign neglect of the specificities of television, in which prescribing the attitude to be taken towards a given programme becomes a substitute for trying to understand how such texts achieve their effects.

The procedural conventions of such a narrowly conceived approach can engage neither with television as a medium nor with the sheer diversity of its content. Less gloomy critics have therefore gravitated towards an emphasis on one or the other of these latter features, with their preference shaped according to whether they have been impressed by television's uniformity or by its variety. Two of the best-known, but contrasting, stances were those adopted by Marshall McLuhan in the 1960s and by Clive James in the 1970s. McLuhan (1964: 32) fleshed out his well-known claim that the medium is the message by describing content as, 'the juicy piece of meat carried by a burglar to distract the watchdog of the mind'. Food for thought, no doubt. In his column for Britain's *Observer* Clive James was no less sardonic (he once described an Ingmar Bergman teleplay as 'muesli without milk'). He saw in the content of television a rich feast of critical possibilities, a cultural smorgasbord which perfectly catered to his overdeveloped sense of wit. The result is a marvellous source of after dinner one-liners. James has a gift for puncturing cultural pretensions, a talent for quipping against the pricks. If read against the high seriousness of his essays on Russian literature (James 1982), however, then James' response to television seems glib and formulaic, and the medium's distinctiveness seems neglected. When, for example, the theatre critic Kenneth Tynan suggested to him that television criticism was impossible because it required you to 'know everything', James was initially nonplussed. It was rather like inviting a long-time street fighter to think like a referee. His belated but characteristic response was to declare himself heartened by a recognition that even though he could not claim omniscience, nor could anyone else (James 1977: 20).

The episode is instructive. When George Bernard Shaw purportedly observed of a particularly disastrous theatrical first night that, 'This play had everything, but is everything enough?' he was being no less pertinent than Tynan and no less witty than James. What Shaw's remark relies upon is a readership attuned to the indispensable role of theatrical convention. In like fashion it is the conventions of television which provide a way into a critical understanding of the medium. What Tynan overlooks is the distinction between the language *of* television and the language *on* television (Silverstone 1981: 38). It is precisely this difference between the (restricted) forms of discourse that are distinctive to television and those which are characteristic of the profusion of voices, subjects and themes that it appropriates which both McLuhan and James are inclined to neglect. They also neglect the ways in which the component features of this bewildering plurality interact both with each other and with the expectations of the audience. Their respective emphases (on the global properties of the medium and on the details of a given programme) means that their engagement with such considerations is, at best, oblique. What is missing is a recognition that the structure of television discourse is conditioned, but not determined, by the technology of production, and that it is expressed through signifiers whose promiscuity it regulates but does not prescribe.

It is this determination at the level of discourse which accounts for television's very intelligibility – the fact that it can be read by so many – and this is both a measure of its cultural achievement and the basis of a critical approach. Far from being impossible, television criticism is splendidly democratic. Not only do most of us do it, but most of us *can* do it. Where Tynan views this in terms of the limits it places on the idea of the professional critic and the privileged interpretation, the opportunity it offers is for a realignment of critical practice, in which the question 'how (well) does it work?' assumes priority over the puzzle of 'what does it mean?'. This intrinsically sociological stance depends upon probing the ways in which the cultural habits of both audience and producers intersect so as to produce a possible meaning. The subject of such a criticism is the forms of tacit knowledge on which this cultural interaction depends, and its purpose is to subvert television's 'blissful clarity', (Barthes 1973: 143) to recover a sense of its strangeness.

Which edges us a little nearer to *The Singing Detective* in that, like the exchange between Tynan and James, the series was produced in Britain (with Australian support). The most appropriate critical path is that line which charts the text's conditions of legibility. We need to recover not just its encoded (or preferred) meaning, but to probe into the cultural and material circumstances which made the series possible; to consider what made it possible for us to read it, and to try and identify the audience for which it selects and to whom it might speak.

The series was first screened in Britain in November and December 1986. It might well have been termed 'the BBC's Christmas present to itself', had not *Edge of Darkness* previously attracted such an epithet (Penman 1986: 76). It was a Christmas present in the sense that the BBC was very much in need of just such a flagship series, given the pressures to which public service broadcasting was subject in Thatcher's Britain of the mid-1980s. And it was also a present in the sense that, within a broadcasting organization in which the claim (if not the fact) of autonomy is given more forceful institutional expression than is usual within television, the BBC was also prepared to grant a greater than usual measure of discretion to the writer. This was, in part, explicable in terms of the particular history of writer Dennis Potter's relationship with the BBC. That history had included the banning of his play *Brimstone and Treacle* some ten years previously. This episode had, in its turn, contributed to Potter and his producer staking a claim to independence by setting up their own production company, moving to London Weekend Television, developing feature film scripts, and so on.

Both the critical response to *The Singing Detective* and the BBC's own profile of Potter[1] suggested that here was something special. For example, under the heading 'Is the Year's Best Film on TV?', it had prompted an enthusiastic and influential review by the *New York Times* film critic Vincent Canby. More specifically, *if* the notion of *auteur* status is capable of migrating to television from its origins in the study of film, then it seemed that Potter could plausibly be invested with such a title. Such a claim was contested by Rosalind Coward (1987) and yet by 1996 there would be three book-length critical studies of Potter's life and work (Stead 1993; Cook 1995; Gilbert 1995) and he had also been featured in a book series that was otherwise devoted to interviews with, and commentary on, the work of members of the contemporary pantheon of film directors (Fuller 1993). Ten years after it was first shown *The Singing Detective* remains the most acclaimed of the works with which his name is associated. The series could conceivably have been made for Britain's Channel 4 (an organization whose existence is itself predicated upon the prior presence of the BBC). It could not have been made for the American networks.

It does, however – and however obliquely – exhibit the signs of the networks' presence. My suggestion is that the discourse of British television during the 1980s can only be understood in relation to its American counterpart. Probing the properties of American television at that time is thus a preamble to isolating what was, and is, distinctive about the British.

First, and most obviously, the American networks are simply too intent on reconciling audience targets with corporate control to relinquish very much of the latter to a production team, let alone to a writer. It is, however, a misleading and sentimental conceit to read this in terms of a distinction between the BBC's principled support of culture and the American networks' venal commercialism. Each country's television may bear the distinctive trace of their very different theatrical and film-making traditions, but all television discourse is permeated by both contemporary market pressures and hierarchical controls (cf. Farnsworth 1992). What is problematic is the way these factors articulate so as to produce variations in programming and in typical modes of inflection. That process resists being reduced to a contrast between art and commerce, a distinction which simply cannot provide the leverage to explain such minor miracles as the early *Hill Street Blues*. Here was a network series distinguished by open and complex multiple plotting (derived from the soaps), characterization of some depth, and a knowing and affectionate reworking of film noir conventions. The art/commerce contrast also precludes any recognition, or engagement with, the visual accomplishments (derived from rock videos and commercials) of so resolutely non-literary and politically retrograde a series as *Miami Vice*.

The terrain between post-liberal blues (Gitlin 1983: 308) and postmodernist vice (Fiske 1987: 118) was the location for a strategic skirmish, part of the contested ground in a wider battle to define the agenda for a popular culture which may be American in origin but has become global in its reach. In the associated struggles for audiences what is incidentally at stake are the forms which notions of cultural centrality might take. The success of *Miami Vice* suggests just how far the terms of such engagements has become weighted towards the image rather than the word.

Consider, for example, *LA Law*, which as its title suggests, could be seen as not just the other side of the country to *Miami Vice* but as the other to the codes (both moral and semiotic) which informed the latter. It was a series produced by the team responsible for *Hill Street Blues* and although it embodied some of *Hill Street*'s virtues, it altogether lacked the visual texture of that earlier series. Gitlin (1983) documents how *Hill Street* was conditioned by the injunction to 'make it look messy'. Hence the graininess, the shadowy, imperfectly lit scenes, the occasional use of hand-held cameras, the frequent dislocation of privileged narratives by the movement of other actors within the frame, the emphasis on sombre-toned blues, greys and browns. In *LA Law* the only messiness was interpersonal and it had no visual correlate. Yet it was possible to envisage how the settings and the way they are shot, could, as in both *Hill Street* and *Miami Vice*, (and subsequently in such series about professional working practices as *ER* and *Law and Order*) be employed to consciously mirror or disrupt the dominant narrative. Thus although *LA Law* made use of sight gags, it seems visually retrograde by comparison. Not because it had too many suits and too many suites, but because of how they were shown. The ingenuity with which the designs of its protagonists were explored was not matched by a comparable visual exploration or critique of corporate design.

None the less *LA Law*, like *Hill Street* and *Miami Vice*, was indebted, and gave textual expression, to the organizational continuities between network television and Hollywood cinema. It was, of course, Hollywood in its heyday which had prefigured the world market in images, developed the authoritative narrative models, and orchestrated appropriate conceptions of visual literacy. It was, moreover, Hollywood which had effectively constructed the very idea of America by way of the classic genres of the western, the thriller and the musical. The subsequent metamorphosis of the forms of dominant cinema into the forms of dominant television, structures the field on which the BBC is obliged to play. What further distinguishes that field is how a hyperreal conception of America is routinely but continuously generated from the megatext (Browne 1987) that is that nation's television. A crucial characteristic of this conception is that it is both eminently accessible and extraordinarily complex; at once easy to recognize but yet impossible to define.

A schematic outline of just how this occurs can be inferred by combining themes derived from the analysis of soap operas with some observations drawn from studies of cultural transmission and conceptual acquisition. The place to start is with the modal television text – any single episode of any established soap opera series. Viewed on its own, it may well appear almost inexplicable, being characterized by narrative redundancy and repetition and yet nevertheless curiously opaque. Action and characterization within such an episode acquire – or rather are invested with – their meaning and significance only in relation to those sedimented understandings which have been laid down by the antecedent episodes. It is therefore through watching a particular soap opera over time that the notion of a soap community comes to be constructed and the audience becomes implicated in it. It is in recognition of the resulting structural complexities (as manifested in the multiple inflections of any given narrative line, a plurality of plots, open form, temporally layered characterization, and audience engagement) that the soaps – in an inversion of literary-derived hierarchies – have acquired a privileged position amongst television academics (e.g. Hobson 1982; Geraghty 1991).

In this sense it is the soaps which most clearly exemplify tendencies which are at work across a wide range of television's serial forms, from situation comedies to cop shows, from cartoons to hospital dramas. The soap's seriality, and its associated construction and invocation of its own phenomenologically distinctive sense of historical time is, in turn, located within the temporal uniformities and impersonal ordering of the television schedule, with its commercially ordained rhythm and its daily, weekly and seasonal patterns. The schedules are thus the discursive means for achieving connections between the broadcasting organizations' overall political and economic project and the textual, cultural and social specifics of a given series. Different programme types and textual forms which select for different audiences are thereby articulated by the schedules. Within the type of commercial television system represented by the American networks the manifest intention is to deliver audiences to advertisers. Nevertheless the very form of the schedule corresponds to a *simulation* of social integration, to a pluralism of appearances. A time-travelling De Tocqueville might therefore have been interested in how an incidental effect of the schedule is to create an imaginary realm in which there is a continuous attempt to reconcile the maintenance of (discursive rather than social) order with the diverse characteristics and divergent (textual) interests of individuals and groups.

It is the routine operation of commercial imperatives, rather than any conscious conspiracy, which encourages attempts to build upon the intertextual tendencies that are characteristic of the series form. These involve the combining of seriality with that repertoire of tactics which Raymond Williams (1974) has called television's 'flow' and with such programming strategies as 'hammocking' (placing a minority interest programme between two popular ones) and 'tent-poling' (hanging less popular programmes around a high-rating peak prime-time one) (Selby and Cowdery 1995: 226–35).

It is through its simulation of the temporal dimension of community that the series as a *form* facilitates the construction of a community of interest(ed fans) over time. And because the schedule discursively organizes the articulation and integration of such simulated social groupings, its *form*, in its turn, signals a model and a modelling of the wider social order to the audiences which coalesce around particular series. American television's formal simulations of temporal and social organization are further invested with a sense of *place* through their deter-minate settings, that is, through an aspect of programme content. *NYPD Blue* and *Chicago Hope* notwithstanding, this nowadays seems less likely to be explicitly signalled by the programme titles themselves (such as *LA Law* and *Miami Vice*, *Dallas* and *Streets of San Francisco*, *Hawaii Five O* and *WKRP Cincinnati*). *Seinfeld* nevertheless signals a New York location just as *Cheers* had signalled Boston (and a multi-million dollar boost to that city's tourism). In terms of programme plausibility, place matters. What if , for example, *LA Law* had been *Green Bay Law* and hence set in my wife's home state of Wisconsin? Then, as she wryly indicated at the time, and as *Picket Fences* subsequently confirmed, it would be obliged to have plots, characterization and ambience that might seem to have almost as much in common with the defunct Scottish series *Sutherland's Law* as with the corporate world of metropolitan California.[2] Here again, however, it is not so much particular programmes as the overall structuring of the field that I wish to emphasize, with its mosaic-like patterning which provides for the incorpo-ration of (simulated) locations from frontier Alaska (*Northern Exposure*) to retirement Florida (*Golden Girls*). It is in this megatextual sense that network television is America, having transmuted/reproduced the nation which Hollywood had invented.

No matter whether the actual production location is Acapulco or Vancouver, American television is television 'made in America' for Americans. Yet although each programme may insinuate some definition of America and Americans, no verbal definition of what America is, or of what it means to be American, reaches across the programmes themselves. I nevertheless said earlier that the resulting conception of America is both accessible and complex, both recognizable and undefinable. There are some affinities here with that process through which Benedict Anderson (1983: 39–40) saw the newspapers and novels of 'print capi-talism' as having generated an imagined national community, a fiction which derived from the understanding of the individual act of reading as communally shared with anonymous others. What differs, however, is the notion of the text, which is not the (relation with a) discrete, bounded, material artifact that is a particular work of print but the continuous, plural, open, endless flow of sounds and images that is all of television. Hence notwithstanding the enormous variety in the *content* of America as idea amongst viewers, my suggestion is that the *form* of such a notion will be strongly isomorphic with the form of the television mega-text itself. Amongst the televisually literate an innovative programme is therefore expected to be densely inter-'textual' and innovative viewing may consist of channel-hopping (compare Mark Poster's (1990: 65) suggestion that 'decon-struction may better be defined as TV viewing applied to books'). More generally, the attendant sensibility is one in which the boundaries between television textu-ality and other modes will be experienced as highly permeable.

If the very notion of 'America' is, importantly, a consequence of Hollywood and subsequently the American television networks, then 'England' and 'Englishness' is, by contrast, above all a literary invention (Colls and Dodd 1985). As Dick Hebdige (1982) has documented, the hostility of Britain's opinion-makers and cultural custodians to the 'Americanization' of popular culture goes back at least as far as the 1930s. The terms in which such fears are couched have remained remarkably constant for more than half a century. An indigenous and authentic Britishness (or more often Englishness) is set against the corrupt and corrupting influences which American culture purportedly embodies. Its a pattern of response which links the writings of a misanthropic high Tory like Evelyn Waugh to George Orwell's 1940s essays on popular culture, to Richard Hoggart's *The Uses of Literacy* in 1957 and to Martin Esslin's *The Age of Television* in 1983.[3] Its impact in and on the BBC has been most evident in quality English drama (or QED[4] in Alex Calder's (1987) felicitous acronym), but its influence has been pervasive.

Such sentiments have proved remarkably resilient in the face of their continual subversion by popular taste. They are, however, incorporated in a body of thought which, like Marlow's body at the beginning of *The Singing Detective*, was in crisis by the 1980s. When being British meant watching *Dallas*, it also meant that a literary conception of culture was faced with a crisis of representation, and a nationalist conception of culture was faced with a crisis of jurisdiction. One response to the presence of so many cultural space invaders was to imperiously bemoan cultural imperialism from the foxholes scattered throughout publishing, higher education and the quality press. Thus Mike Poole's (1984) survey of the backgrounds of British television reviewers showed how such criticism read like a conspiracy of the literary against the laity. By contrast, those British intellectuals who had chosen to work in television were confronted on a day to day basis with the incentive to work the crisis through. And that is precisely what *The Singing Detective* attempts to do.

Like Marlow's own long, slow process of deterioration, the onset of such present difficulties can be traced back to, and was triggered by, indisputable evidence of betrayal and an end to innocence. With the arrival of commercial tele-vision in the mid-1950s the BBC, like Marlow's father, was cuckolded.

Furthermore the British public, like Marlow's mother, proved to be willing participants in their own seduction. Both they and she decamped. Thus Jane Root notes that by September 1957 British commercial television had gained 79 per cent of the audience. She goes on to cite Peter Black's observation that 'The audience's goodwill towards the monopoly turned out to be an illusion. Once they had a choice, the working class left the BBC at a pace which suggested ill will was more deeply entrenched than good' (Root 1986: 61). Both the British public and Marlow's mother had been subject to the austere constraints and the dead weight of an authority which (whether in the form of in-laws or control of broadcasting) had sought to regulate their domestic activities. Each of these authorities had sought to legitimate their control in the name of a common culture and common decency. But each expressed a conception of the past, rather than their subjects' own sense of the present or their image of the future. Neither the British public nor Marlow's mother wanted any part of it. Their anthem was American – 'Don't Fence Me In'. Their actual seducer had less to offer, of course, but was none the less just sharp enough, possessed just enough of the requisite amount of gloss, to be a vehicle for their suppressed desires and their impulse to escape.

Although in each case the entire process of seduction was observed, it was only imperfectly understood at the time, whether by Marlow or by the British cultural establishment. Its implications were, however, clearly disturbing. In each case there was a need to believe that the prevailing conception of identity (whether personal or national) was still intact, that nothing had really changed. In each case this depended upon a lie at the centre; and upon allocating blame for the public presence of one's own shit to someone else. There it lay in the schoolroom of the nation, disrupting the authorized lessons. It could not be ignored. Authority, whether in the shape of a patriotic schoolmistress, or cultural apologists for BBC 'standards', was receptive to the idea that it was the least intelligent who were at fault (in the accents of such an authority 'mess' could even sound like 'mass'). The denied and dirty little secret, however, was that the threat to identity came not from without, but from within. Such a secret could only be spoken obliquely, refracted through fictions, manifested in signs of disturbance, transformed into a foreign body (whether by Marlow or by the British cultural establishment).

Thus for the adult Marlow, his mother's villainous suitor subsequently appears in two different guises. In his detective story he is the (upper-class) agent of a foreign power, a betrayer of secrets; in his interpretation of the present he is a go-between for Hollywood interests, the seducer and betrayer of Marlow's ex-wife. Acts of personal betrayal are thus fused with the repudiation of Britishness, in which villainy consists of an embracing of alien elements, a denial of community membership. But the childhood Marlow offers a much more ambiguous interpretation of the community response to the original seduction, the event from which these later fictions derive. Like his perception of family and of self, his perception of community is split. It is therefore seen by him – and shown to us – as at once comforting and threatening. For example, he and we see the village pub as the site of communal sentiment (orchestrated by his father), as a location for (his mother's) uneasy duplicity and as a place of collective menace.

For the adult Marlow striving to come to terms with the debilitating effects of this split, story telling is a psychic necessity; part therapy, part evasion. The matrix from which a solution to crisis can be constructed is that psychic and cultural territory which lies between what he is and what his hero is, between his story and his detective('s) story. Marlow was, of course, the name of an earlier psychological investigator and cultural explorer, the narrator of Joseph Conrad's *Heart of Darkness* (the BBC having explored its edge the year before). Like Conrad's protagonist, Marlow as hospital patient embarks upon a journey into his own past. But in any such exploration a guide recruited from the ranks of literary high culture is in danger of being either too quixotic or of travelling in only the narrowest of channels (however deep they may be). His indispensable *aide-mémoire* and Sancho Panza is therefore Marlow as singing detective, and this Marlow has a trans-Atlantic namesake (albeit with an 'e') in the form of the private-eye hero of Raymond Chandler's novels. Chandler's work occupied a profoundly ambiguous position in relation to the contrast between being British and being American. His novels were set in Los Angeles and steeped in the American vernacular, but his detective was imbued with moral principles that critics variously interpreted as commendable English integrity, as hard-boiled decency, or as a somewhat improbable public school propriety. Marlow's singing detective signals such cultural ambiguity in a much more conscious fashion. His musical tastes (which, given the 1940s setting, predate television) are both popular and British (whereas Marlow's mother was shown as preferring Bing Crosby and the Andrews Sisters). But his laconic patterns of speech nod towards Hollywood, and although his accent is hardly mid-Atlantic it is manifestly off-shore. *The Singing Detective* therefore incorporates a recognition that 'Americanization' was an identifiable aspect of British popular culture by the 1940s. George Orwell was amongst those who had deeply objected to this development and in 'Raffles to Miss Blandish' he identified the crime story as symptomatic of what had changed. But as Orwell (1957) himself had pointed out, the English author of the 'Americanized' book which offended him (*No Orchids for Miss Blandish*) had never been to America.

What is implicit in the cultural argument of *The Singing Detective* is that Orwell had chosen the wrong writer, focused on the wrong book and drawn the wrong conclusions. Chandler may have lived in America, but he was an English-educated Anglophile whose hardback sales and literary standing were much better in Britain than in America (cf. Gardiner and Walker 1962: 149, 169, 173). Above all, he had provided a critically important solution to the problem of how to reconcile a popular cultural form with the aesthetic standards of high culture. That is a preoccupation which *The Singing Detective* knowingly replicates. For example, the death of the 1940s villain in the final episode of the series is unexplained, but we learn that a note beside the body reads 'Who cares who killed Roger Ackroyd?'. *The Murder of Roger Ackroyd* is an Agatha Christie story in which the narrator is the murderer, but the reference is to the title of an Edmund Wilson essay (1957). That essay singled out Chandler for positive comment, and together with some comments by W.H. Auden, was important in helping to bring his work to the attention of high culture critics.

Chandler's solution to these Anglo/American and high culture/popular culture dilemmas was a literary one. But as the film critic Dilys Powell noted in her review of *Double Indemnity* (for which Chandler and Billy Wilder had written the screenplay) 'Chandler's writing at its best is sharply visual, getting its effects by observed detail' (cited in Macshane 1976: 108).[5] What Chandler's books depend upon is a way of writing in which the imagery is rather more memorable than the convolutions of the plot. For example Phillip French (1977: 71) notes that when Howard Hawks was directing *The Big Sleep* he and his screen-writers got in touch with Chandler to find out who had killed General Sternwood's chauffeur. They gave up worrying about it on discovering that not even he could remember. One consequence of Chandler's cinematic literary style is that his cultural significance and impact have been rather different between Britain and America. That first screenplay secured his reputation in Hollywood, and his work prefigured that developed visual sensibility which is characteristic of contemporary American television and popular films.

I have briefly indicated the ways in which *Hill Street Blues* and *Miami Vice* give expression to this and suggested something of its implications for the BBC. It also helps to explain the huge popular success and critical disdain which greeted a film like *Flashdance*. I want now to suggest how the dancing welder in that Hollywood film can be used to comment upon the singing detective in the British television series. The film is transparently constructed around the principle of having something in it for all possible audiences. This activating principle may seem remote from the cultural debates and concerns which underpin the BBC production. It is, however, precisely this (commercially induced) drive to embrace contrasting social practices which provides the point of common contact. From this standpoint the film's very different solution becomes a means of pointing to what is specific about *The Singing Detective* considered as discourse.

Flashdance is part romantic fairy tale, part peep show. The literary derived conventions of a strong narrative line and of characters who possess some internal coherence are decisively undercut. The star is a woman welder from a repressed religious family background who dances in a night club/strip joint and is practising to get a place in a classical dance academy. She resents her employer's sexual harassment but falls in love with him, asserts her independence but benefits from his patronage. She thus oscillates between such disparate role models as Rosie the Riveter, Gypsy Rose Lee, Rosemary Clooney and *Cider With Rosie*. And yet these inconsistencies are held in check by the narcissistic energy which the film generates, and which derive from its video-inspired fusion of popular music and visual images of dance. Like *The Singing Detective* it therefore constructs, against the odds, a conception of the person. But unlike *The Singing Detective* it constructs that conception not from the (male) mind but from the (female) body – and in ways which render the body as at once the subject of female action and the object of male gaze. The film therefore achieves that improbable integration of identification and objectification which its title implies. Thus 'Flash' could be said to denote both the female subject's inner states (flash/backs) and a male audience's sexual pleasure (flash/flesh), and 'dance' is both an accomplishment to be identified with and a spectacle to be looked at.

Unlike *Flashdance*, *The Singing Detective* is grounded in a pattern of cultural debates and practices which prioritizes literary criteria. This is evident not only from the long list of books and plays adapted for television by the BBC, but from the status accorded to writers generally, including not just dramatists but, instructively, the authors of comedy series. Thus in Britain the names Ray Galton and Alan Simpson (*Hancock*, *Steptoe and Son*), Dick Clement and Ian La Frenais (*The Likely Lads*, *Porridge*) and Johnny Speight (*Till Death Us Do Part*) were almost as well known as 'their' shows. By comparison, innovation in American television is linked to the production house (e.g. MTM Enterprises) or to the producer/director (e.g. Stephen Bochco, David Lynch). Moreover, that dense intertextual referencing that is characteristic of innovative American television (much accelerated through such series as *The Simpsons*, *Twin Peaks* and *Northern Exposure*) typically involves the invocation of other television programmes and films rather than books. *The Singing Detective*'s refusal of a visually and musically accomplished integration (*pace Flashdance*) is consistent with the British pattern of prioritizing the literary. There is a routine interrogation or disruption of any presumption as to the veracity of the text's visual images. The consoling and integrating force of popular songs (of the 1940s) is nostalgically accorded full recognition *and* subverted. Doctors suddenly become participants in a lavish musical entertainment, a nurse suddenly becomes a night-club singer, pyjama-clad hospital patients watch as a body is recovered from the river, an elderly candidate for a heart attack begins to sing like Bing Crosby. From the outset the text oscillates between disparate *mise-en-scènes* which invoke *The Third Man* and the conventions of Jack The Ripper movies, war time pin-ups, contemporary hospital dramas, soap opera style family conflicts and images of community life. It is therefore particularly instructive that in an otherwise strongly *auteur* influenced account of Potter, Cook (1995: 217–22) chooses to credit the productive tensions and constructive relation between Potter and director Jon Amiel with the effective 'authorship' of the series. Bringing these strands together so that the series was both a critical and a popular success was not all down to the writer.[6]

All of these dislocations do none the less come to be understood as consistent with narrative integration and as the expression of the central character's own view of the world. At the centre of this disordered pastiche is an author/patient (Marlow) trying to avoid death. His only power is in language, and this linguistic resourcefulness contrasts with, and is threatened by, his deteriorating physical condition and social dependence. What is signalled is a hierarchical ordering of the discourses within the text (childhood, detective story, hospitalization) so as to privilege the position of Marlow-as-author/patient. The apparent narrative disorder is designed to ensure that the viewer, as bewildered as Marlow-as-patient, and as concerned to establish coherence, is moved to identify with his crisis. Apart from the off switch there is really nowhere else to go. This initial identification is reinforced through the accumulation of verbal evidence that Marlow-as-patient controls the activities of Marlow-as-detective, and through the accumulation of indications that Marlow-as-patient supplies and suppresses information about Marlow-as-child.

The text's narrative organization is revealed as not so much linear as paratactic (cf. Richter 1974: 17) i.e. dependent upon a circular structure such that the 'plot' seems to go round and round. Although it can, with hindsight, or on a second viewing, be reconstructed in linear terms, it employs a free approach to time, being structured more in accordance with the principle of progressive revelation than with regard to historical sequence. Far from being open, therefore, the text vigorously encodes a preferred reading. The viewer is drawn into the text as a problem-solving accomplice of its fictional author. As such, the viewer comes to recognize that the breaching of boundaries between Marlow's various worlds is a routine accomplishment. The absurd can be made to make sense (and what could be more absurd than the two villains in raincoats and trilbies, an Abbott and Costello duo who seem to have been scripted by Harold Pinter).

Having firmly secured support for a narrative which privileges Marlow as a patient, all that remains is to kill him off. In this way the viewer can come to recognize the author of this achievement. Like the absurd, the happy ending thus makes sense. The operation was a success. The patient died but the author lives, the patient is shot but the author is saved – and by his own fictional creation. And secure behind him are the *other* authors of the text (the literate viewer and the production team), co-conspirators in the preservation of a threatened body of thought about culture in general and television in particular. The question raised by the resulting small fictional disturbance to the surface of television's hyperreal megatext is whether that threatened body of thought is experiencing its last gasp or rehearsing a creative revival. If I am right what is at issue is: am I rite, or am I write?

3

POST-PICTURES AND EC(H)O EFFECTS

What is it that distinguishes the Benetton adverts? Perhaps it is the intentional play on 'united colors' as, for example, in the image of a global (nuclear) family. The colour photograph of a Chinese child wrapped in the same green blanket as its black and white 'parents' achieves, in the realm of iconic representation, a purely formal harmony of composition that both contradicts and is contradicted by the social realities of racial categorization and ethnic division. Or perhaps it is that although these adverts rely upon images that consciously strive to be universal in subject matter (for which read global), they are specifically Italian in conception. Like that studio shot of brightly coloured condoms arranged like children's party balloons, or the photo of a nun kissing a priest. Such images could be read as a tentative and deliberately whimsical exploration of Italianate catholicity, as a not-yet-dangerous first sip out of that same well from which Madonna draws.

Well, maybe. But if so, then what had begun as no more than faint traces of such a sensibility's darker depths, of its engagement with blood, sacrifice and death, seem to have gathered ground with each new Benetton campaign. Thus beginning in 1992, Benetton started to go beyond its own in-house, studio produced colour photographs in order to cull black and white images from the realm of photo-journalism. These included a photograph of the emaciated figure of David Kirby, surrounded by his family and dying of AIDS, an image which Oliviero Toscani, Benetton's creative director, referred to as a 'modern Pietà' (cited in Rosen 1993: 23). And in their 1994 campaign the same kind of symbolic values were mobilized in the choice of a photograph of the blood-stained clothing of a soldier killed in Bosnia.

In so far as Benetton advertising is different it is, of course, different within the limits of consumerism and in accordance with the commercial potential of novelty and exoticism. Thus although these black and white (if sometimes colourized) photographs are placed in magazine advertisements and on billboards they – unlike those studio produced colour images – do not appear in Benetton's shops. And although Benetton arranged for photo shoots in the Gaza strip, in which ordinary Palestinians modelled the clothes for its 1995 Spring/Summer catalogue, the company – which has more than 7000 retail outlets in 120 countries –

does not have a shop there. Benetton's ontological understanding of commercial realities would therefore seem to be well and truly discrete from its representations of realism. My suggestion is that these adverts are nevertheless of interest, both as a general guide to the changing rules of advertising and as a distinctive and specific articulation of the incidental flows of cultural traffic between catholicity and commercial strategy. Before briefly considering the latter claim let me sketch a conventional interpretation of the former.

Under the old rules, the first maxim of advertising was 'don't sell the sausage, sell the sizzle'. In the garment business this quickly became 'don't sell the clothes, sell the body'. (By 'old rules' is meant those operating up until around the onset of the 1980s – the now bizarre notion of advertising as primarily a source of product information belongs firmly to the prehistory of the discourse and to the history of its apologetics.) The purpose of this classic maxim was twofold. First of all, to forge a link between a particular commodity (sausages, clothes, whatever) and a particular cultural meaning (mouth-watering sizzles, attractive bodies, whatever). Second, to make this claimed relation between a given object and a specific cultural value appear to be a natural, taken-for-granted one, to literally fix the meaning in ways that Roland Barthes (1973) sought to elucidate. In this way traditional advertising acted as an unlicensed broker between the circulation of commodities in the market and the circulation of meanings in the culture. It none the less interpreted the movement as going one way, as flowing from the culture to the commodity. Advertisers didn't have to make the meanings – and they didn't have to pay for them. Meanings were just *there*, waiting to be appropriated. Any consequences for culture as a system were seen as no more than accidental and incidental by-products of adding value to the product.

With the development and expansion of a fully fledged consumer culture, however, advertising became more and more knowingly constitutive of culture as such. There wasn't a sausage that didn't sizzle superbly or clothes that weren't attractively embodied. And consumers knew it. And because advertisers knew that consumers knew, advertisers have been impelled to further colonize and cannibalize extant cultural meanings in their attempts to construct the signs of distinction. Commodities and meanings, things and ideas about things, have therefore come to seem hopelessly confounded. One of the correlates of such expansion is that there are fewer and fewer locations in which culturally valued meanings might be constructed outside of the market. Those that are – or at least those whose claims to cultural authenticity rest upon such outsider status – are now either subject to determined efforts at cooptation, or revealed as already implicated, or constructed on the cusp of such a contrast. Examples of this latter now proliferate, ranging from some of Kurt Cobain's lyrics to Andrew Wernick's (1991) ambivalent awareness of how his book on promotional culture is a manifestation of the phenomenon that it critiques.

As a consequence advertisers have become less inclined to focus only on the achievement of specific meaning/commodity linkages. Increasingly they have come to emphasize the relevance for their endeavours of that wider cultural system through which meanings are generated. The object of advertising discourse has therefore not only tended to shift away from the particular commodity and towards the brand name, but also away from the specific meaning and towards the cultural codes through which meanings are generated and consumers are constituted. This dual development is particularly marked in those industries, such as fashion and cosmetics, whose economic logic depends upon the idea of novelty and change. It is now the name (Benetton, or Doc Marten's, or whatever) which must endure, and this name displaces a particular product as the item to which value has to be attached. In Oliviero Toscani's aphorism, 'Products change, images capitalize' (Rosen 1993: 21). The advertiser's problem thus becomes one of identifying and securing a privileged position for the name, on the assumption that the resulting sign value in the culture will translate into exchange value on the market. When making names meaningful is the means of making money, then making such meanings means playing with cultural codes generally and with those governing the processes of representation in particular. Nowadays it can sometimes seem as if such second order signification has become the norm. Adverts are increasingly engaged in interrogating their own conventions, and/or problematizing taken for granted signifier/signified linkages in the wider culture and/or flattering the readers of such adverts for their cultural competence (Goldman and Papson 1994; Perry 1994: 80–96).

In so far as these contemporary advertisers can be said to have learned from Barthes, they have done so by effectively turning him on his head. Barthes' innovation in *Mythologies* (1973) had been to show how, in the passage from language to myth, what was a first order sign within language, might function as a second order signifier within myth. In this way the specific and the particular were not just linked to the dominant social values of myth but served to naturalize them, thereby contributing to the reproduction of the existing social order. Barthes thus provided a methodological basis for reading traditional ads critically. One of the correlates of advertising and media saturation, however, is that media literacy and critical readings are increasingly widely diffused. Consequently advertisers themselves now seek to construct adverts which purport to display a shared sense of scepticism and knowingness as between the image producer and the putative consumer. The evolving logic of such developments is towards an ever more explicit signifying of cynicism concerning the practices of representation, a marking of them as dead myths. Such signs of cynicism are in their turn, however, second order signifiers for the only notion of authenticity that such a discourse permits, namely, the illusion that one is without illusions, that one knows the score. There is thus an ahistorical naturalization of the present through the myth that myth is at an end.

What characterizes Benetton's advertising is that it is constructed across both the earlier, product recall formulas and these more recent modes, in that it simultaneously affirms a universalist myth through its content, whilst elaborating a form which works to render that myth problematic. Thus the images which Benetton have recently employed are akin to the kind of photographs which regularly appeared in the pages of *Life* in America or *Picture Post* in Britain during the pre-television heyday of these now defunct magazines (Jeffrey 1981: 178–203). Benetton's retrograde innovation is to relocate these otherwise traditional representations within another discursive context. Benetton may draw from anywhere in the global cultural archive, but what their chosen images bring with them is a penumbra of critique, an association with diffusely progressive sentiments, although not necessarily a link with progressive politics. Their choices are none the less obliged to pass through that filter which the very idea of advertising provides. So although what counts as advertising may be challenged – as in these photographs – advertising itself cannot be. And the position which advertising occupies within culture works to invest these images with its own inherited set of meanings. So on the one hand there are formal similarities between some of Benetton's latest *Life*-like pictures and an earlier, photo-journalism tradition – they now help to sell clothes as they had formerly helped to sell magazines. On the other, there are substantive contrasts which derive from their different positioning within culture as, for example, between the historical narrative of such photo-journalism and the associational logic of advertising images. The Benetton sponsored magazine *Colors* is symptomatic of the shift towards the latter. Subtitled 'a magazine about the rest of the world', it is identified in editorials as 'a global magazine about local cultures'. Each issue has a distinctive theme, such as sport, the street, tribes. What serves to police the resulting display of material and social differences is that the images through which these themes are realized are assembled in accordance with either a 'Family of Man' premise[1] or through a foregrounding of purely formal shared properties, properties that we are induced to read off from the design and composition of the images themselves. Published in bilingual editions, of which one is always English, the advertising slogan on its subscription form reads 'big pictures! not many words! lots of ideas!' (which might be read as either suggesting its use as an aid to second language acquisition, or as evidence for anxieties about the demise of literacy as such).

What Benetton means by ideas is given expression by the cluster of practices which have gathered around their advertising campaigns, practices which their publicity handouts are concerned to document. Their adverts win prizes, get hung in art museums and are the subject of formal critical scrutiny. And the adverts also get banned from publication in various well-known magazines, the billboards get complained about on talkback radio, and both get talked about in letters to editors. Whether due to happenstance or conscious intent, it would seem that Benetton believes that for members of its targeted constituency, such a ritualizing of controversy is tantamount to a consumer report 'seal of approval', a means of securing a 'best buy' recommendation.

For the same images to stake a claim both in the street and in the gallery is not itself new, but it does suggest a certain interesting indeterminacy about their cultural status. Toscani's claim that 'Products change, images capitalize' might therefore be set alongside the resolutely non-Foucauldian maxim (and – presumptively – the knowingly paradoxical sign) of art critic Robert Hughes that

'Signs discipline; pictures educate'. So where are these adverts to be located? Do they limit, or do they extend? In the street, Benetton's images might be said to imply something more than discipline, a fleeting provocation to reflect on the discourse of advertising, a gesture towards a gestural politics (Finkelstein 1994: 4–6). In the gallery, however, they offer something less than education (mode[rni]st pictures! not enough words! too few ideas!). They suggest something old, like *Picture Post* perhaps, but they offer something new only by way of the change of context. More than signs, but less than pictures. Post-pictures.

More than twenty years ago John Berger's television series *Ways of Seeing* (1972) critiqued the juxtaposition of images of starving refugees from East Pakistan and of Western consumerism in the colour magazines of British Sunday papers. For Berger, a culture that displayed and tolerated such a contradiction had manifestly lost its way. But as Goffman (1974: 475) had presciently observed in a lecture series first delivered in 1970, both the starkness of such a contrast and the security of the distinction between the representation of material realities and consumer mythologies had already begun to blur. In an anticipation of the hyperreal, Goffman referred to the emergence of 'a sort of interaction pollution' in which advertisers employed framing devices (childrens' voices, street noises, false starts, interruptions of commercials with Orson Welles-style news breaks) in order to give an appearance of naturalness.

Berger had polemically prised the images of refugee poverty loose from those written texts and historically located narratives which invested them with their editorially prescribed meanings. He had sought to recruit both them and the surrounding adverts to a totalizing critique which foregrounded the material contrasts which they depicted and the global system which generated them (Bruck and Docker 1991). But in the very act of, as it were, 'flicking through' such images in the name of history, Berger was complicit with ways of reading which deprived them of their respective histories (the big picture! not many words! lots of ideas!). It wasn't that words didn't matter; it was just that the magazine's words didn't. In substituting his own words, Berger enjoined us to contemplate the dislocative contrasts in the content of the images as the contrast between the real world and a dream world. But although grainy, black and white photographs might then have signified documentary realism as against the fantasy world of colour advertising, in the care with which *both* categories of images had been cropped, composed and commodified there was already the suggestion that their effective and shared subject matter was the modes of representation themselves. Since that time, confidence in photo-journalism as a faithful recording of the truth has given way to questions about both the methods by which truths were constructed and the motives which informed them. Benetton, in foregrounding the contrast to which Berger wished to draw our attention have, like Berger,[2] positioned themselves as concerned with social issues, but have done so under circumstances in which there is no longer any confidence in the presumption of a linkage between the realism of the images and a critical form of discourse.

Thus the form of Benetton's concern has much more in common with the catholic commercialism of what Umberto Eco (1995: 267–82) refers to as Italy's 'thaumaturgic underground' than it has with what Bruck and Docker (1991) describe as the 'puritanic rationalism' of Berger's English Marxism. The thaumaturgic underground consists of the literally millions of magazines which are sent free of charge by orphanages, missionary societies and sanctuaries and circulate throughout Italy. 'Despite differences in approach', says Eco:

> all these publications have one thing in common: the publication is a kind of outer wrapping for the payments slip . . . . The mediated objective is the support of orphans, the acquisition of an altar for a mission in the Congo and so on. The immediate objective is the future attainment of grace or recompense for grace received.
>
> (1995: 267)

Eco points out that these magazines are easily the biggest publishing business in Italy, one which is dependent upon tens of thousands of small donations and thus at pains to establish and maintain close links between readers and the publications themselves. The magazines have made a commodity of grace received, readers send in money because they were *not* injured in a car crash, or because their child *did* pass an exam, or an operation *was* a success. The model of virtuous conduct which these magazines construct is presented as generated from a three-way relationship between the devotee, the relevant saint and the orphans (or paupers, or sick children). Eco notes that history is missing from their discourse:

> Swimming in pity . . . none of these magazines ever asks why there exist abandoned children, children in poverty and sickness . . . the existence of evil and poverty is established as an unchanging background that ultimately makes possible the commercial enterprise which prospers on that basis.
>
> (1995: 277)

This is just the kind of milieu out of which a Benetton style advertising campaign might be expected to emerge. But whereas Eco's analysis is designed to reveal the commercialization of the supernatural, the movement of Benetton's social issues campaigns is towards the sanctification of consumption.

In effect then, Eco interprets the nexus between these magazines and their readers as not so much founded upon the gift of grace as upon the exchange of favours. Generating donations in this way is a very competitive business and this has prompted some sanctuaries and charities into inventive strategies. Amongst those which Eco (1995: 274) mentions is San Domenico Salio who offer, via the *Bollettino Salesiano*, a garment with thaumaturgic properties that is meant to be worn in moments of extreme pain. Benetton's advertising, by contrast, makes no such directly efficacious claims for its clothing – it is organized around a more secular, more modest, more immediate fantasy of consumer pleasure. It is, however, a pleasure that acknowledges, is mediated through, and constructed against, the Manichean representation of a world in which there is pain, distress and suffering. But by the grace of Benetton, the sweater purchaser-cum-suppliant-cum-postulant will be endowed with a public sign of private virtue.

Eco (1995: 280–82) looks to America for evidence that there is a secure future for what he interprets as the wedding of thaumaturgy and technology. He finds it in such enterprises as the Oral Roberts University in Oklahoma. This features such achievements as regular remakes of Genesis (in technicolour) and the transubstantiation of Coca-Cola – this latter adding a further metaphysical twist (and profitable spin) to the ontologically indeterminate, but materially beneficial and globally copyrighted claim that Coke is the 'real thing'. It is Eco's (1987: 1–58) own (spirited) attempt to define what, for Americans, the real thing might be which leads him to include such displays, along with Oral Roberts' television appearances, wax museums, Disneyland, the Getty Museum, Marineland, and the Forest Lawn–Glendale cemetery, as instances of the hyperreal.

For Eco the hyperreal is that which is more real than real, the copy which is more perfect than the original. It is also American, since 'the American imagination demands the real thing and, to attain it, must fabricate the absolute fake' (Eco 1987: 8). It rests upon a conception of knowledge as iconic and a commitment to the obliteration of the distinction between sign and referent. Although Eco's account is critical, he is above all interested in how the hyperreal works. He thus eschews gloomy moralizing and is discriminating, astute and wide ranging in his response to the hyperreal's various manifestations. His tone equivocates between bemused condescension (the Madonna Inn) and evident respect (the Getty Museum), between enjoyment and disorientation (Marineland), between recognition of technical virtuosity and a measured anxiety about its implications (Disneyland).

Eco chooses to entitle his essay *Travels in Hyperreality*. Inasmuch as this is indicative of his general stance and overall intention, it implies that the European-made baggage which he knowingly brings with him might merit inspection. For Eco's text can, in turn, be read so as to amplify what it seems willing only to whisper, namely the flourishing of the hyperreal within Europe itself. This latter is expressed, for example, in the 'ploughman's lunch' syndrome. *The Ploughman's Lunch*, which is the title of a Michael Ayres' film with a screenplay by Ian McEwan, proves to be a metaphor for Thatcherism. It is a meal identified and sold as traditional and authentic pub food and it purportedly harks back to a defining English pastoral; it turns out, however, to be a wholly contemporary fabrication invented by a marketing executive. The nostalgic evocation of 'plain and simple' qualities is in accord with the principle of minimizing the costs of preparation and maximizing returns. It is a fake which tells the truth about the social order which produced it.

In Eco's account the main narrative function of hyperreal America is to provide a contrast with Europe. But it is a subtle contrast. He continually refers back to European examples, but these do not therefore serve as some secure and unchanging benchmark against which to measure deviation or register indeterminacy. He wonders if one can meaningfully distinguish between the European tourist's pilgrimage to the Pietà of St Peters and that of the American to the Pietà of Forest Lawn, and he ponders on the status of a remade Duchamp 'ready made' at Cologne's Goethe Institute (Eco 1987: 39). Whether with respect to audiences, artifacts or artistic production the effect is to dissolve any notion of an absolute distinction between the old world and the new. Above all, however, 'Europe' comes to be defined by the still visible sedimentations of its long history and high culture – and for Eco this is closer to what 'authentic' means. Hence the passage in Eco's essay at which the distance between the two continents is at its narrowest is where he recognizes the legitimacy of the Getty Museum's hyper-reconstruction of the Villa of the Papyruses at Herculaneum. Eco writes:

How can a rich man, a lover of the arts, recall the emotions he felt one day in Herculaneum or in Versailles? And how can he help his compatriots understand what Europe is? It is easy to say: Put your objects all in a row with explanatory labels in a neutral setting. In Europe the neutral setting is called the Louvre, Castello Sforzesco, Uffizi, Tate Gallery[3] (just a short walk from Westminster Abbey). It is easy to give a neutral setting to visitors who can breathe in the Past a few steps away, who reach the neutral setting after having walked, with emotion, among venerable stones. But in California, between the Pacific on the one hand and Los Angeles on the other, with restaurants shaped like hats and hamburgers, and four-level freeways with ten thousand ramps what do you do? You reconstruct the Villa of the Papyruses.

(Eco 1987: 33)

If there is any irony in Eco's capitalization of the 'Past' then it is a gentle variant of the trope. This is because for him, those stones still speak, and he sees the merit of Getty's version of the hyperreal as lying in its imaginative translation of their script into the American vernacular.[4] But such hyperreal reconstructions and the translation of their meaning into another discourse also have a long lineage within Europe – of which a project such as London's Globe Theatre is only the most recent manifestation. They range from the nationalist symbolism with which the post-war reconstruction of Warsaw's medieval square was explicitly invested (cf. Steiner 1971: 51–2) to the technical virtuosity and loss-leader marketing strategy of Josiah Wedgwood's Romanesque copy of the British Museum's Portland Vase (Wernick 1991: 1–21). It is, however, the ploughman's lunch syndrome which is most symptomatic of how a received conception of authenticity is increasingly subverted by the uses made of the idea of the authentic within what Eco (1987: 39) sardonically refers to as 'the European sanctuaries of the Genuine'. When framed and bracketed by the tourism and heritage industries, authenticity functions as a code name for marketable. It is a product of discourse rather than an intrinsic property of objects, buildings and practices. The stones may still speak to Eco, but without his highly developed sensibilities (which are tantamount to a hyper-historicity) they cannot be heard above the noise of the traffic or the respectful whispers of the bourgeoisie worshipping themselves. This 'Europe' is no longer simply a given material reality; it is now as much an effect of its prior representations as is 'America'.

The European and American variants of these discourses make their way to their various sites by different routes. One way to summarily sketch their respective paths is to suggest that whereas Walter Benjamin's (1968: 217–51) 'The Work of Art in an Age of Mechanical Reproduction' could only have been written in Europe, Herman Melville's *The Confidence-Man* (1989) could only have been written in America. The former acquires its force from the *contrast* between the aura associated with a single, original artifact to which one must travel and the more secular plurality of a series that is able and available to circulate to multiple points of reception. Compare this with Melville's story. It is in no way predicated on the distinction between the original and the copy; its focus is not on the authenticity of the artifact but on the plausibility of the performance; a performance for which spatial mobility is a necessary condition. Where Benjamin emphasizes the transition from original to copy as a movement from religiosity to politics, Melville probes the moral import of the relation between making it and faking it at the frontiers of a money culture. His novel pivots on the closing words of Chapter 43, in which the river boat barber William Cream, having been creamed by Frank Goodman, philanthropist, citizen of the world (and of course con-man) tells of an encounter with Goodman such that 'all his friends united in thinking him QUITE AN ORIGINAL' (capitals in original). Chapter 44 is entitled 'In Which The Last Three Words of the Last Chapter are Made the Text of Discourse, Which Will be Receiving More or Less Attention From Those Readers Who Do Not Skip It'. This latter chapter interrupts the narrative, plays with the relation of fact and fiction, and interrogates the veracity of the phrase as employed by the barber's friends – in a form which exemplifies what it attempts to describe – that there are no guarantees of authenticity. In other words, the meaning of 'original fake' was known to Melville in 1857. His zestful, vertiginous story is, moreover, part of that long, long line which threads through American popular culture (Lindberg 1982) up to Gordon Gekko, the public personae of Oliver North, Ronald Reagan and beyond.

Both the Benjamin and Melville texts can now productively be applied to understanding conditions on the side of the Atlantic other than their own. Read this way, what Eco could be said to find appealing about the Getty museum is that it is informed by Benjamin's sense and sensibility of transition. And what could be said to be disturbing about the fictional 1980s British television journalist who is the duplicitous protagonist of Ayres and McEwans' *The Ploughman's Lunch* is his resemblance to Melville's American con-man from a 130 years earlier.

It would seem that the presence of a diffusely sedimented agedness (Eco's 'the Past') helps to sustain the presumption of authenticity, and since this is a terrain on which America finds it difficult to compete, it forms part of Eco's explanation as to why the hyperreal flourishes there. But he also recognizes that the relation between the two terms is a contingent rather than a necessary one, prompting him, for example, to question whether a bronze recasting of a sculpture can meaningfully be called a fake. To which should be added that the distinction between restoration and reconstruction has likewise come to appear increasingly permeable. A traveller in England might therefore wonder how Eco would adjudicate as to the status of restored Tudor houses which are so pristinely black and white as to evoke not so much the notion of austerely pre-modern Elizabethan as waywardly (and hence perhaps post) modern Mondrian.

For Eco, authenticity is, finally, a judgement on the integrity of a practice rather than a property which is immanent in material artifacts. In his brief contrast between the Hearst Castle at San Simeon and that of King Ludwig at Neuschwanstein he refers to the latter as 'a total fake (but thus more authentic)', proclaiming it to be 'completely Gothic as Gothic was understood in the later nineteenth century' (Eco 1987: 34). Eco's own virtuoso reasonableness distances him both from Hearst's compulsively eclectic, voraciously acquisitive megalomania and from Ludwig's unremittingly single-minded, bankruptcy-inducing madness. But as between them it is Ludwig who comes off best, notwithstanding that it is the Hearst castle which contains a great many genuine artifacts.

Yet despite Eco's accomplished casuistry, Ludwig's Neuschwanstein does nevertheless pose some unsettling questions, questions which arise from the intersection of its historical meaning and its present use. It is the most popular tourist attraction in Bavaria and the very icon of German romanticism, its image displayed on anything from Japanese telephone cards to British chocolate bar wrappers. It was also, together with the cathedral of Notre Dame, the inspiration for Disney's cartoon (and subsequently theme park) representation of the Sleeping Beauty's fairy-tale castle. The physical site at which these two clusters of associations can most clearly be seen to meet and merge is the Meguro Emperor 'love-hotel' in downtown Tokyo (Crescimbene 1991: 32) whose exterior is a full-scale replica of Bavaria's own original fake. This building literally signals a cementing in place of the discursive interdependency of what are, respectively, these manic and Magic Kingdoms. It is a localized material confirmation of a globalized conjuncture of images, ideas and practices whose nodes are sited in Hollywood and in Germany, in cinema and in tourism, in theme parks and in national imagining.

It is, however, Neuschwanstein's foundational fakery rather than its more recent appropriation which, for Eco, brings it within the orbit of his essay. The French have their own version of such a historic simulacrum. More than two centuries before the construction of Euro-Disney, Marie Antoinette had arranged for the Queen's Hamlet to be built at the Petit Trianon at Versailles. It consisted of a dozen architect-designed thatched cottages grouped around a lake in an imitation of the native Austria of her childhood. It was here that she and her friends played at being peasants by eating (cake rather than ploughman's lunch?)

out of doors, minding sheep and making butter. In their hyperreal simulations of the past an eccentric German king's folly and a French queen's amusement park predate their American counterparts. In America their originating principles of aristocratic restrictedness were not so much democratized as commercialized. It is when such hierarchical orderings of taste engage with the operation of markets that a concern with authenticity becomes particularly pressing. Eco's essay explores such clashes in America, but with a sub-textual awareness of their European workings. It is this latter which I have chosen to foreground. For if his account of Italy's thaumaturgic underground demonstrated just how extensively the myths of the supernatural have been commercialized then, as Benetton's advertising insinuates, can the histories of the real now be far behind?

4

ON FIRST BUYING INTO
MUNICH'S BMW 325iA

C. Wright Mills owned a BMW. So did Professor Siegfried von Tirpitz in David Lodge's satirical novel *Small World* (1984). And so did I.

Together with Hans Gerth, Wright Mills might be said to have translated the machinery of Frankfurt School thought into an American academic idiom. As far as the American popular press was concerned, however, his more immediate achievement consisted of using Munich's machinery to puncture the conventional image of the academic. They began to publish photographs of him, suitably clad in goggles, leather jacket and boots, riding his BMW motorbike to classes at Columbia (Scimecca 1977: 17), no doubt with an eye to invoking that cluster of rebellious associations which was given paradigmatic expression by Marlon Brando's portrayal of *The Wild One*.

David Lodge makes a no less conscious use of the social semiotics of modern means of transportation. It is, for example, important to the narrative development, character delineation and dust jacket design of his novel *Nice Work* (1988) that his English businessman drives a Jaguar and his female English Literature lecturer drives a Renault. In the airport lounges, hotel rooms and lecture theatres which form the landscape of *Small World*'s academic conference circuit, however, the inhabitants are for the most part obliged to indicate difference by other means. Professor von Tirpitz's distinctiveness is thus first demarcated not by his car, but by a perpetually black-gloved hand. Amongst the inhabitants of the conference circuit, this is widely understood to signify something unspeakable in his past. The effect on the reader of such a sleight of hand – or should that read slip of the tongue – is that the professor is transmuted into Dr Strange(g)love. It is nevertheless by way of the impassive Teutonic aggression with which he drives his black BMW 635CSi coupe that this purportedly unspeakable past is transcribed into astonishment and terror in the present. For von Tirpitz speeds along the autobahn at a steady one hundred and eighty kilometres an hour, moving so swiftly, so silently and so intimidatingly close to whatever vehicle is ahead of him as to entirely fill its rear view mirror with the BMW's looming bonnet and windscreen.

It is an image which both derives from, and subtly deconstructs, a series of advertisements which the company ran in Britain during the 1960s and 1970s under the copyline 'Move Over For BMW'. Described by Stephen Bayley (1986: 73) as 'loutishly assertive . . . pushy and irresponsible', it was subsequently replaced by a campaign which centred on an altogether less aggressive Milton Keynes professional who lives in an architect designed house, understands electronics and likes to go skiing. In Lodge's appropriation and reworking of the theme of the earlier campaign, he explicitly excises the adverts' recourse to a rear view mirror filled with glaring lights on main beam. His Professor von Tirpitz intimidates, 'not by flashing his lights (which is forbidden by law)' (Lodge 1984: 111) but by stealth. The effect, which is barely leavened by the satirical tone, is to sardonically amplify, rather than dampen down, the sense of threat by making it more nearly official than merely anti-social. For the imagery of power, speed and unexpected menace is now wedded to a clinically controlled aggression that is expressed through the exercise of a disturbingly impersonal, state-sanctioned, or at least formally legitimated, technical efficiency.

At one level this contrast between BMW as the signifier both of a romantic, radical academic populism and a villainous aristo-technocratic elitism is little more than the contrast between 'Two wheels good, four wheels bad', a cyborgian permutation on, and reversal of, the 'Four legs good, two legs bad' formula of George Orwell's *Animal Farm* – albeit with not a hog in sight. But what if the signs were to be reversed, and we were to put Wright Mills behind the wheel of that black 635CSi, so that he becomes a P.J. O'Rourke of the Left? What remains intact is the notion of a rebellious or deviant taste, of a break with the implicit cultural principle that BMWs and academics from the humanities cannot be made to mix. Wright Mills (1963: 568–576) may once have cryptically suggested that IBM + Reality + Humanism = Sociology, but there is no corresponding equation for BMW + Representation + The Humanities. The latter simply does not compute. In the relevant faculties of the English-speaking academy a (safe, reliable, Swedish, expensive) Volvo may be permitted – can even be aspired to – but not a (fast, reliable, German, expensive) BMW. This is because it is only from within a social category which combines relative affluence with social estrangement that an ageing rustbucket can be made to represent an aesthetic of resistance/indifference. A rust-resistant Volvo offers a somewhat less positively sanctioned but manifestly more practical permutation on this culturally prescribed aesthetic that also just happens to be more upmarket. This is congruent with one of Volvo's advertising slogans in America as 'The car for people who think', and with it the invocation of what one of Volvo's British advertising copywriters called 'the prestige of intellect rather than the prestige of money' (Bayley 1986: 89). Its correlate is an eschewing of visual appeal in favour of a positive valorizing, even fetishizing, of a dour, plain look that is both an intrinsic value and a proxy for sturdiness, depth and dependability. A Volvo is not – at those prices – classless, but – semiotically, at least – transclass; a workhorse with an expensive pedigree. Four wheels better.

This is to arrive at a familiar location by way of a circuitous route. The point is, of course, that the specific technical purpose of a vehicle may be to act as means of transportation but that this instrumentality is intertwined with its more general cultural function of acting as a carrier of social meanings. It is what prompted Wolfgang Sachs' (1992: 219) exasperated and environmentalist-sanctioned observation that 'High-performance motorization has as much to do with transportation requirements as Gothic cathedrals did with shelter from inclement weather. Speed machines are the material expression of the religion of progress'. This intentionally nods towards Roland Barthes' earlier and less ecological, more obviously wry and ironic, suggestion that cars are the contemporary equivalent of Gothic cathedrals, 'the supreme creation of an era, conceived with passion by unknown artists and consumed in image if not in usage by a whole population which appropriates them as a purely magical object' (Barthes 1973: 88). What may be experienced as 'purely magical' is, however, not simply given but must be won. It not only depends upon the complicity of the target audience but is also the product of both elaborate staging and tacit assumptions. Cars may have come to be identified with such enduring verities as power, sex and money – and the magical strategies that the desire for them provokes – but these associations are not intrinsic and nor do they come ready made. Such meanings must be fabricated.

Consider nationality. What Barthes (1977a: 32–51) called the classical 'Italianicity' of a Panzani advertisement – with its image of a string shopping bag containing pasta, onions, green peppers and ripe red tomatoes in the appropriate national colours of the Italian flag – has a modern counterpart in the contemporary 'Germanness' of a BMW or a Mercedes Benz. The richly coloured ingredients which surround the tin of Panzani concentrate are intended to forge a link between a manufactured object and organic materials, by investing them both with the myth of naturality and the colours of nationality – stilled life perhaps, but still life.

The Germanness which these cars signify, however, whether as object or as image, involves no such cooptation of nature in the service of culture. On the contrary, they unequivocally proclaim themselves as artifacts, as made. Moreover, throughout the 1980s what helped to signify that they were German-made was not so much their colours *per se* but rather the engineering of an internal consistency in the relation *between* colour and the cars as technical artifacts. That is to say, nationality was indicated by a design logic in which their body colour, like the body work itself, seemed to be built into the vehicles, rather than something applied to them. What we were intendedly induced to see was not so much a covering of paint as a burnishing of metal (gunmetal bronze, steel grey, lach silver) or the repudiation of the principle of colour as decoration, or as something added (black, white). It is a design feature which could generate in most of us that plausible circularity by which colour deviations from this modal tendency did indeed seem deviant. The engineered effect, as with BMW's canting of the central control panel towards the driver, or as with its (robot-welded) doors which obliquely call attention to their (laser-determined) goodness of fit, was a signalling of the vehicle's seriousness of purpose. Accordingly, and flatteringly, this corresponded with a discursive positioning of the driver, both as someone to also be taken seriously and as someone who incidentally, but none the less axiomatically, was as well groomed as the car itself. Such an inflection and secularization of what might be called the Lodge/von Tirpitz principle of combining control and menace strives to fuse the technical attributes of the vehicle with a political presumption about its class of owners and their characteristics. Both the vehicle and those who drive it are constructed as custodians of a combination of power to spare and a disciplined restraint in its exercise.

From within the singularity of this upmarket, German design philosophy, however, what BMW also sought to do was to position their vehicles, and by implication and extension their owners, as sportier, as solid but not stolid, as both materially and semiotically less heavy and less obviously Teutonic than the corresponding Mercedes Benz models. The company's own market research in the American, European and Japanese markets points to a pattern in which BMW buyers are, on average, younger (by five years in Japan, eleven in America), more likely to be graduates, less likely to be married and to earn somewhat less (around 75 per cent in America, around 90 per cent in Europe) than the buyers of the equivalent Mercedes model (BMW 1991a). Wolfgang Sachs' (1992: 117) acerbic suggestion that 'the ambitious prefer high performance vehicles [in order] to score a victory, and the successful [in order] to avoid having to accept a defeat – that is the difference between BMW and Mercedes owners', may be at odds with the tone in which such findings are presented, but it nevertheless seems congruent with their substance. Within Germany itself, such a process of distinguishing the two brands from one another is further facilitated by the cultural associations of BMW's Bavarian location (Olins 1989: 90).

In the rest of the world, the extent to which BMW and Mercedes Benz have come to stand for both German automobiles and for Germany, suggests that we have travelled some distance from that time when Volkswagen (VW) first sought to establish a market for its (now classic) small car in America. At that time the American norm was a huge saloon with tail fins and lots of chrome, embraced by consumers but disdained both then and now by critics (cf. however, Armi 1988). VW relied upon a (now classic) advertising campaign which consciously played upon the scepticism of American car buyers by picturing the Beetle as a lemon. Volkswagen's lemon was an altogether more whimsical image than Panzani's pasta, peppers and onions. It was, of course, intended to be read as a knowing and wholly metaphorical reference to popular slang rather than to actual fruit; to another discourse rather than to the natural world. For inasmuch as the humble VW was in any way lemon-like – as, for example, was affectionately insinuated by the Disney studio's waywardly auto-kinetic Herbie – then it was none the less a lemon that ran like clockwork. Thus although it may have been marketed in America (and duly appropriated by Hollywood) as a cheap fun(ny) car, it is none the less genealogically linked to its more contemporary and more upmarket compatriots by the designer Ferdinand Porsche in particular, but more generally by that discursive thread which foregrounds engineering know-how and functionality of design. That same thread metonymically marks the rise of West Germany to a position of economic power and a role as a major player in the world economy.

Herbie was an anthropomorphized image of playful German machinery which could run and run and run, an image which travelled around the world by courtesy of the cultural hegemony of the American film industry. By the 1990s, something like the kind of affection which Hollywood had earlier bestowed upon the VW Beetle was discernible in *Go Trabi Go!*, a film made with a kind of ironic nostalgia by an East German studio. It centred upon the (post-1989) holiday travels and mishaps of an East German family in an East German car, the two cylinder Trabant (Wark 1994: 92–3). After the fall of the Berlin Wall the poorly designed, fault prone and underpowered Trabant was identified by the media of the West as an icon of the failure of the system which produced it. The film mocks the car too, but in a tone that is warmer and without condescension.

By contrast with Trabi, Herbie had always been *productively* wayward, located firmly on the side of (mechanical) reliability rather than ridicule. But for those subsequent cohorts of children for whom *Star Wars* had provided the defining images of magical machinery, Herbie's basically 1930s look might nevertheless appear as more nearly quaint than cute. Thus when the American designers and programmers of 'Where in Time is Carmen Santiago?', an early and best-selling example of educational computer software, required an absolutely reliable means of time travel and rapid global transportation, then a Herbie clone would not do. They were instead led to construct, from within the archive of science fictional possibilities, something called a Chronoskimmer. This machine's 325i suffix, however, linked it semiotically to the realm of extant German engineering fact, a fact whose material embodiment as a BMW 3-Series sports saloon might well grace the driveways and express the culture (cf. Rogers and Larsen 1984) of the software's affluent and technology conscious designers.

Such a choice of insignia by the Californian counterparts of that (no doubt Californian-influenced) Milton Keynes professional may have been the result of a deliberate stratagem of product placement, akin to that by which a BMW was subsequently to displace James Bond's Aston Martin in the film *Goldeneye*. This was assuredly a somewhat shrewder marketing ploy than the rueful acknowledgement by the chairman of Aston Martin Lagonda that, 'a BMW is as well engineered as one of his own cars when the price differential can be as much as $100,000' (Dormer 1990: 124). But perhaps that 325i suffix was simply a serendipitously matter-of-fact by-product of processes of evaluation within the relevant high-tech occupational community. After all, Steve Jobs, the co-founder of Apple Computer, was in the habit of parking his BMW – which, like C. Wright Mills' was a motor cycle – in the lobby of his company's Macintosh building. For Robert Cringeley (1993: 194), the micro computing industry's unofficial historian, it thus constituted 'an ever present reminder of who was boss. It was a renegade operation and proud of it' presided over by 'the most dangerous man in Silicon Valley' (Cringeley 1993: 182).

Read one way, these are illustrations of the multiple paths along which the prestige of the BMW company has seeped incrementally into the wider culture. Read another, they become examples of the multiplying traces of its rise to a position of global significance as a manufacturer of upmarket automobiles and motor cycles.

The beginnings of BMW were as a manufacturer of aircraft engines, an origin which leaves its trace in the stylized propellers of its blue and white badge work and identifying motif. The company began to concentrate on car and motor-cycle production when it was subject to prohibitions on armaments production under the Treaty of Versailles. This move resulted in the introduction of their technically innovative flat twin motor cycle in 1923 (Bayley 1985: 100), a design classic by Max Friz which was to commend itself to C. Wright Mills, and which was to remain basically unaltered until its replacement by the K100 RS in 1984. During the 1930s and the 1940s BMW became an influential arms producer whose plants were seized at the end of the war. But as the company was privately owned the plants were soon returned to their owners and civilian production was resumed.

The post-war *Wirtschaftswunder* or German economic miracle is closely identified with the success of the German automobile industry. Yet for some fifteen years after the war BMW's performance proved to be disastrous. Badly managed and short of capital, the company recorded a loss of DM12 million in 1958 and by 1959 its market share had slumped to less than 2 per cent. Faced with impending bankruptcy it approached Daimler-Benz in the hope of a merger. The negotiations prompted a takeover offer from the British firm GEC at a price which Daimler-Benz could not match. Whereupon the Bavarian state government stepped in, bought the company, and then orchestrated a successful bid from the German firm NAM which matched GEC's offer. Under the new management the company began to prosper. By 1967 this formerly unprofitable maker of endearingly quirky bubble cars under licence had transformed itself into a company which had doubled its share of the German car market and massively expanded export sales of its motor cycles (Reich 1990: 254–7).

Throughout the 1970s, and OPEC price rises notwithstanding, BMW was the fastest growing car company in Europe, and began to reap the benefits of having a strongly networked, single large shareholder (the Quandt family) with a long-term outlook (Womack *et al.* 1990: 19). It entered into this major expansion phase with the launch of its 5-series in 1972, the same year in which Munich had hosted the Olympic Games from a newly built stadium that was close to the car maker's own new headquarters building. This was followed by the 3-series in 1975 and the 7-series in 1977, thereby establishing a core pattern of three distinct principal model lines. The 6-series coupe which lasted from 1976 to 1989, and the 8-series which followed it, were sports cars selling in small numbers and designed to compete with Porsche and the relevant Mercedes models. Both the core pattern and the 3–5–7 nomenclature have persisted up until the present day. Since the life cycle of these model lines has been about eight to ten years, each of them and the overall tripartite structure have now been reproduced through into a third generation of models. Around 65 per cent of these have been 3-series, some 25 per cent have been 5-series, and the 7-series has made up about 10 per cent, with the precise ratios varying as new models were introduced or old ones neared the end of their cycle (Dymock 1990: 185). What has also been established along with this pattern has been the principle of overlapping engine sizes (and overlapping prices) as between the 3- and 5-series, and between the 5- and 7-series.

As a consequence this model range, and the marketing strategy which informs it, effectively represents not just the pyramidal structure, but also the functioning, of a stratification system. Vehicular and social mobility are semiotically linked; social categorization is signalled through mechanical performance and bodily appearance. The strategy itself had first been developed in the 1920s and implemented in the 1930s by General Motors (GM) against Ford. As Alfred Sloan, the then head of GM had put it, 'The core of the [GM] product policy [lay] in its concept of producing a full line of cars graded upwards in quality and price' (cited in Rothschild 1974: 38). In the BMW version, this is refined into a system which signals common but differential membership through its combination of discrete designs and integrated design philosophy.

At the same time, however, all BMWs are what Hirsch (1977: 27–54) calls 'positional goods'. These are goods whose value to their owners depends importantly upon the fact that most of the population does not have them. Or as Hirshman (1979: 38) is prompted to observe in response to a BMW advert, 'such cars are precisely meant to enhance the stimulation function in relation to the want satisfaction function (by offering) a somewhat superior driving experience and the satisfaction of feeling superior to the great mob of motorists'. Where satisfactions are relative to others in this way, then they decline as more people acquire them. To the extent to which the formal democracy of money and an expanding material economy leads to an extension of ownership, then this has the effect of threatening values in this positional economy. The BMW model range is constructed across just such a structural dilemma and this finds expression through a balancing act between seeking to expand membership of the system (i.e. increasing sales) and maintaining the exclusivity on which the survival of the system depends (i.e. limiting sales). The hierarchical ordering of models thus becomes both a means of control and a channel of upward mobility, in which there seems to be an inverse relationship between the ever more nuanced gradations of vehicular refinement and the price to be paid for their acquisition. The steps from the entry level 316i to the 750iA at its apex, chart the route, and the boundary-blurring overlap between series signals both the openness and fluidity of the system and the option of choosing to trade off a measure of effective power for an enhancement of formal position (or vice versa). In such a refined milieu, however, excess must be understated. Its arcane correlate is the 'badge culture' of the insider, through which those small external signs of internal difference, the raised, chromium plated cod-pieces which specify engine capacity and type, provide the basis for the evaluation of the owner. A knowing permutation on this practice was recently directed at the readers of the high-tech magazine *Wired*. It featured an advertisement for Lexus cars in which the photograph foregrounded the company's web-site address by rendering it as the relevant chrome-plated insignia on the rear of one of their otherwise unadorned luxury saloons.

Such badgework, together with the entry of Japanese cars into this sector of the market – exemplified by that 'otherwise unadorned' Lexus – highlights a further problem which besets the design and marketing of artifacts which seem to be so explicitly and expensively devoted to the achievement of absolute standards and the realization of a modernist aesthetic. For whilst these cars are more or less intendedly dedicated to the material representation of social difference, they are also predicated upon and gravitate towards expressing the pure uniformities of scientific and technically-based design. For German manufacturers the latter's Bauhaus/Ulm School antecedents have now been wedded to the converging logics of CADCAM (computer-aided design and manufacture) and the wind-tunnel, in what Baudrillard (1981: 185–203) cryptically refers to as the Bauhaus-initiated escalation of 'political economy into cyberblitz'. Yet the market forces which were responsible for the exertion of this gravitational pull into the orbit of the modern also place limits on such entry going below the rarefied atmosphere of modern society's upper (social) levels. The fundamentals of high performance and precision engineering remain a necessity for the vehicles which populate these upper reaches, but in themselves these attributes are no longer sufficient to ensure the maintenance of such an elevated position.

This has become a pressing problem for German car makers in general and for BMW in particular. What presently distinguishes the German automobile industry is that it has the lowest level of industrial concentration in Europe, the highest costs of production and a low volume output of high margin products. All of the manufacturers are export orientated and from the mid-1980s through to the early 1990s all of them, from VW to Porsche, experienced declining sales in America, which is their largest and most crucial overseas market (Morales 1994: 116). This has accelerated the erosion of the traditional pattern of market segmentation in which the various German firms occupied largely discrete niches. This pattern had begun to come under pressure in the 1970s, when Mercedes and BMW each began to seriously encroach upon the traditional terrain of the other. In its turn, this blurring of boundaries is now overlaid by the extensive overlap between the top of the VW and Audi model ranges and the entry and mid-level Mercedes and BMW models (Reich 1990: 317–18). This latter development was, moreover, accompanied by advertising initiatives which, in Audi's case, made play with the phrase *Vorsprung durch Technik* (Progress through Technology) in a British campaign that was no less astute than Volkswagen's earlier American one (Bayley 1986: 93–100).

Read one way, the Audi advertising slogan might be understood as ironically harking back to Hitler's insistence that the Volkswagen be identified as the KdF or *Kraft durch Freude* (Power through Joy) vehicle. The slogan's efficacy did not, however, depend upon a knowledge of such historical specificities. Rather it served to invest the brand with a diffuse Germanness that the name 'Audi' had been perceived to lack, whilst the associated campaign acknowledged British ambivalence about Germany's post-war economic ascendancy. The Audi campaign thus sought to both capitalize upon Germany's reputation for technical efficiency and yet, by ironically playing with the associated imagery of a humourless thoroughness, to subordinate it to (the xenophobic conceit of) a more pragmatic, more hedonistic, more balanced, discourse of Britishness. It is therefore analogous to the principle at work in the purportedly Jewish humour of 'How did they lose?', comedian Mort Sahl's one line response to the German Pavilion at the New York World Fair, or in advertising man Jerry Della Femina's (1971) not entirely tongue-in-cheek suggestion that the slogan for the Sony account in America should be, 'From Those Wonderful Folks Who Gave You Pearl Harbor'.

Like these examples, Audi's campaign might be said to have been not just positioned, but poised, between Umberto Eco's light-hearted but exemplary definition of postmodernism and Dick Hebdige's necessarily more sombre reading of punk usage of the sign of the swastika. Eco had suggested that what distinguishes postmodernism is that it revalues the past 'but with irony not innocently'. It is expressed in the attitude of

> a man who loves a very cultivated women and knows he cannot say to her 'I love you madly' because he knows that she knows (and that she knows that he knows) that these words have already been written by Barbara Cartland. Still there is a solution. He can say 'As Barbara Cartland would put it, I love you madly' . . . (he) will have said . . . that he loves her, but he loves her in an age of lost innocence.
>
> (Eco 1985: 67)

Hebdige's (1979: 116–17) interpretation of the punk swastika is couched in a very different tone, in recognition that something much more sombre is at stake. But he likewise points to the wearing of a swastika as, in context, an instance of just such a second order signifying practice, as a recognition and exploitation of its efficacy as a sign which gives offence. Hebdige thus understands punk usage as polysemic, as an invocation of decadence, as a means of disrupting taken-for-granted cultural codes, and as signifying a loss of meaning, rather than as a signal of support for the practices and beliefs with which the swastika has been historically associated. The Audi campaign is predicated upon that related cluster of war time associations which 'German technology' still invokes in Britain, but it frames them with that light-heartedness which is at work in Eco's example. This in turn, however, is further framed by the very notion of advertising which, as Chapter 3 sought to demonstrate, is a discourse which carries its own set of historical associations and imposes its own limitations, so that it lacks that positive sanctioning and additional layering which Sahl's Jewishness gives to his rhetorical question.

Nevertheless, through its incremental extension of the language of advertising

on to such terrain, the Audi campaign did not just initiate a flow of material benefits to the company; it could be seen as a constitutive tracer of changes in the
culture of consumption. For example, by the end of the 1980s the Rover car
company was advertising its flagship Sterling sports saloon to would-be British
buyers by displaying it against the background of the Stuttgart Art Gallery – as
designed by British architect James Stirling. In what proved to be an ironic –
because unanticipated – anticipation of the subsequent purchase of the company
by BMW in 1994, the commercial consists largely of a conversation, in German,
between the car's new German owner and a suitably impressed colleague.

From the mid-1970s onwards what had been discernible in BMW's responses
to the build up of such market pressures was a series of incremental shifts in the
company's competitive centre of gravity and an associated loosening up of the
hegemony of Bauhausian modernity. For inasmuch as the universal and the true-
once-and-for-all leads to the same set of answers from competing enterprises with
lower margins and cost structures, then it becomes harder for a high cost, high
price producer to sell. The movements have therefore been from hardware
towards software, from materiality towards image, from the realm of mechanical
reproduction to the realm of simulation, from gravity to play. To trace the erratic
trajectories of these processes is to slide unobtrusively from the real to the hyperreal. But no matter how labyrinthine the milieu and how attenuated the
connection with the real world may have become, the thread back to it remains
unbroken, and is exemplified by those imperatives which have subsequently led
BMW to adapt and reorganize the production process itself. During the 1990s
the company's organizational response was to both further flatten its already hori-
zontal structure and to commit itself to a more international system of
production. First of all, some 55 to 75 per cent of total production costs are now
outsourced, mostly in the form of collaborative work with specialist subcontrac-
tors. Second, a new American plant has been established on a greenfield site in
Spartanburg, South Carolina, able to either subcontract to the established
European suppliers, or to link up with revitalized American firms or the newer
networks established by Japanese manufacturers in America (Morales 1994:
118–19). To hold on to this thread allows us to enter into the play of signs and
images, in the knowledge that they are not the monster at the heart of the system
but rather the products of a real Minotaur that is at once elsewhere and determinedly pulling strings of its own.

In their tactical flirtations with the hyperreal BMW have therefore not just
drawn upon German engineering in the design and manufacture of their cars; on
the densely networked infrastructure of a high skill tradition that is anchored in
co-determination and a developed system of vocational education (Streeck
1989). The very architecture of their Munich headquarters, in which the main
administration building, or the *Vierzylinder*, is shaped like four vertical cylinders,
suggests how they have also been willing to draw on the *idea* of German engineering (see Figure 4.1). The building's proximity to the city's Olympic stadium,
the near coincidental launch of the 5-series and the 1972 Munich Olympics,

Figure 4.1 The *Vierzylinder*, BMW's administrative building, Munich

suggests how they have knowingly played the German card as a marketing ploy. Almost from the beginning of BMW's upward accelerating sales curve, the Bauhaus/Ulm aesthetic was already placed in quotation marks. Not as a move beyond that notion of modernity for which it now stands, but as both a recognition of its (commercial) possibilities and as a hint of a preparedness to interrogate its (commercial) limits. It is a hint which is also given architectural expression. Standing next to the headquarters building is the BMW museum, a more modest edifice which takes its inspiration, and its spiral interior, from Frank Lloyd Wright's Guggenheim Museum. For those new car buyers who choose to collect their BMWs in Munich, a choice which includes an invitation to visit the factory itself, the museum is where the factory tour begins and ends. It not only houses vehicles from the company's past, not unexpectedly it displays the image of itself that the company wishes to convey in the present. Within this more general process of image production, the BMW collection of 'art cars' – cars which various well-known artists have been commissioned to paint – takes pride of place. As of 1996 there are fourteen such vehicles with the most recent addition having been painted by David Hockney, complete with stylized dachshund and driver.

These works of mechanical reproduction in an age of art now tour the world. They are intendedly auratic but designed to travel; regularly on the move but no longer driven. If Walter Benjamin (1968: 217–51) is read as seeking to grasp the meaning of industrialism and the effects of mechanical reproduction for and on the 'aura' and religiosity associated with art, then one can see why in another life this collection might have attracted his interest. For these cars point to the meaning of post-industrialism and the effects of sign values for, and on, mechanical perfectibility as a commercial ideal and its subtext of emancipation through the machine. Read one way they can be shrugged off as ephemera, the detritus of upmarket advertising; read another, they become indicators of a discourse functioning at the very limits of its applicability and showing signs of disturbance as a consequence.

The first of the BMW art cars dates from 1975, when the Frenchman Hervé Poulain, who had entered his BMW 3.0 CSL for the Le Mans 24-hour race, had the idea of having it decorated by a professional artist. In addition to being a racing car driver, Poulain was an auctioneer and the author of a book called *L'art et l'automobile* (1973). He was also a friend of the American sculptor Alexander Calder, who was resident in France at that time, and when BMW agreed to the art car idea it was Calder who was commissioned to do it. He was already well known for those artifacts for which Marcel Duchamp had been inspired to coin the term 'mobiles'. The word and the concept passed quickly into the language, and in 1973 Calder had attracted further attention as a result of his design for the exterior of a commercial aircraft for Braniff Airlines. Calder painted the car in those bright primary colours which were characteristic of his sculptures, but in a pattern that accorded with his own principles of composition rather than following the streamlining of the vehicle itself (see Figure 4.2).

The vehicle prompted sufficient interest and attention for BMW to follow it

Figure 4.2 Alexander Calder art car

within a year with another art car. A ferociously quick and powerful 750 bhp, turbo-charged version of the 3.0 CSL, this was also an entrant at Le Mans. The artist was Frank Stella (see Figure 4.3), an American best known for hard edge, non-figurative works painted on distinctively shaped canvases. Stella's early 'black' and 'aluminium' pictures had attracted critical attention for their mini-malist aspirations to an absolute flatness, but in the 'protractor' series of the 1960s (the reference is to the shape of the canvases) he had retreated from such a theoretically ordained imperative. In these works he thus allowed for the legiti-macy of illusion. It was, however, illusion understood as something purely visual, as the invocation of a sensation of depth rather than the representation of solid objects (Walker 1975: 7).

What Stella did with his art car was to superimpose an overall black and white grid of squares on to its metal external surfaces so that it had the appearance of being covered with outsize graph paper. A series of geometric shapes were then painted on to this grid in bold black lines, not as a preamble to the work, but as its substance. The effect is one of technical drawings which faithfully follow the outlines of a draughtsperson's aids (such as protractors), of patterns for cutting the metal into alternate shapes. At one level Stella's car could thus be seen as a commentary on Calder's. Calder was a sculptor who had been confronted with the intractability of an object that was (al)ready made. He had painted his car in accordance with his own developed artistic style, as if seeking to subordinate its shape to the shapes and colours that he painted on it, to resist the logic of the

Figure 4.3 Frank Stella art car

medium. Stella's response had been to think through the implications which such givenness had for his objectives as a painter. Hence his use of that most elemental of a modernist painter's methods, the grid, so as to create the explicitly illusionary flatness of a black and white, two dimensional graph paper motif on such a 'strongly' three dimensional object. In Rosalind Krauss' definitive formulation:

> The grid states the autonomy of the realm of art. Flattened, geometricized, ordered, it is antinatural, antimimetic, antireal. It is what art looks like when it turns its back on nature. In the flatness that results from its coordinates, the grid is the means of crowding out the dimensions of the real and replacing them with the lateral spread of a single surface . . . . The grid declares the space of art to be at once autonomous and autotelic.
>
> (1986: 9–10)

Read in this way, what the BMW catalogue (1991b: 15) interprets as Stella's reserved and modest observation that 'The resulting colored pattern should be regarded as agreeable decoration' becomes a conscious, deliberate and thoroughly painterly aspiration. In Stella's car an autotelic, aesthetic modern*ism* engages with an automobile, Bauhausian modern*ity*.

In 1977 the chosen artist was Roy Lichtenstein; his canvas was a racing version of the 320i (see Figure 4.4). It debuted as a race car at the 24-hour race at Le Mans and as an art object at the Pompidou Centre in Paris (the Calder and Stella

Figure 4.4 Roy Lichtenstein art car

cars having been exhibited at the Louvre). The Lichtenstein vehicle featured a stylized image of the sun, road markings and comic strip style 'speedlines', interspersed with the Benday dots which had been characteristic of his best-known pop art paintings. The Andy Warhol car (see Figure 4.5) which followed in 1979 was also a Le Mans entrant. Warhol broke with the established pattern of doing a preliminary painting on a scaled down model which was then duly transposed to the vehicle itself by the spray painter Walter Maurer whom BMW had commissioned to work to the artists' design. Warhol both painted everything himself and did so without recourse to a draft or mock-up version. The entire process took less than half an hour, with Warhol employing just one brush and using his fingers to smear lines into the blocks of colour that he had applied to the M1 series coupe. In breaking with this methodological convention, Warhol's method of working also contrasted with the approach that had come to be associated with The Factory, the artist's New York studio in which the production of art had been organized (and hence problematized) along industrial lines, by being made reliant upon photomechanical reproduction and teams of assistants. Confronted with so consummate a work of mechanical reproduction, both Warhol's artistic practice and his verbal response were tantamount to confirming the irrelevance of the traditionally modern conception of the artist. When BMW (1991b: 23) asked him if he was pleased with the outcome, Warhol observed that 'I adore the car; it's much better than a work of art'. By not deigning to do the expected, Warhol had made of 'disappointment' a statement of sorts. Not unexpectedly, the company nevertheless attempted to recruit the resultant product and to position its producer within a conventional high modernism discourse by emphasizing spontaneity, directness and the imprint of character and personal style, although it is the absence of the latter which might be said to define the work.

The first four art cars were thus all Le Mans entrants and all had been produced by American artists with established international reputations. Not only were the cars introduced at a time when the discourses of art and advertising were still recognizably discrete from one another, they also combined the high culture cachet of art with the selection of artists with a reputation for works whose surfaces were either decorative, or accessible, or both. Moreover, although the direct advertising of sponsors' names was already an established feature of race cars in America, it was only just beginning to appear on European race tracks. Through the operation of that general principle by which taste classifies (Bourdieu 1984) the art cars, by proclaiming their distance from (the more vulgar characteristics of) the market, served to position BMW at the upper end of the market.

The art cars of the 1970s were intendedly racing vehicles which had incidentally been decorated; extensions of a competition programme that was, in its turn an extension of marketing, research and development programmes. But even before they were retired from the race track they had begun to acquire a different kind of momentum in another set of circuits. The Calder car may have been powered largely by the value of novelty and a proper name, but the Stella car had made its wit and intelligence so widely accessible as to no doubt confirm the

Figure 4.5 Andy Warhol art car

potential benefits of the art car theme to BMW. As for the Lichtenstein car, there was something almost symmetrical about the happenstance by which it debuted in the same year as the Pompidou Centre itself. For the car seemed well nigh made for the building in which it was first displayed, a building that, in defiance of Baudrillard's (1982) bizarre reading of it, became almost from the outset an icon for the notion of a bridge between high and popular culture (Sudjic 1994: 55). During the 1970s the art cars thus became constitutive cultural tracers of a blur-ring of the boundaries between advertising and art, the museum and the market, European and American culture, the high and the popular, in a process to which not even Warhol's studied blankness was immune.

The art cars of the 1980s and early 1990s were characterized by further shifts of emphasis. The idea of decorated race-cars was displaced either by the painted versions of pristine production models or by racing versions of production models that were only painted *after* they had ended their time on the race-track. There was also something of a hiatus, with the Warhol car of 1979 and Robert Rauschenberg's 635CSi of 1986 separated only by the 635CSi which the Austrian Ernest Fuchs painted in 1982. This latter presaged a more explicitly globalizing strategy, both in the sense that the cars began to travel to exhibitions in such loca-tions as Tokyo and New York, and in that the Rauschenberg vehicle was to be followed by cars painted by Australian, Japanese, Spanish, German, South African, Italian and British artists. This was presumably not unrelated to that falling off in American sales which occurred during the mid-1980s, just as the rapid growth of the 1970s had previously established America as the single most important export market. By the mid-1990s American sales were again on the rise (albeit after dipping dramatically in 1993) and global sales of BMWs have continued to expand (Taylor 1996).

Much the most critically important of this second generation of art cars was that painted by Michael Jagamara Nelson – and his wife – in 1989 (see Figure 4.6). Jagamara Nelson is a member of the Papunya group of artists whose work has been responsible for first securing an established place for Australian Aboriginal art within the international art market. In the opening words of Eric Michaels' essay on 'Bad Aboriginal Art', 'During 1987 the Australian press reported frequently that Aboriginal art, especially Western Desert acrylic "dot paintings", had become flavour of the month in New York, Paris and Munich' (1988: 47). Michaels argues forcefully against the positioning of Western Desert acrylics and their Aboriginal painters ethnographically, as leading to a valorization of primitivism and with it an interpretation of the use of acrylic paint and canvas as somehow less authentic. Michaels points out that authenticity is not the issue. His thesis is that these works engage with the (post)modern world at every level, in ways that are at once thoroughly contemporary, legitimate, knowing and counter-appropriative. They do so by drawing upon a body of distinctive creative and authorial practices. Michaels summarizes these as involving; first, an ideology of *re*production and the repudiation of individually based creative authority; second, the principle that rights to paint certain designs are earned or inherited, they do not die out with the death of a particular artist; third, the notion that although unauthorized appropriation is both possible and a problem, plagiarism is not; and fourth, design traditions are held collectively. Michaels' specific focus is upon Warlpiri acrylics from Yuendumu, but he builds his case by drawing upon the overall affinities with, influences of, and detailed differences from, the nearby Papunya artists. For example, he contrasts the 'muted, cerebral' neatness of Papunya with the 'sloppy, gestural' Yuendumu product and plots this distinction against the relations between the two communities, their links to art advisers, and the concomitant temporal shift from minimalism to neo-expressionism in the international art market. Such differences matter, but the crucial commonalities are, as Bob Lingard (1989: 20) puts it, that, 'Aboriginal art is neither authorial, representational nor "inspired". Rather it is conceptual in the fullest sense of the term'.

That BMW chose to commission not one, but two Australian art cars at the same time prefigures their exoticizing of the Jagamara Nelson car. Jagamara Nelson was both initially selected and subsequently positioned as a 'native' artist, as against that reassuringly familiar 'typically Australian . . . vitality and optimism' (BMW 1991b: 39) represented by Ken Done and the car that he painted. The Jagamara Nelson car resists the cosiness and closure of such a categorization. This is *not* because it lies outside it as its other – the 'other' to 'typical Australian vitality and optimism' sounds alarmingly like Carlyle's advice to 'lie still and think of England'. Nor even because the decision to choose two Australian artists tacitly

Figure 4.6 Michael Jagamara Nelson art car

testifies to that social division between indigenous and colonial which such 'typical' terminology strives to efface. And certainly *not* because so thoroughly social and communally sanctioned a work is somehow explicable as the product of an estranged, alienated, individual(istic) artist at odds with his culture. Rather it is because the work straddles so many discourses as to expressly bring into question such traditional ways of reading and offers an aesthetic challenge to the distinctions which a conventional critical language strives to maintain, such as modern/primitive, novel/derivative, artist/laity, authentic/complicit, representation/simulation.

For example, the usual reading of the dots as the characteristic which defines and distinguishes such acrylic paintings sits uneasily with the routine, matter of fact way in which the task of adding them to the work may be delegated to others. Moreover, the dots were often not a feature of the ground and body painting from which these works evolved. Michaels (1988: 57) refers to them as 'background, mere fill' and this is consistent with the remarks which Michael Jagamara Nelson makes about the art car in a 1990 documentary film called *Market of Dreams* which Kate Kennedy Smith had directed for the Australian Broadcasting Corporation. Nelson both recruits his wife's aid to the time consuming task of dot making on the vehicle and offhandedly indicates that the acceptability of this practice derives from the dots being incidental to the main design.

He also observes that the specifics of the art car painting were prompted by the experience of flying across the Australian landscape. This resurfaces in BMW's (1991b: 35) catalogue notes as the suggestion that 'Papunya paintings be understood as aerial views of landscapes' which nevertheless 'simultaneously embody religious myths ("dreamings") which have been handed down . . . for thousands of years'. Thus even before taking account of the car as a canvas, and its manufacturer as patron, the painting is already a conceptually elusive and allusive bricolage; both history *and* myth, both contemporary *and* archaic, both contingent *and* archetypal. The effect is not so much to shrug off definitions as to straddle them – pre-colonial, post-colonial; this worldly, other worldly; global culture, local culture; of the market and a commentary on it. Notions of authorship and originality are likewise confounded by the painting practices themselves, so that in the very process of consummating a work which BMW (1991b: 35) designates as a 'masterpiece', the terms and terminology of the exchange between artist and patron are interrogated.

With respect to all of the BMW art cars it is clear that any understanding of this exchange between artists and patron must be seen as powerfully skewed in favour of BMW, an exchange in which congruity, whether pre-existing or otherwise, is represented through the modal tendency toward the tastefully decorated object. What distinguishes the Jagamara Nelson and Andy Warhol cars is that they constitute the limit cases, the works which are most explicit in signalling the relations in which they are implicated. Thus the Warhol car had been produced through practices which were at odds both with The (Warhol) Factory's postmodernist working conventions of reproduction and imitation and with BMW's expectations of how the work should proceed. The entire process had taken some twenty-eight minutes – slightly beyond the duration of Warhol's now famous maxim that 'in the future everyone will be famous for fifteen minutes' – but nevertheless altogether too quick for the television crews who had gathered with the intention of recording the event. It was all over by the time they had set up their equipment. By comparison it is the Jagamara Nelson car which emerges as inventively postmodern in its attempt to negotiate the contrasts and contradictions between the conditions of its production and the circumstances of its reception – not by (a)bridging them but by displaying them. And it took a full seven days to paint.

It is therefore instructive to compare the questions posed by such a Michaels' influenced reading of the Jagamara Nelson car with Tom Wolfe's (1968: 63–85) innovative account of the custom-car milieu and its artifacts as they emerged in Los Angeles in the 1950s. For what distinguishes Wolfe's interpretation is his willingness to consider such custom cars, and the practices through which they are produced, as something other than subcultural curios or ethnographic exotica. They are instead seen as both an aesthetic challenge to all that Detroit and its products are seen to represent and yet nevertheless implicated in a complex exchange with the industry and its representatives. Wolfe's (1968: 70) notorious antipathy towards aesthetic modernism leads him into a perverse, strained and hostile characterization of Detroit's cars and their designers as 'pure Mondrian'. Its correlate, however, is a receptiveness to the practice and products of customizing which allows him to see its constitutive cultural and aesthetic vitality as both responsible for its subsequent impact upon the main manufacturers and as necessarily grounded in an estrangement from them. The relevant affinities between the foregoing account of Aboriginal art and Wolfe's excursion into the car culture of California customizers are, of course, affinities of method; any similarities in the social organization and cultural practices of their respective subject communities are either wholly fortuitous or decidedly tenuous. But inasmuch as they coalesce around the car as a cultural icon and art object, then the method does reveal suggestive analogies and shared concerns. Thus Wolfe (1968: 75) casts the customizers, their customers and their culture in the role of Dionysians, 'who feel alienated and resentful when confronted with the (sophistication of that Apollonian) Anglo-European ethos' that is professional automobile design. And he documents, celebrates and anxiously contemplates the future of the customizers' negotiated resistance to the blandishments and cooptation strategies of Detroit, seeing that resistance as of a piece with the cultural milieu which sustains customizing as a practice. A closely related, and updated, concern appears in one of Eric Michael's other essays on Aboriginal art. It closes with the observation that:

> Contemporary production processes are so highly evolved that they can be programmed to vary slightly each product of an assembly line, so no two 'designer' Chevrolets are exactly alike ... The frightening possi-

bility involves the attempts to turn Aboriginal painters into manufacturing machines of a similar order.

(1989: 34)

It is indeed the case that every BMW now produced at the Munich factory has a computer chip attached to its chassis which allows it to be 'customized' from within the full range of available specifications and in accordance with the requirements of individual purchasers. It is also the case that Wolfe and Michael have justifiable and legitimate fears as to the future of, and for, those practitioners for whom they speak. But both such novel production processes and such well-grounded fears derive from the system-wide and systemic uncertainties that are generated by precisely that enhanced reliance/dependence upon image production which Zukin (1991) has theorized as the transition *from* the world of Detroit *to* Disneyworld. BMW's development provides a tracer of how one specialized car company has sought to accommodate to, and to capitalize upon, that process.

Wolfe's main informant had been George Barris, a custom car maker whose body shop was responsible for Herbie, the first Batmobile and the hot rods which had featured in the film *Rebel Without a Cause*. James Dean subsequently commissioned Barris to add speed stripes and the logo 'Little Bastard' to his silver-bodied Porsche roadster, just days before the actor's fatal crash (Bayley 1986: 54). At that time the combination of adolescence and money was a still recent cultural invention, an invention to which the film and its star themselves bore testimony. So at that time such amendments to the expensive, late model Porsche's paint job could still be construed as a semiotic affront, as an offence against symbolic order through the unauthorized defacement of a sublime artifact, as a well nigh sacrilegious act of adolescent vandalism. Such things belonged only to the arcane realm of hot-rodding and customizing; they did not and ought not to happen to real dream cars. At that time the cars which so astonished Tom Wolfe (1968: 77) were typically graced with translucent colours which had lots of brilliance and depth, 'purple, carnal yellow, various violets and lavenders' and the 'Kandy-Kolored tangerine-flake' which provided his essay with its title. By the 1990s, similar but more discretely named colours began to appear on BMWs. Such traditional options as arctic silver and bronzit beige have now been joined by Dakar yellow, along with what Wolfe's customizers might have referred to as 'Krushed Kardinal Purple' or 'Velvet Penthouse Green'. In like fashion the photographer Helmut Newton, clothes designer Karl Lagerfeld, and the Las Vegas magicians Seigfried and Roy began to appear in the BMW owners' magazine, alongside the usual vineyards, castles and technical features.

What BMW is caught up in is a localized manifestation of a global shift. The old antinomies of art and commerce no longer grind against each other like tectonic plates. Each has been obliged to give ground to the expanding terrain which lies between them, to the more recently created, more fluid and shakier territory on which fashion, entertainment, advertising and publicity play. Because the force which drives that territorial expansion is the generation of commodified differences, the multifarious specific manifestations of this foursome are always on the road to somewhere, but it is a somewhere that could be anywhere.

As a guide to such a landscape, a car helps. Not, as in a Baudrillard (1988: 54) paradox, because 'The point is not to write the sociology or psychology of the car, the point is to drive'. Rather the point is to figure out the game – and for that purpose I have argued that it helps if the car is a BMW. More generally, however, a car helps because the car/driver hybrid has a grammar of its own. It is a grammar that is most discernible in America, where it triangulates with more than 40,000 miles of freeway and a national(ist) aesthetic (Eyerman and Lofgren 1995). It provides a cusp for what Anne Friedberg (1992: xi–xii) calls the 'mobilised virtual gaze', a concept which gathers together the phenomenologies of cinematic and televisual spectatorship, train journeys and shopping malls and links them to her daily experience of seeing the topography of the southern California freeway system reconfiguring itself through her windscreen. The explicit cerebrality of such motorized *flânerie* is, however, an altogether less popular modality than that evoked by Joan Didion (1979: 83) and Reyner Banham before her. It is an experience not of driving, but of being caught up in 'the only secular communion which Los Angeles has', an experience in which 'the mind goes clean, the rhythm takes over and time distorts'. By comparison, there is something strikingly unrepresentative about the amount of attention devoted by such otherwise very different thinkers as Jameson and Baudrillard to the socially – and critically – privileged interior space of that city's Bonaventure Hotel. Perhaps then, a car helps because the experience of driving with the windows (or, better still, the top) down at night – at once enclosed and looking out, and open and looking in – seems so strangely tangential both to such architecturally induced, and supposedly paradigmatic postmodernist disorientation and to modernist panoptic power. As such, it is not reducible to either that rebelliousness and resistance which C. Wright Mills' BMW serves to symbolize, or to that fantasy of technical domination which Siegfried von Tirpitz's 635CSi represents. It is a feeling somewhere between escape and participation; a location between the machinery of dreams and a technology of representation; an awareness of being knowingly suffused with and positioned by myth; an experience that is understood as both individually chosen and widely shared. Hence the force of Norman Mailer's (1968: 174) perception, in an echo of that other, very different Thomas Wolfe, 'that it is the moment for which Americans live, that collective journey through the dark when strangers are brought close by the wind and the sound of the tires, the lights on the highway, the compass of the night'.

5

THE EMPORIUM OF SIGNS

Jean Baudrillard (1983b: 1–4) introduces the notion of hyperreality by way of a story by Jorge Luis Borges. In the latter's 'On Rigor in Science' (Borges 1964) the cartographers of an empire produce a map so detailed that it exactly covers the territory of which it is a representation. With the decline of the empire there is a deterioration of the map. During the 1960s Guy Debord (1994: 23) had also drawn upon just such an image in his *The Society of the Spectacle*. He observed that what he called 'the spectacle' could be thought of as a map, a map of a new, oxymoronic world of autonomous representations; a map that is drawn to the scale of the territory itself. What Baudrillard further suggests, however, is that for Borges' fable to serve as an allegory of the hyperreal it must be inverted, so that it is the map which precedes and engenders the territory, and it is the territory rather than the map which is now rotting and decaying. Or rather, says Baudrillard, what has now disappeared is the very notion that maps and territories, representation and reality, might be ontologically discrete. Both have been displaced by simulacra.

Debord's Situationist colleagues could be said to have offered one of the better commentaries on, and guides to, the resulting cultural situation. They knowingly employed the map of one city as a means of finding one's way around the built environment of another. If this ploy is understood in terms of a routinized alertness to the contingent intertwining of metaphor, method and the material world, then it hints at how one might navigate within the hyperreal. The incidental coordinates of my particular version of such a venture are provided by French nuclear testing, Disneyland, Japanese consumerism and the structure of academic careers. On their own these particular lines of sight can do no more than provisionally identify a specific location, but the general intention is to illustrate a replicable technique; to insinuate a pragmatic approach to the hyperreal which is altogether less apocalyptic and more secular than Baudrillard's.

Borges may have prompted an allegory of the hyperreal but it is Disneyland which provides the model. For the most part, however, Baudrillard's (1983b: 23–6) brief analysis of the California theme park is not 'about' Disneyland at all. Its liminal focus is on the 'absolute solitude' of the Anaheim parking lot and on the mystery of Los Angeles. Nevertheless for Baudrillard, Disneyland *is* America, an imaginary place which feeds reality and reality energy into that 'endless unreal . . . immense script and perpetual motion picture' (1983b: 26) that lies beyond its perimeter.

Roland Barthes drew inspiration from an imagined empire of a different kind. The *Empire of Signs* (1982) is the title and theme of a book length essay on Japan which he regarded as his most successful work (Barthes 1977b: 156). He introduces it with the disclaimer that it is not 'about' Japan at all. Rather what Japan offered was 'a situation of writing' (Barthes 1982: 4), the prospect of travelling in a fictive nation without maps and an incentive to perforce read a language that he does not know. For Barthes this offers a means of critiquing modernity in general and a series of opportunities to challenge or otherwise problematize the metaphysical 'fullness' of Enlightenment discourse in particular, undertaken through a prose style which refuses the opposition between sensuous and cerebral.

The Japan that Barthes invents and takes delight in is a nineteenth-century Japan. It is a country that is outside the modern, a country filled with signs, but in which all those signs are empty. He observes that the food a cook (who cooks nothing at all) prepares is 'reduced to a tiny clump of emptiness' (1982: 24); that 'the streets . . . have no names' (1982: 33); that in the face of a Bunraku master 'there is nothing there to read' (1982: 62); and that 'the haiku's flash illumines, reveals nothing' (1982: 83). Invocations of an unequivocally contemporary Japan are rare, but here too even that violence which accompanies a student protest against the Vietnam war is interpreted as 'expressing nothing' (1982: 103), just as the students' red white and blue helmets 'refer to nothing historical' (1982: 106). At the very centre of the book there is a photographic image of the Shikidai gallery in Kyoto's Nijo castle. This image is accompanied by a caption whose closing words are 'nothing more, nothing else, nothing' (1982: 51) and the final words in Barthes' essay refer back to it as an *un*centred and reversible space in which 'there is nothing to *grasp*' (1982: 109, italics in original).

What is intriguing is the ways in which these two analyses move across one another; of how the pleasure which Barthes takes in the empty signs of his imaginary Japan articulates with Baudrillard's fascination with the end of the real in that fiction which is his America. How, for example, might their respective accounts of 'Japan' and 'America' be understood when filtered by an awareness of the subsequent phenomenal success of Tokyo's Disneyland? Not only was the Tokyo version of the theme park visited by more than 13 million Japanese in 1988 (Brannen 1992: 216) but Iyer (1989: 383) cites a Japanese public opinion survey in which more than half the respondents identified Disneyland as having given them most happiness in life.

This opens up the prospect of reading these canonical French texts through the West-t(a)inted spectacles of modern Japan. I said reading *through* rather than reading from modern Japan, because my interest is in the accompanying processes of refraction, the ways in which such spectacles break open the taken-for-granted manifestations of modernity and reassemble them into new patterns. The effect is not just to construct a location at which these texts can productively be brought to bear upon each other. It is also to point to a discursive position from which they might constructively be critiqued. For modern Japan is a strangely familiar country which, through its own ambivalent exoticizing of the West, has at once inflected, resisted and reversed the binaries of Orientalism (cf. Miyoshi and Harootunian 1993) in a pattern of doubling that Borges might relish.

My version of modern Japan is therefore no less imaginary than Barthes' traditional one. It too is constructed from outside and it too is orientated towards the Occident. It does, of course, matter that my Japan is read from within a tiny outpost of the West, a former British colony that is now cross cut by both post-colonial and postmodern discourses. Just as it does, of course, matter that Barthes' knowing conceit is to write for, and against, the West with, and from, the security of a centre that functions to valorize the process of identifying, patrolling and problematizing its own margins. This contrast is, however, not introduced in order to enter yet another wearily familiar plea for, or vindication of, the virtues of any particular marginality, but rather as a preamble to a more layered notion of the centre/margin distinction.

What is available to my (New Zealand-based) way of reading contemporary Japan is a productive absence, a lack of that reflex of diffuse anxiety which derives from the threat of economic competition. In this sense it is thus open to the kind of ambience which Barthes reserves for the Japan of tradition. Barthes' essay is, however, manifestly written so as to repress (as *ultra* textual) any consideration of those feudal social relations which sustain the Japan in which he takes such pleasure. By contrast, the explicit premise and sustaining condition of my reading is the pattern of modern(ist) capitalistic relations between New Zealand and Japan. New Zealand is, to be sure, a small nation with a developed awareness of vulnerability, replete with concerns about its external relations, concerns which derive from having been thrust into new economic orbits by those global realignments which are the result of the working out of the post-war settlement. But not only does the volume, significance and rate of growth of the country's trade with Japan now much exceed that with the whole of Europe (let alone Britain); it also enjoys a long-standing trade surplus with what has become its second most important trading partner after Australia. There is an obvious structural asymmetry in overall economic power, but this is a generic feature of the external relations of a small capitalist economy, albeit now edged with a post-colonial tinge. The point for present purposes is that local commentaries on the economic relationship with Japan are in no way overlaid with Euro-American preoccupations about Japanese competition (or for that matter with Australian concerns about levels of direct investment). Rather it is characterized by attempts to enhance the existing pattern of complementarities in the structure of the trading relation through the construction of mutualities in the realm of cultural translation. The legacies and effects of war, together with a conventional enough panoply of East/West differences and contrasts, are still at work, but rather than being amplified by the trade relation they are muted by it. What such an economic position vis-à-vis Japan therefore facilitates are readings of that country that might better be described as pragmatically utilitarian rather than Orientalist. This is not to embrace some global fantasy such as the IBM mantra of world peace through world trade, or the transparently loopy declaration of a New Zealand Prime Minister that the country over which he presides is a part of Asia. What are here designated as 'pragmatically utilitarian' readings are, of course, interested, selective and no less vulnerable to criticism, not least for blurring the line between an openness to cultural difference and a blindness to social division; but they are also less predisposed to be exoticizing, fearful or condescending. What they hint at is the availability of a location which is productively complicit with such a determinate economic and political relation but not merely reducible to it; at the possibility of occupying a position from which to eschew Japan-bashing but to affirm critique.

It is, however, more difficult to avoid intemperate responses in relation to France. From such a location it is, *contra* Barthes, Japan which presently looks (reassuringly) modern and France which looks (retrogressively) feudal, a France that, unlike Barthes' Japan, is responsible for generating material problems rather than subversive pleasures. Not an empire of (empty) signs, but the signs of (the hollowing out of) empire. It is, moreover, an empire that is all-too-knowingly anxious about its own deterioration. So no matter how pristine the condition of its metropolitan maps and how elegant its linguistic and diplomatic casuistry, what also distinguishes my France is its anachronistic territorial claims, its shabby acts of state-terrorism and its bully-boy tactics. In a limited and circumscribed respect, therefore, the geo-political implications of Japanese ascendancy appear as countervailing and hence less threatening than the *raison d'état* of a France in decline. (Limited and circumscribed, in that it must be calibrated against the Japanese sanctification, both official and unofficial, of amnesia and myopia with respect to the historical record of its treatment of, and relations with, its neighbours in general and Korea and China in particular.)

Although the details vary from location to location, the contrariness of this kind of positioning, deriving as it does from being a bit player in a global script, has increasingly come to seem more nearly paradigmatic than idiosyncratic. In this sense reading against the grain becomes a cultural given rather than something that has to be struggled for, and reflexivity is not about the attempt to escape location but rather about the attempt to realize it. This assuredly does *not* mean that anywhere can become a centre, but rather that the specifics of marginality have assumed a new relevance for the metropolitan centres themselves. Marginality is both opportunity and threat; something that they need to understand in order to better maintain centrality and extend influence, and something that they may experience as overall control passes away from what Castells (1989) calls the space of places and towards the space of flows. There is at once an acceleration of global inequalities and an imperative for centres to recognize that globalization has meant the development of new networks of power, such that it is the systemic structuring of the latter rather than specific nodal locations which have effectively become hegemomic. Those complex processes of structuring which are a consequence of the global flows of capital, technology, peoples, images and ideas (cf. Appadurai 1990) are both densely layered and highly specific in their local forms of articulation and sedimentation, such that no one place is assuredly a centre for all purposes. Traditional centres may thus come to experience the stirrings and recognize the discourses of their own particular versions of marginality.

It is the attempt to somehow repair the attendant inter-discursive disorderliness which might be said to connect French nuclear explosions in the Pacific with one Gallic critic's designation of the Paris Disneyland as a 'cultural Chernobyl' (*The Times* 1992). In the former case Paris behaved with all the traditional imperiousness of a militarist centre. In the latter, the condescension becomes etched with all the anxiety of a culture that is threatened with marginalization by the bomb in its own backyard. Part patrician-aloofness, part gonzo-journalism, it reads like the response of a culture that (belatedly) knows itself to be outmoded but is determined not to be usurped. Both examples move across a territory whose institutional ground is signalled by Crozier's (1964) classic definition of (French) bureaucracy as 'an organization which cannot learn from its errors' and Lemert's (1981) account of the social foundations of the 'tout Paris' principle. As befits the nation which gave the words *dirigiste* and *de rigeur* to the world, both instances are premised upon a somewhat brittle conception of the contrasting positions associated with centre/margin power relations. It is thus a model which oscillates erratically between taking up the position of a centre whose reflex is to post the (undesirable) consequences of its decisions to the margin, and a margin which interprets its marginality as deriving wholly from exogenous forces.

This is itself a cavalier simplification in the Gallic mode. So too is the observation that France remains a major actor in the global flow of armaments – but is on the slide with respect to EU leadership. Or that Paris is a global capital of (theorizing and) high culture – but marginal with respect to (the production of) popular culture. It is just such topographical and off-the-top-of-the-head peculiarities, and the institutional forces which they represent, which invests French theory with its informing tone. This does no more than hint at how the myriad specific connections and overall configuration of the associated inter-discursive cultural field actually operate, of just how they help to shape – and to limit – the tenor and temper of its constituent discourses.

But if French theory is so institutionally embedded, then how has it succeeded in becoming global in its reach? Perhaps the most informed and informative response is suggested by Lamont's (1987) carefully detailed study on just how the reception accorded to Derrida in America was related to the organization of cultural markets. In like fashion one might point to a structural isomorphism between the specifics of that highly schematic and sketchily drawn French culture pattern offered above and the general organization of academic careers. To suggest such an elective affinity may seem less bizarre and less prone to a slide into reductionism if it is set against an observation by Clifford Geertz. What he points to is the quirkiness of university career systems, in which the modal tendency is to spend several (early) years at the perceived heart of things, and subsequently to be scattered to the perceived periphery and thus experience a sense of downward mobility in 'differing degrees and with different speeds' (Geertz 1983: 159). It should be noted that Geertz's references to the 'centre of things' and the 'heart of things' happens to fudge any consideration of internal stratification by blurring the distinction between those cognitive and discursive resources which are available at such central locations and the social and material precariousness of temporary, impecunious and lowly status positions. None the less it is only outsiders who might see 'downward mobility' as a slightly odd way to describe the transition from temporary centrality to tenured marginality. For what Geertz clearly signals is the phenomenological plausibility of distinguishing between security of tenure and peace of mind through his observation that, 'The physics departments of the whole country are dotted with people who were "around MIT (or Cal Tech) for a while"; and to study English history at Princeton and teach it at Louisiana State can lend a particular tone to your life' (1983: 159). There is, I suggest, a resonance between that tone and the 'tout Paris' principle; a shared conception of centre/margin relations. It is, however, a conception that is proving to be insufficiently layered to do justice to the ramifying consequences of globalization for the very meaning of such terms.

For with globalization comes the bemusing prospect that the obligatory excursions of the hitherto marginal into such indeterminate territory are being transformed into assets. This means that social theory, understood as a form of cultural capital, is now obliged to generate its own permutation on the real estate litany of 'position, position, position'. The exploration of the place from which 'we' read is now central, a foregrounding of background has become indispensable. With it comes an acknowledgement of the methodological importance of circling around what Foucault (1972: 50) identifies as the first question, i.e. 'Who is speaking'? In the spirit of Rozencrantz and Guildenstern, however, (or, more nearly, in accordance with Tom Stoppard's elevation of their marginality to centre stage) my suggestion is that this should promptly be shaded into the supplementary (in Derrida's sense) question of 'Who is asking'?

Galtung (1981: 838) offers a less elevated, but not unrelated, permutation on Foucault's maxim in his sardonic – and not entirely whimsical – discussion of cross-cultural differences in intellectual style as between British, American, German, French and Japanese social investigations. He observes that what distinguishes Gallic methodologies is that the first question is not about performativity (the American), or evidence (the British), or first principles (the German), or mentor's credentials (the Japanese), but effectively, 'Peut-on dire cela en bon français?' (Is it possible to say this in French?). There is then, an endearing consistency about the Gallic conceit of Baudrillard's amplification and exaggeration of just such a question when he observes that, 'To see and feel America . . . . You have to have wondered, at least for a brief moment, "How can anyone be European?"' (1988: 104–5).

What can be said in French (and with both theoretical lucidity and empirical subtlety, notably, for example, by Pierre Bourdieu) is that some measure of complicity with popular culture is a precondition for understanding it *as* culture. This thereby allows it to be theorized as something other than simply and tauto-logically high (or even folk) culture's *other*. This is why it is of some consequence that France (for which read Paris) is the global capital of high theory, *haute cuisine* and *haute couture*. For these are practices whose very refinements tend to be acti-vated by their combining of the discrete structural principles of resistance to whatever is most general in the wider society and the interrogation of their own tradition. What this therefore allows for is a pattern of intermittent and tactical accommodations to the popular. Such accommodations are characteristically achieved by the transformation of the popular into 'the popular', that is, a know-ingly selective recruitment and translation of popular culture into a discourse that is determinedly external to it. The filtration of American gangster movies through the rhetoric of existentialism is an exemplar of this process.

Such encounters can prove to be productive. When it comes to popular film, for example, continuing French achievements in the thriller genre serve to signal the possibilities, potential and actual benefits of a long-standing engagement with, and recognition of Hollywood's accomplishments. When it comes to contemporary street culture, popular music and television, however, France seems marginal – almost off the map – although it is (importantly) saved from such a location in popular literature by Simenon (and Zola before him). The revival of the notion of *flâneur*, like the notion of cinematic *auteur*, is explicable as an interesting example of a (in this case, Franco–German) cross-cultural attempt to bridge these different realms and yet retain a high modernist subject(ivity). Interesting in that, even more than was the case with the *auteur* principle, it is clear that those refined, individuated sensibilities (whether under-stood as Baudelaire's or Benjamin's) which are associated with the concept are simply being asked to bear far too much weight (cf. Wolff 1985). The recognition of the associated institutional transformation of both publics and of public space is subordinated to the evocation of an experience that is culturally delimited and selectively distributed. It is an analysis in which the populace is there, but the popular seems to be absent. A comparison with a comparable British response to the changing city, substituting Dickens for Baudelaire, and Raymond Williams for Benjamin, would prove illuminating. For it is noticeable that the defining British accounts of popular culture (Thompson, Williams, Hoggart) have the emergence and consolidation of modern working-class lives as their object and focus. By contrast the corresponding texts (corresponding that is, in the sense of having successfully travelled and been widely cited) on specifically French popular culture have been pre-modern in their subject matter (Ladurie on carnival, Bakhtin on Rabelais, Darnton on cat massacre). The accomplished poetics and elegant formalism of Certeau's (1984) analysis of everyday life are, no doubt, both specif-ically French and contemporary, but his subject matter is not.

Nevertheless there are moments, both in the late Baudrillard of *America* (1988) and *Cool Memories* (1990) and the early Barthes of *Mythologies* (1973), when these authors seem to be reaching for a recognition of, and even an accommodation with, the popular, rather than treating it as the occasion for Orientalist-style (i.e. wholly external) theoretical conceits. What had made *Mythologies* so nearly exemplary had been the tension between its somewhat austere and formalized theoretical allegiance to a *marxisant* structuralism and that intermittently open and affectionate playfulness which distinguishes the best of its specific studies. By contrast, Barthes' material on Japan is so ultratextualist, so fully committed to the (purely) critical virtues of (pure) emptiness as to axiomatically exclude any consideration of the social relations which sustain its multiple manifestations. Barthes knowingly and wilfully refuses to analyse or engage with the social order in which the signs appear. Thus as Shortland (1989: 17–18) notes, *Empire of Signs* has received rather perfunctory treatment from commentators on Barthes, tending to be read as a series of footnotes to his *Writing Degree Zero* (1984) (which literary readings of the Barthesian canon are predisposed to privilege over *Mythologies*). But a recuperation of Barthes' own conception of the Barthesian canon suggests that what Japan allowed him to do was to go beyond the ideology-critique of *Mythologies*, to write in a way that was uninhibited by his antipathy to consumerism. His aristocratic distaste for doxa, as it is manifested in the popular culture of the West, is still there as a sub-text, but a merit of *Empire of Signs* is that it allowed Barthes to indulge in his most sublime celebration of the ordinary and the everyday.

Yet the preoccupations of *Writing Degree Zero* are manifestly at work, in that Barthes reiterates that these Japanese signs are not anchored by any transcendental signified, but are in the end empty. This assertion is echoed by the epistemological elusiveness of *Empire of Signs* itself. Thus it does not claim to be an ethnography about Japan, and when read as such it tends to have been found wanting, prompting Moeran (1990: 4), for example, to identify 'occasional flashes of welcome illumination, but more generally pangs of regret'. Nevertheless its title and its theme have been borrowed by Japanese semioticians (Ikegami 1991) and it has proved to be a precursor of recent concerns about the relation between ethnography and writing (Clifford and Marcus 1986). Most plausibly, then, it is about writing (about Japan), writing which might yet be read as an ethnographically-influenced empirical claim about a particular semiotic system, or a general epistemological claim about the properties of all such systems. If the former, then what merits investigation is the kind of social order in which such free floating signifiers circulate and the social functions and interests which they serve. Such an inquiry would no more than echo a general observation of Gellner's (1970: 141) on the sociological role of absurd, ambiguous, inconsistent or unintelligible doctrines and their possible connections with the exercise of social control in any society. With respect to the specifics of the Japanese case, it might therefore draw attention to the interpretation of, and debate around, the social functions and cognitive status of the literature of *Nihonjihron* or 'Japanese distinctiveness' such as Dale (1986) has offered.

But although Barthes' Japanese essays *can* be read as empirical demonstrations, this seems altogether incidental to their role as a commentary on the very notion of representation; as both signals of epistemological instability and as devices for promoting an acknowledgement of it. Yet in recognizing writing as both message and control, as at once a carrier of meaning and a barrier to its recognition, Barthes is none the less obliged to rely on (another kind of) writing, a writing which, in its turn, refracts its own enabling (but otherwise repressed) social conditions. Thus in his *Roland Barthes* (1977b: 156) Barthes refers to *Empire of Signs* as his most successful book, acknowledging that his experience in Japan of 'a happy sexuality doubtless finds its corresponding discourse quite naturally in the continuous, effusive, jubilant happiness of the writing'. And in an interview on his work he observed that 'Japan greatly liberated me on the level of writing by furnishing me with quite ordinary subjects, daily occasions, that are happy subjects, in contrast to those of *Mythologies*' (Barthes 1985: 229).

The book is also in accord with that coterie-like tendency which Lemert identifies as characteristic of French *maîtres à penser*, the distinctive way in which their writings are explicable as responses to one anothers' work. Hence they characteristically take as given, and routinely invoke, that wider cultural field on which they aspire to play, but like novelists, they rarely provide footnotes or documentation of the process. Thus the title and theme of *Empire of Signs* plays with, and against, Lefebrve's (1971: 135) maxim in *Everyday Life in the Modern World* that 'we are surrounded by emptiness, but it is an emptiness filled with signs'. Barthes' observations on Japan can therefore be understood as a rhetorical opportunity to unsettle Western categories and concepts and as such they are explicable primarily as critique rather than as observation. It is a critique that is inimical to the presumptions of contemporary high modernity as, for example, this latter finds expression in that formal criterion of perfect singularity of communication which is the premise of Habermas' ideal speech situation. It is so distinct from such a conception as to all but constitute its other. For the point of Barthes' critique is not to establish the prerequisites for truthful exchange but to amplify the possibilities for rapture. It is, quite literally, a fucking metaphysic – a utopia grounded in an aestheticized model of fleeting, non-possessive, and abstract intimacy. This latter (always and already) is that oxymoron which anticipates and echoes the radically indeterminate, dispersed, pluralistic play of signifiers, signifiers which are in their turn a proxy for erotic practices which, whether actual or idealized, are for Barthes distinguished by their (liberating) para-sociality.

At the level of textual organization it is therefore the generic sign systems of the West which are effectively Barthes' subject matter. For example, Barthes suggests that (the Imperial Palace as) the 'empty centre' of Tokyo is, paradoxically, both Japan and a marker for the absence of a transcendental signified. This contrasts with what he calls 'our synesthetic sentiment of the City, which requires that any urban space have a center to go to . . . (moreover) the center of our cities is always *full*' (1982: 30, italics in original). In passing, however, Barthes acknowledges that lying outside and problematizing this contrast are 'Quadrangular, reticulated cities (Los Angeles, for instance) (which) are said to produce a profound uneasiness' (1982: 30).

There is here the hint of Los Angeles as a third term which offends against, and might therefore deconstruct, the very (West/Orient) binary oppositions which Barthes knowingly creates. Baudrillard, in his foregrounding of Los Angeles, interprets the city as no less exotic (that is, no less not European), no less empty of meaning and no less imaginary than Barthes' Tokyo. But the valency of these properties is very different. If, for Baudrillard, the Orient begins in California, then it is an Orient distinguished not by rapture but rather by just that 'profound uneasiness' to which Barthes refers. Yet just as for Barthes it is Tokyo's 'empty centre' which is at once the signifier of a nation and a repudiation of such a meta-physical conceit, so for Baudrillard it is (the original) Los Angeles' Disneyland which is both America and a generator of the hyperreal.

Baudrillard acknowledges that Disneyland is explicable at one level as a play of illusions and at another as a ploy of ideology; as explicitly a fantasy and implicitly a deception. Nevertheless, for his purposes the meaning of the Magic Kingdom is promptly reduced to a single function – that of lulling or otherwise reassuring Americans into believing that the rest of the country is real rather than simulated. But in order that Baudrillard and his readers may be reassured as to the plausibility of his argument for a third level (that is, neither recognizably a fairy story nor an unrecognized fake), Disneyland is perforce obliged to remain *terra*/terror *incognita*. It is identified as an 'imaginary (which) is neither true nor false' (Baudrillard 1983b: 25) in which the details of its internal organization are peremptorily glossed as a collection of etcetera, etcetera. It is a 'deep frozen, infantile world' (1983b: 24) against which the hyperreal is defined, a definition that is secure in, and secured by, an absolute condescension towards the real Disneyland as exem-plifying culture degree zero. In Baudrillard's representation of it, therefore, Disneyland is irresolutely that other which has purportedly been effaced. By an imperious interpretation of it as a deep frozen and infantile world within which 'a whole range of gadgets magnetise the crowd into direct flows' (1983b: 24) Baudrillard debars himself from conceptualizing or otherwise attaining access to the 'inherent warmth and affection of the crowd' (1983b: 23–4). There is the discernible hint of disorder and of a dialectical tension (in the contrasts between deep frozen/warm; infantile/affection; atomized/sociability) in this description, but to build on it might be to threaten the presumption of a third order of simula-tion and the comfortably apocalyptic conceit of the mass as 'a black hole which engulfs the social' (1983a: 4). So Disneyland is condemned to remain empirically mysterious in order that hyperreal America might become theoretically coherent; it is a black box which, by staying shut, opens up the prospect of achieving closure by way of the black hole of the mass.

Baudrillard's (1988) subsequent more mellow and melancholically ambivalent reading of *America*, continues to be sustained by the principle of hyperreality, but employs the desert as a guiding metaphor and the notion of an achieved utopia as its defining characteristic. The desert as an image is recruited to the task of effacing any traces of a dialectic; of permitting Baudrillard to juxtapose disconti-nuities without the presumption of contradiction, of allowing him to blow hot and cold at the same time. Death Valley thus becomes the 'sublime natural phenomenon (and) Las Vegas the abject cultural phenomenon . . . (but) one is the hidden face of the other and they mirror each other across the desert' (1988: 67), so that sixty pages later it is Las Vegas which is identified as 'sublime' (1988: 127). Monument Valley is at once 'the geology of the earth, the mausoleum of the Indians and the camera of John Ford. It is erosion . . . extermination . . . (and) the tracking shot . . . . All three are mingled in the vision we have of it' (1988: 70). Notwithstanding Baudrillard's aversion to employing the term 'culture' in such hyperreal and, let it be emphasized, popular and non-European contexts, the natural and the cultural are said to mirror one another in this first example, whereas they are understood as mingled together in the second. But when he moves to generalize his argument, it is their collision which Baudrillard foregrounds. His claim is that:

> What is new in America is the clash of the first level (primitive and wild) and the 'third kind' (the absolute simulacrum). There is no second level. This is a situation we find hard to grasp, since this is the one we have always privileged: the self-reflexive self-mirroring level, the level of unhappy consciousness. But no vision of America makes sense without this reversal of our values: it is Disneyland which is authentic here!
>
> (Baudrillard 1988: 104)

The point to note about Baudrillard's account of Disneyland is that the theme park is not to be understood as a permutation on Eco's (1987) 'authentic replicas' – and thus derivative, but might rather be characterized as a 'real fake' – and thus original. To be sure, the distinction between the two terms is an analytic rather than an empirical one – and each shares with the notion of an achieved utopia the common status of oxymoron. What further distinguishes a real fake, however, and confers it with a wider significance, are the generative possibilities associated with its epigenetic characteristics. These allow it to function as an exemplary model whose specific properties anticipate the general characteristics of an achieved utopia.

Baudrillard sees America as both pre-cultural (hence primitive and wild) and post-cultural (hence the absolute simulacrum), both natural and artificial. But inasmuch as *all* cultures are made, then America is not to be understood as outside culture *tout court*, but only as outside Baudrillard's sustaining but parochial naturalization of it as European. There is nevertheless something productive to be salvaged from his notion of an achieved utopia. The American manifestation of such a condition is distinguished neither by a fundamental stasis (as Baudrillard assumes – and as Marcuse had sought to demonstrate) nor by a disguised dialectic (as Baudrillard recognizes) but rather by difference (which his mode of theorizing suppresses) and paradox (which such theorizing amplifies). In a society which Baudrillard otherwise defines as on the move, the term achieved utopia thus works so as to collapse any distinctions between social processes and social products, between aspirations and accomplishments. This may be perfectly congruent with his general theoretical proclivities but it is wholly at odds with providing a minimally adequate empirical account of Disneyland as the paradigmatic real fake.

It is, however, possible to couch Baudrillard's insight in a more empirical (but still critical) idiom, such as Stretton's (1971: 264–5) observation that 'America is a society without an imagined alternative'. This shifts the ground sufficiently so as to allow the theme park and its clientele to be rescued from relegation to that *ab initio* and absolute otherness to which Baudrillard (initially) assigned them. For instance, it creates a space for Iyer's specifically social contrast between the Japanese and American Disneylands. In Iyer's (1989: 382) reading, it proves to be the Tokyo Disneyland – 'an eloquent microcosm of modern Japan' – which is informed by that same gloomy and totalizing otherness which had distinguished Baudrillard's account of its Californian predecessor. For Iyer, it is this latter and Florida's Disneyworld which function so as to provide a consciously consoling and reassuring standard, so that he effectively finds something dialectical in the relation between the glitter and technical perfection of America's Disneylands and the excesses and human imperfections of its customers. Read affirmatively, it is as if the collective memory of carnival and grotesquerie were simply too resilient and intractable to be wholly effaced by their purely mechanical simulation. By contrast, the Tokyo Disneyland is 'a perfect box within a box. Immaculate in its conception, it was flawless in its execution . . . with no disjunction at all between the perfect rides and their human occupants' (Iyer 1989: 382–3). Hence the very tension between the social and the simulated which Iyer sees as characteristic of the American theme parks, is precisely what he finds (disturbingly) absent in contemporary Japan – which therefore becomes not so much a utopia achieved as the realization of dystopian desire. Yet Baudrillard (1988: 126) – who classifies Japan as a 'strong culture . . . (which) reflects back to us the image of our degraded one' – had defined that tension as absent in California! As for Barthes, far from being disturbed by the absence of such opposing tendencies in his (premodern) Japan, he had been manifestly enchanted by it. Not, however, because he was intrigued by a Japanese equivalent of a 'crisis of representation' and an associated 'end of the social', but precisely because 'his' Japan was instructively exempt from such preoccupations.

What emerges when these authors are read alongside each other is a set of permutations on Orientalism – although Baudrillard, as befits a Columbus of the media and a heretic of cultural cartography, had set out to find his exotic East by flying westward across the Atlantic. In this playing out of East/West, other/same and modern/non-modern contrasts, Iyer's is the most orthodox, Barthes' the most knowing and Baudrillard's the most (anxiously) innovative. We are all, of course, differentially implicated in such contrasts by our respective histories; they are shuffled and dealt to us in distinctive combinations and the resulting hands may be played in different ways. None of our existing three players was willing to lead with 'contemporary Japan'. But then none of them occupy a location (shared by Australia and New Zealand) that is culturally in the West but in which the compass bearing of the Far East is actually more or less due North. Such (post)colonial cultures are ambivalently positioned between claims to local distinctiveness and cultural forms which derive from the articulation of a British colonial legacy and a subsequent American hegemony.

This may not (quite) be a description under which modern Japan can be subsumed, but it does nevertheless hint at a rather different cluster of affinities than those suggested by the observation of a Bruce Springsteen band member that 'Kyoto was just like New Jersey' (Iyer 1989: 366). This latter substitutes for (and thereby complements) Barthes' wholly other traditional Japan with a contemporary version that is wholly the same. Cumings (1993: 81) interrogates such assumptions when he knowingly and sardonically makes play not with the similarity, but with the contrast, between Mike Davis's nightmarish portrayal of contemporary Los Angeles in *City of Quartz* (1990) and modern

> Tokyo, where the fabric of morality, national development and urban civility are all intact . . . the trains run on time and the kids think drugs are what you buy in a drugstore. And if Marx is dead, no one seems to have noticed.

Cumings' general point is that Japan's rise to pre-eminence is both an embarrassment to any argument based on the Enlightenment project and yet nevertheless profoundly implicated in the West. As such it is chronically neither wholly other nor wholly the same; *Born in the USA* necessarily plays differently in Kyoto – but it assuredly does play. Since this kind of cultural layering is also the defining characteristic of a (post)colonial location this provides an incentive not to discard the modern Japan card in that peremptory fashion which is characteristic of both Barthes and Springsteen's sideman. For on a world stage whose basic rules have long seemed non-negotiable for small players, maybe such a card can be used to open up opportunities for taking a trick or two. It might even provide prospective hints of new patterns of play, patterns which are given metaphorical expression by those Wittgensteinian family resemblances which thread across Japanese baseball, West Indian cricket and New Zealand rugby.

From such a perspective what is therefore intriguing about modern Japan is its Orientalist inflection of the Occident, not its pure unintelligibility but the strangeness of the familiar, as in the routine sight of blonde-haired, blue-eyed models in the major department store adverts, or the matter-of-factness of alien encounters with Sigourney Weaver and Arnold Scharzenegger in the television commercials. This is not Barthes' Japan – his is one without advertising, television, neon, department stores, traffic, *manga* or baseball (cf. Whiting 1989). It might nevertheless be employed, like Barthes' Japan, to help us (get a) fix (on) our own fixations.

Consider pachinko (see Figure 5.1). In one of Barthes' rare excursions into the present, he does introduce us to pachinko (pinball) parlours. Nevertheless, what

Figure 5.1 Pachinko parlour in Kobe

for Barthes is striking about pachinko is the deft hand movement of the players rather than the sheer decibel level of the assembled machinery; the purported continuity with the craft of calligraphy rather than the affinities with the factory system; the delicate trace of tradition rather than the visual and auditory assault of modernity. De Mente and Perry (1968: 100–1) read the meaning of Japan's two million pachinko machines very differently from Barthes, focusing on the 'serious' players who struggle to beat (and may use magnets to cheat) these machines and the attempts to counteract them through surveillance procedures and dubious alterations to the machines. If Barthes seems concerned to write the Enlightenment out of Japan, then De Mente and Perry seem determined to write it in. They thereby manage to avoid both Barthes' knowing predisposition to interpret the Japanese as exotic and Iyer's caricature of them as automata, as extensions of the Disneyland machinery. The De Monte and Perry account is no less of a translation, of course, and in translation something is always lost. But what Geertz (1983: 36–54) has usefully emphasized, what Callon (1986) has superbly demonstrated, and what Bauman (1987) has methodologically sanctioned is that something may be 'found in translation' too. That something cannot be reduced to the conventional cultural reflexes of either the observer or the observed; it is neither wholly discrete from the discourses with which it intersects, nor wholly conditioned by them. That is to say, it is not simply found, rather it is *made*.

Thus for example it is through its combination of careful ethnography and political imagination that Brannen's (1992) study of the Tokyo Disneyland succeeds in restoring agency to its Japanese visitors. Brannen's point of departure is that the Japanese owners both *wanted* and think of it as an exact copy of the Los Angeles 'original' rather than one which incorporates some Japanese features. Brannen's close reading of the Japanese version of the theme park shows that it does nevertheless differ from that which it purports to replicate (one enters, for example, not into Main Street USA but into Global Bazaar). These differences are, however, effectively denied. The apparent paradox of such a construction of cultural consumption is that it is concerned both to keep the exotic exotic *and* obliged to make the exotic familiar. Western simulacra are recontextualized so as to reinforce a Japanese sense of cultural uniqueness. Brannen interprets this as a manifestation of a specifically Japanese form of cultural imperialism, a way of differentiating their identity from the West – and which has the incidental effect of problematizing the concept of hegemony. This is a theme which is echoed in Creighton's (1991) study of the domestication of the cornucopia of overseas goods in Japanese department stores.

In like fashion Edwards' (1989) study of contemporary Japanese weddings points to how the cutting of a 'Western' wedding cake has been incorporated within the modern Japanese ceremony. This is a development which is both recent and widespread. The cake is, however, made entirely of wax, and the ceremony in which it is employed seems to Western eyes to be marked by a positive exuberance for artifice. At the most general level Edwards interprets this as congruent with that context-specific approach to experience which Ruth Benedict had identified as a Japanese culture trait. The modern wedding thus becomes explicable as a series of poses in which, moreover, detail, a concern for composition and the visual integrity of the performance are enhanced by the commercial development of ritual. It is not the lack of a commercial dimension which distinguishes the more traditional ceremony, but rather that the commercial nexus plays little part in defining the status of, and relation between, the priest and the bride and groom. The advent of commercial wedding specialists, however, ensures that the couples' status as customers becomes more consequential. With it comes the development of a ceremony that is highly structured, carefully staged, unambiguously cued and orientated towards maximizing visual impact.

Such a benign attitude and relaxed response towards artifice and simulation, together with their matter-of-fact social assimilation, also emerges from Ikuya Sato's (1991) ethnography of *bosozoku* (Japanese motor-cycle gangs). *Bosozoku* youths clearly recognize that they are playing age-specific, quasi-theatrical roles. Sato reveals how this knowingness is exemplified in the adoption and display of the group names of the gangs. He notes that for gang members 'We are what the name of our group says', but that it is a characteristic of these names that they do not emphasize a single image, but rather involve the juxtaposition of various themes. His discussion of the identifying insignia for the Tarantula gang provides the most striking example of this practice. He points to the contradictory semantic associations which are generated by the combination of the four Japanese characters which go to make up the word 'Tarantula'. Some sense of this in English is conveyed by the meaning of three of the four characters (the fourth is, in context, phonetic) as 'abundance' 'orchid' and 'butterfly'. Sato (1991: 60–1) suggests that the name Tarantula, like other:

> *Bosozoku* group names deliberately subverts self-defining functions. That is to say, the message encoded in group names is not just 'We are what the name of our group says' but at another level, includes the message 'We are *not* what the name says' . . . . The names of *bosozoku* groups presuppose the Batesonian frame of 'This is play' and are a kind of self parody.

The four Japanese characters which go to make up 'Tarantula' evoke strength, evil, beauty, the grotesque, nobility and, through their juxtapositioning, the motifs of mobility and fluidity. The effect is to exceed even that polysemic ingenuity which Hebdige (1979) had identified as the basis of punk's capacity to unsettle dominant cultural codes, although it is an effect which bears little trace of punk's socially subversive stance. *Bosozoku* are (contra Johnny Rotten)[1] into play, not anarchy, into identities forged in and through pleasure rather than from resistance and in anger, a pleasure predicated upon commodities and fully within consumer culture. What Sato calls their 'outrageous paraphernalia' is neither an oblique refraction of class division nor the signal of an attenuated link to strategies of class struggle.

In each of these studies participation in consumption is interpreted as consequential for and congruent with the construction of identities – and Japan is a society which has an enormous range of consumption sites. It is the latter which prompts John Clammer (1992: 212) to suggest, wryly but without irony, that for many Japanese 'shopping . . . is freedom'. In his account of the relation between shopping and Japanese images of self he notes that, particularly for an older generation with experience of post-war deprivation, it is nothing less than marvellous that through shopping they can choose and create alternative identities within the framework of a conservative society.

In the interpretation of consumerism amongst the young, the commercial success of Yasuo Tanaka's novel *Somehow, Crystal* has come to provide the paradigm case for discussion (cf. Field 1989; Klopfenstein 1984). The text spans two weeks in the life of its Tokyo college girl heroine and consists largely of detailed descriptions of brand-name goods in the form of food, music and clothes. Its critical notoriety derives in large part, however, from the combination of the book's best-seller status and its 442 footnotes with their detailed advice on where particular commodities might be obtained. As a novel which sold some 800,000 copies (Field 1989: 170), it was something of a literary phenomenon. If, however, the book's commercial success is located alongside the enormous sales of the etiquette manuals with which it might be said to share some attributes, then even such a substantial figure assumes an altogether more modest status. Edwards (1989: 78) notes, for example, that a best-selling *Introduction to Ceremonial Etiquette*, first published in 1970, had gone into its 195th printing by 1982.

More generally, in probing for the social structural effects of consumption, Clammer resists an interpretation of it as compensatory, as an index of alienation. Rather he emphasizes the expanding range of possibilities, enhanced public roles for women, a distinctive youth culture, developments in the arts and so on. In Clammer's version of a postmodern Japan, avant-garde experimentation, pragmatism and tradition coexist in a social order that is without a history of meta-narratives and that is premised upon a construction of self and sociality which may no longer be wholly discrete from that of the West, but remains importantly distinct from it.

This predisposition to interpret Japan through categories derived from discourses on the postmodern has been sardonically satirized by Akira Asada (1989) and explicitly critiqued by Yoshio Sugimoto (1990). Rather than employing the conventional tropes of early, mature and late capitalism, Asada makes an ambivalently ironic reference to its elderly, adult and infantile versions as exemplified by, respectively, Italy and France, England and America, and Japan. Sugimoto's emphasis is on the persistence and consequentiality of Japan's traditional social relations of production. Even within the realm of consumption, however, the postmodern image of 'shopping as freedom' does need to be set against shopping as a traditional and obligatory routine, a routine that is over-whelmingly the responsibility of Japanese women, many of whom are obliged to shop almost every day (Fields 1985: 53–7). Likewise, the connection between the multiple-layered reciprocities of Japanese gift-giving and their elegantly wrapped manifestations and carefully studied routinization by department stores would seem to be more about the reproduction of the traditional order than its transfor-mation. Nevertheless, if the intention is to explore not just 'their' culture, nor even 'ours', but rather the instability of such a contrast, then the wanton plurality of such a densely saturated consumer culture can provide a continuing series of provocations and pleasures. Thus the translucent thickets of night-time neon street advertising are not just rendered bereft of their specific exhortatory func-tions by the inability to read that language for which they nevertheless seem to have been made. They can also enhance an appreciation of how (another kind of) cultural work might none the less still get done through signifiers that have all but floated free of their conventional signifieds, as, for example, in the Japanese use of English, so that the inverted A in a word like BLACK (see Figure 5.2) is invested with a purely formal visual appeal.

Yet something more than this seems to be at work in the fortuitous and felicific ambiguity of 'Spiritual Bond for Women', as the slogan inscribed on a white sail which advertises a women's fashion boutique in Tokyo's Roppongi district (see Figure 5.3). For whether such a 'Bond' is here read as meaning supportive, constraining or even Jamesian, the English meaning of the slogan also intersects with the aesthetic properties of the artifact which it embellishes, with its no less serendipitous juxtaposition of the sail's airy, silk delicacy, the dumbbell-like metal weights which anchor it and the small, chisel-like red heart which decorates it. There are echoes of such small surprises throughout modern Japan; in the improbable combination of manhole covers in which pastel-coloured images of flower blooms are inscribed upon a heavy metal 'canvas' (see Figure 5.4), or in a shop front festooned with cheery, cherry-red 'Tommy Blak' boxing gloves (see Figure 5.5).

A further case in point is a 1992 prime-time television commercial for a Honda Vigor convertible. It shows a young couple preparing and being prepared for what is clearly a big night out – she in off-white ball gown and he in black tuxedo and red-lined cloak. When they meet up and drive away together it is she who is behind the wheel. The camera pans around so that we finally see his face (and not just the back of his head with its slicked-down hair or the extreme close-up shot of his moustache being trimmed). Only then does it become evident that 'he' too is actually a she. Yet it is not so much the cross-dressing *per se* which is particularly noteworthy as it is the generation of an ambience of shared and non-binary plea-sure which accompanies such 'playing with the frame'. The commercial at once firmly secures the closure of its syntagmic chain yet succeeds in signalling the permeability of the very categories that it displays. It not only insinuates that each role consists of a repertoire of gestures rather than the manifestation of an essence. It also implies that their actual allocation is arbitrary and interchangeable,

Figure 5.2 Advertisement in Tokyo subway

Figure 5.3 Sign outside a fashion boutique, Tokyo

Figure 5.4 Manhole cover, Tokyo

so that either party could have played the other part, or played the same part another way.

At one level, such a commercial becomes explicable in terms of a thoroughly traditional structure of gender roles and family life. The term 'OL' (office ladies) refers to those typically college educated, young, unmarried women in Japan who are in paid employment. They are likely to continue living at home and their career prospects and remuneration are less than that of their male counterparts. They can, however, expect to pay little or no rent and they therefore enjoy a level of discretionary income which makes them a key target audience for commercials for overseas holidays and expensive consumer goods of all kinds – up to and including cars. In this context then, the commercial is premised upon a brief interlude in the life cycle of these young Japanese women, a purportedly carefree interregnum between schoolwork and housework. Where Clammer might fore-ground the changes that this commercial signals, Yoshio Sugimoto might want to emphasize the associated continuities. Thus the commercial might be interpreted

Figure 5.5 Shop front, Tokyo

either as a proto-feminist symbolic challenge to this social pattern, or as substantively functioning to reconcile its audience to the requirements of those traditional roles and imperatives which it (purely) formally contradicts. Or it might be understood as a gendered permutation and extension of Barthes' (1984: 91) suggestion that the Japanese male transvestite 'does not play the woman, or copy her, but only signifies her', and hence acts as a sign of pure difference, of 'man' and 'woman'. Or, and perhaps most plausibly, it might be read as a 'pleasurable' contemporary articulation of the enduring tensions between socially distinct subject positions and the discrete readings which they sanction.

To read Tokyo's Disneyland, Japanese weddings, *bozosoku* and car commercials outside of the context of their production and reception is a way of keeping the exotic exotic, positioned somewhere between inscrutability and condescension along one axis, and between delight and apprehension on another. There are problems too in seeking to make the exotic familiar – since a distinguishing characteristic of these cultural practices is precisely that they are constructed across the instabilities of the exotic/familiar contrast. Thus a reading which approaches them solely in terms of their articulation of, and continuity with, extant local meanings, can achieve closure only by (over)emphasizing either their matter-of-factness or their ineffable mystery. It is, however, just because they tack back and forth between the(ir) exotic and the(ir) familiar, with a concomitant making of new meanings, that they make claims on our attention. Not as products, but as practices. In terms of manifest content there are rapidly proliferating, multiple overlapping features as between Japan and the West. 'Their' hybridity is, however, manifestly and stubbornly not 'ours'. It has a different genealogy and it generates novelty in accordance with a different grammar.

Hybridity with respect to content is therefore not somehow *outside* of what Harvey Sacks (1974: 218) (in a felicitous phrase which is part Raymond Williams, part Michel Foucault) refers to as 'the fine power of a culture',[2] with its matter-of-fact entry into the minutiae of everyday life. Read one way, this phrase is an acknowledgement of a culture's liberating productivity with respect to the generation of possibilities; read another, it is an acknowledgement of that culture's limits and limitations with respect to the construction of selves and social organization. 'Content hybridity' might then be interpreted as a form of cultural repair work that is constructed across such a distinction. It thereby incidentally signals both the resilience and the leakiness of cultural controls, as well as obliquely hinting at their principles of assembly.

At its most sublime, this is what activates the engagement of film director Akira Kurosawa (often read in the West as 'Japanese' and in Japan as 'Western') with the plays of Shakespeare. But it also routinely informs more prosaic practices and settings. For example, in June 1991 there was a report in the *Mainichi Daily News* of how high school couples have attached more than 500 metal padlocks (bearing such messages as 'I'll love you forever') to a metal fence at the base of a Hiratsuka City broadcasting tower (see Figure 5.6). The newspaper notes that the local authorities are still trying to figure out a way to easily remove the locks, many of

91

Figure 5.6 'Locked in Love': news item, *Mainichi Daily News*, June 1991

which are made of solid brass. There is a clear continuity with that traditional practice in which the pictorial wooden votive charms known as *ema* are inscribed with wishes and desires addressed to the gods, and which are offered at shrines and temples throughout Japan (see Figure 5.7). But where the temple has become a television mast, the *ema's* wood and knotted cord has become a brass padlock, and the authorities have become exasperated, then such conduct also begins to display some affinities with (New York) graffiti writers and the practice of 'tagging', albeit in the form of romantic postmodern prayers rather than semiotic guerrilla warfare.

Such practices may easily be dismissed as trivia, or perhaps first categorized and then filed away through the use of some such paradigmatic notion as (Jameson's) pastiche. This can, however, only be accomplished at the cost of foreclosing on

Figure 5.7 Ema at entrance to shrine, Kyoto

the recognition of a certain demotic ingenuity, a downplaying of their novelty so as to emphasize a more general continuity. Yet as with Kurosawa's transformation of Macbeth in *Throne of Blood*, they invite a less determinate interpretative stance, an acknowledgement of the extent to which they have become something that nobody had hitherto thought of, expected or counted upon.

That novelty 'stirs things up' is a tautology, but what remains contestable and contested is just how novel are such instances of content hybridity. This kind of debate should, however, now be seen to be overlaid by a second order activity, as instances of such content hybridity are increasingly being introduced (as here) into milieux other than those in which they conventionally circulate. What I have been edging towards is an active promotion of this collusion and collision of cultural meanings so as to make for the construction or amplification of a critical space that is somewhere between seduction and reduction; a plausible counterfactuality which might permit a recognition of 'fine power' without necessarily submitting to it. It might also shift an understanding of the terrain on which hybridity is constructed away from content and towards processes.

A tentative analogy for such a distinction may be derived from linguistics, more particularly from Bickerton's (1995) account of the contrast between pidgin (cf. content hybridity) and creole (cf. process hybridity). Pidgin is the product of contact between two groups who do not share a common language. Bickerton argues that the collection of words which may result is not itself a language since the associated juxtapositions do not create propositions. It is instead 'on the way to language', rather like the first utterances of a child. A creole, by contrast, is produced by a child who is learning a language for the first time and is exposed to a pidgin. The child posits a syntax and then uses it to generate new propositions. It is thereby in at the birth of a language, a language that it at once creates and by which it is itself created. Barthes' attempt to facilitate a novel way of writing by reading a culture as a language that he does not know is on the cusp of such a contrast. So too are those interpretations of 'Japlish' (i.e. the exoticizing use of English words by Japanese in Japan) which celebrate its surrealistic serendipity instead of simply referring it back either to its local meaning or to its departure from standard English.

Norma Field's *In the Realm of a Dying Emperor* (1993) is a recent example of an attempt to create a critical space through engaging in such second order activity. It knowingly combines the West's privileging of the claims of individual dissent with a knowledge of Japanese culture that is both scholarly and indigenous. She therefore insists on 'the possibility of declaring a complicated love' (Field 1993: 280) for Japan by both documenting and celebrating instances of political dissent. These latter are read as both a problematization and a realization of what it is to be Japanese, over and against the oppressive singularity of a 'common-sense Japaneseness'. The same deliberate courting of a more layered analysis is discernible in Anne Allison's *Nightwork* (1994), an ethnography of a hostess club in Tokyo. Allison combines a feminist critique of salary men and the corporate culture of masculinity with a structurally informed and generously sympathetic reading of their predicament. The resulting text is both more tough-minded and more nuanced than, for example, those more widely known observations on being a bar girl which Angela Carter gathered during her two years in Japan, an experience to which she attributed her radical credentials (1982: 28).

Inasmuch as the conceit which anchors such studies is the notion of critique as universal, then the *de facto* effect and movement of these works is towards a privileging of the West over Japan. By contrast, Barthes' essay on traditional Japan is manifestly a critique of the contemporary West – although it might nevertheless be read as offering so accomplished a repudiation of such a universalizing tendency as to tacitly all but confirm it. Confronted with the prospect of a universalizing tendency towards consumer culture, however, then the critical response can come to seem gloomily formulaic. Certainly, if Japanese consumerism is compared with its Western counterpart then there is the same familiar reproduction of market relations, and a similar flow of utopian promises. Such global uniformities are, however, interwoven with something more than the distinctively local obligations of gift-giving. What emerges from amidst this highly developed, guiltless and guileless promiscuity are glimpses of something that is playfully demotic and affirmative. I would not want to claim anything quite so exoticizingly symmetrical as that 'they' can teach us something about (the aesthetics of) consumption whereas 'we' can teach them about (critique and) politics. My purpose is not to uncover some 'authentically Japanese' structural or aesthetic principle, but to make use of Japanese images and effects – that appear as more than merely random when they are read through Western eyes – for a semiotic politics, as imaginative antidotes against 'our' own forms of closure.

Suntory's 'Beer Nouveau 1991 Natsu' (Natsu means summer) seems almost made for just such a purpose (see Figure 5.8). With its (French) allusion to wine vintage, its use of Australian ingredients and the 'reversed seasons' that they permit, its Ken Done design work and day-glo colours, it relies upon Western imagery and materials but departs from Western conceptions of how beer might be marketed. In Japan, Done's designs mean Australia. But as with the cover of Fiske *et al.*'s (1987) study of the *Myths of Oz*, there are souvenir shops from Perth to Brisbane which testify that those designs signify Australia not just within Japan, but in their country of origin too. That beer and beer drinking are also metonyms for Australia has long been a central motif in both the domestic and overseas advertising of Australian brewing companies. Suntory's brew is likewise 'Australian' in both ingredients and imagery, and moreover it has a taste that bears a passing resemblance to the iconically entrenched can of Foster's. Yet even a cursory awareness of the position which beer occupies in Australian culture, or the most casual acquaintance with the studied, sardonic boorishness and obligatory Ockerdom of Australian beer commercials, suggests that as a product 'Beer Nouveau' might be rather hard to move within the island continent. As a sign out of place, however, it can be made to run and run. For it delicately subverts that

Figure 5.8 Suntory's 'Beer Nouveau 1991 Natsu' with design by Ken Done

deliberate eschewing of delicacy which Australian brewers are at such pains to amplify in their fabrications of Australian cultural nationalism.

Done's version of nationalism draws upon Australian images and motifs for its content, but this advertising man turned painter is probably best categorized as a Neo-Fauvist or Neo-Impressionist. This is to say that the most discernible formal influences on his work are those same turn-of-the-century European painters whom the Japanese most admire. These painters were, of course exposed to, and much influenced by, classic Japanese wood block prints – just as more than a century before, such Japanese printmakers had absorbed some of the techniques of perspective from the Dutch (Wilkinson 1990: 110). This opens up the prospect that what the Japanese may find appealing about Done's work is that in its hybridity they can glimpse a complexly refracted version of their own culture.

This is no more than a sketchy documentation of the 'content hybridity' of such a beer can, a cursory laying out of the cultural materials from which it is constructed. But although this points to the sources of its familiar component images and elements, the principles of combination and assembly none the less remain elusive. To be sure, Ken Done's Japanese beer can is altogether less mysterious than Jorge Luis Borges' bogus Chinese encyclopaedia, whose internally contradictory and conceptually puzzling classifications had provided the inspiration for Michel Foucault's *The Order of Things* (1973). For present purposes, however, it is as an incentive to infer a 'process hybridity', as a provocation to posit a generative syntax, that the former artifact might none the less assume a more general significance. Understood as a device for prompting the taken-for-granted to appear strange, such a felicific combination of exoticism and familiarity facilitates a generalizing of Foucault's impulse to interrogate the given categories of thought. It is altogether less radical than his, but not to the point of freezing such an impulse into a pedagogy.

Put another way, inasmuch as it prompts the question of what are the kind of cultural conditions which make such a design possible, then this promptly opens out into questions about the changing relations between cultures and the status and cognitive efficacy of those categories that are purportedly internal to them. For example, Moeran (1990), Hendry (1990; 1993) and others have productively employed 'wrapping' as a metaphorical guide to Japanese culture, suggesting that how something is wrapped often assumes more cultural significance than what is being wrapped. To promote the reading of Suntory's beer can 'out of place' and without opprobrium, and thus to ask not what it might mean to 'them' but what it can be made to mean for 'us', is not to generalize such a methodological principle. Rather it is to posit a process hybridity through which it might articulate with a more obviously Western recourse to the contrast between surface and depth, so as to provide leverage both on the changing phenomenology of consumption in the West and on some of the traditional conceits by which we strive to understand it.

To conclude. I have noted that Baudrillard had recognized and used a short fable by Jorge Luis Borges as an allegorical anticipation of the hyperreal and that

Foucault had drawn inspiration from the Argentinean writer in seeking to understand the order of things. There is yet another bravura Borgesian fiction whose version of the hyperreal both evokes what I have referred to as process hybridity and throws light on the emporium of signs that is 'modern Japan' as seen from the West.

Borges' *Tlön, Uqbar, Orbis Tertius* (1965) is a sustained and densely written provocation, a literary detective story and vertiginous semiotic puzzle which effectively resists summation. Its cryptic opening sentence, 'I owe the discovery of Uqbar to the conjunction of a mirror and an encyclopedia' (Borges 1965: 17) signals the play on, and with, the relations of fact, fiction and theory, of same and other, which is its theme. The story which follows is an elaborate and disorientating sequence of duplications, inflections and variations whose effect is to repeatedly undercut the emerging premises of the narrative.

It matters for my purposes that the one point of stability in Borges' story, and the anchor from which it develops, is the *Encyclopaedia Britannica*. It matters because Endymion Wilkinson's (1990) study of relations between Japan and the West makes use of the earliest editions of the *Britannica* as a rough measure of the extent of Western interest in and knowledge about Japan from the late eighteenth to mid-nineteenth centuries. As just one of a range of authors (cf. for example, Miyoshi and Harootunian 1993) who have sought to document historical shifts in Western perceptions of Japan, Wilkinson (1990: 106) notes that *Britannica's* first edition (1771), 'simply contained an abbreviated geographical entry stating, "Japan, or Islands of Japan are situated between 130° and 144° of E. long. and between 30° and 40° N. lat.". In contrast, the same edition had no less than eight double column pages on China'. By the seventh edition of 1842, however, articles on Japan had consolidated into the stereotypical imagery which was to later become inseparable from the Western view of the country. In Wilkinson's (1990: 109) summary,

> an isolated impenetrable world; earthquakes, volcanoes, Mt Fuji; suicides; a clean, hard-working, nervous people anxious to learn, characterised by extreme virtues and extreme vices; a tantalising market for manufactured goods.
>
> In the second half of the nineteenth century this cluster of images was enlarged to include . . . Japan as a land of artistic refinement and intriguing geisha.

Brought up to the present, this theme becomes Holborn's (1991: 15) acknowledgement that 'the fantasy which we call Japan' is always already there, existing as chains of images bounded by 'the frame of cinema, the television screen, the edges of a page, the viewfinder of a camera, or the border of a flag'.

In Borges' fiction it is the idea of the *Encyclopaedia Britannica* as a real source of reference which functions like that concise factual entry on Japan which Wilkinson reproduces from the first edition of this standard work. In each case they serve as starting points from which to display the construction of an imagined world. For Borges, this process is initiated by his inventing a literal, if inadequate reprint of the original encyclopaedia. The two extant copies of this reprint differ only in that one of them contains a brief article on the land of Uqbar, a country about which we are informed that its literature never refers to reality, but only to the imaginary regions of Mlejnas and Tlön. Tlön subsequently appears in another work, namely volume 11 of *Orbis Tertius*, and as Borges' narrator puts it, 'It was two years since I had discovered, in a volume of a pirated encyclopaedia, a brief description of a false country . . . . Now I had in my hands a substantial fragment of the complete history of an unknown planet' (Borges 1965: 21). It is a planet whose nations are 'congenitally idealist' although a scandalous and heretical doctrine of materialism continues to circulate. We learn that the effect of such idealism on reality is 'to add small fictional objects to it, such as stories' (Sturrock 1977: 120). As the story develops, however, and after a second (and again amended) copy of *Orbis Tertius* is discovered, this time as part of a complete forty volume set of *The First Encyclopaedia of Tlön*, then:

> reality gave ground on more than one point . . . contact with Tlön and the way of Tlön have disintegrated this world . . . . Now the conjectural 'primitive language' of Tlön has found its way into the schools. Now the teaching of its harmonious history, full of stirring episodes, has obliterated the history which dominated my childhood. Now, in all memories, a fictitious past occupies the place of any other. We know nothing about it with any certainty, not even that it is false.
>
> (Borges 1965: 33)

As the story moves to its conclusion, Tlön does more than attract adherents. It assumes the scale, scope and dynamism of historical change, threatening to annihilate the narrator in the process, whose inference is that eventually the world will be Tlön, and that 'in a hundred years from now some one will discover the hundred volumes of the Second Encyclopaedia of Tlön' (Borges 1965: 33).

The implication, which grows throughout the story, is, of course, that Tlön is the (hyperreal) world which we (erratically) inhabit and which (erratically) inhabits us. As such, it goes beyond that territory/map Borgesian fable on which Baudrillard had drawn. For the *Tlön, Uqbar, Orbis Tertius* story does not presume the hyperreal as given, but rather it allegorizes the pattern of its expansion. Moreover in the trajectory of that process through which Tlön has been invented, and in the anxieties to which it gives rise, there are also echoes of the ways in which a country like Japan has been constructed, has assumed, and has been allocated, a more central place in the material and imaginative world of the West. What also distinguishes Borges' narrator's tale is:

> the dismay of the teller, who feels that his everyday world . . . his past . . . (and) the past of his forefathers . . . (are) slipping away from him . . . the

subject is not Uqbar or Orbis Tertius but rather a man who is being drowned in a new and overwhelming world that he can hardly make out.

(Irby 1971: 42–3)

This is further overlaid by the way in which the structure of Borges' narrative, by doubling back upon its own premises, is designed to both disorient and initiate, to induce in the reader that sense of metamorphosis which is the subject matter of the story itself.

And the moral? Borges was an Argentinean – and thus axiomatically an exotic, both partly constituted by, and by definition attuned to, the material effects of fictions produced elsewhere. He wrote from within a nation which was able to introduce the tango – its impassioned iconic dream of itself – to Japan, only after 'it had been Frenchified, Anglicized, or Americanized once or several times en route' (Savigliano 1992: 237). His response to the rhetorical methodology of Baudrillard's 'How can anyone be European?' might therefore be to ask, with an irony that is no less ambivalent than Akira Asada's (1989) but with much more sophistication than most of us can muster, 'How can anyone avoid it?'

6

INDECENT EXPOSURES
Theorizing whistleblowing

Introduction

The term whistleblowing is a relatively recent entry into the vocabulary of politics and public affairs, although the type of behaviour to which it refers is not wholly new. It is employed here to mean that process in which insiders 'go public' with their claims of malpractices by, or within, powerful organizations. This restricted sense of the term is in line with Bok's (1984: 210–29) usage and distinguishes it from such related practices as in-house criticism, official and unofficial 'leaks' and the like. This nevertheless allows 'blowing the whistle' to be interpreted as a form of conduct which has a long, if decidedly uneven, lineage. The history of whistle-blowing is uneven, in that such practices are intermittently dispersed in time, erratic in their trajectories and indeterminate in their form. Yet there is a clear sense in which they are available to and for a narrative of historical continuity. For such conduct bears witness to, and otherwise supports, those influential and long established discourses whereby the West proclaims the distinctiveness of its own political tradition (and especially those arguments concerning individual rights, the claims of conscience, the responsibilities of citizens, the emancipatory power of reason). A consequence of our ineffable complicity with that tradition is that what might otherwise be read as random incidents of criticism are raised to the status of critical indices of freedom. If interpreted at this rhetorically enhanced level of evaluation, then whistleblowing episodes may be said to dramatize the very foundation of the Enlightenment project, i.e. the possibility of combining individual autonomy and social rationality, or of reconciling the claims of truth with the practice of politics.

When filtered through such a discourse, whistleblowing is therefore more than just a new name for an old practice. The use of the term facilitates an active consti-tuting and re-ordering of the historical record. The notion of an affinity between the activities of, for example, Daniel Ellsberg and Martin Luther is both made visible and rendered plausible. This in turn permits a link to be forged between the publication of *The Pentagon Papers* via *The New York Times* in 1971 and the public nailing of the Ninety Five Theses to a cathedral door in 1517. What is thereby achieved is a concise, rhetorical gathering together of the early stirrings of 'the modern' and its mature, ambivalent, densely textured but still developing, legacy in the present. And what is also affirmed thereby is the stubborn recalcitrance of reality, a reality which remains impervious to the purportedly totalizing simulations of the hyperreal. In seeking to contextualize the controversies which gather within and around the phenomenon of whistleblowing, this chapter therefore reads them as competing cartographies, as contrasting maps of the hyperreal's jurisdiction.

There is a burgeoning literature on whistleblowing, from Peters and Branch's (1972) nod towards the muckraking tradition of journalism to the academic Marxism of Rothschild and Miethe (1994) (cf. also, for example, Nader *et al.* 1972; Mitchell 1981; Westin 1981; Brabeck 1984; Graham 1986; Glazer and Glazer 1989). All of these studies are premised upon the availability of a political equivalent to Greenwich, that is, an Archimedean point from which they may contribute to the unproblematic reproduction of the Western democratic tradition through the replication and naturalization of its narrative conventions. For what is foregrounded in these analyses is; the principled ethico-political stance of the whistleblower versus the governing realpolitik of the system; moral wo/man against immoral organization; the spirited resistance of the precariously sovereign individual against repressive social control.[1] Interpreted in this way, 'blowing the whistle' thus becomes a colloquial and contemporary characterization of the enduring verity of Enlightenment ideals. These texts may impart a vernacular gloss to such venerable oppositions and such venerated terminology, but they none the less carry the message of their durability and persistence.

It would be churlish not to recognize and respond to the appeal of such approaches and the conduct which they celebrate. But it should also be recognized that the empirical content of these studies stands in an uneasy relationship to their narrative form. Substantively, such writings serve to locate and document the development of a social problem; procedurally, they emphasize the pertinence of enhancing a regime of legislative protection; formally, they define the problem as explicable within the terms of the existing narrative order. It is, however, through their implicit grounding in a humanistic ontology of freedom that these texts serve to smuggle in a consoling and therapeutic insulation against those more awkward theoretical, structural and political issues which are raised by the bleak statistical record on the social fate of whistleblowers.

The fate of whistleblowers is characteristically bleak in that if they have not already decided to resign, they can expect to be dismissed from their employment. This was the norm amongst the (overlapping) fifty or so cases discussed in the 'first wave' studies assembled by Peters and Branch (1972) and Nader and his colleagues (1972). The ten whistleblowers in Westin's (1981) study were all sacked and only one succeeded in winning reinstatement. Mitchell's (1981) more obviously journalistic account of seven cases also documents job losses, along with arrests, marital breakdown, and ostracism. There is the prospect of being blacklisted and Bok (1984: 212) notes that the (Soviet-style) pattern of routinely referring (American) public service whistleblowers for psychiatric evaluation is increasingly being emulated by private sector employers. In the more recent and most comprehensive study by Glazer and Glazer (1989) over two-thirds of the sixty-four whistleblowers interviewed had lost their jobs. Lennane's (1993) brief analysis of thirty-five Australian cases also documents long-lasting health, financial and personal problems.

But no matter how disturbing the factual material may be, the very familiarity and continuity of the tropes through which it is expressed acts so as to provide a reassurance of sorts. The presumption of a stable linguistic order both generates and anchors those counterfactual ideals against which the social experience of whistleblowers is evaluated. It is, however, precisely such a presumption which is rendered problematic by the trajectories of actual whistleblowers' 'careers'. What is therefore signalled by these attempts to reconcile narrative continuity with the requirements of descriptive adequacy is a discourse functioning at the very edge of its applicability. The tensions in these texts provide a permutation on the Gramscian theme of 'pessimism of intellect, optimism of will'. As such, these analyses do *not* hold out the prospect of a 'get out of jail free' card – but only the chance of one. For although 'is' and 'ought' may formally remain stubbornly separate, would-be whistleblowers are in effect cautioned against going public by the same authors who commend the integrity of those who do (e.g., Glazer and Glazer 1989: 206–7 and *passim*). The rhetorical subtext may be 'don't let the bastards grind you down', but the empirical message is that they almost certainly will.

Some writers on deviancy (for example, Cohen 1974: 27–8; McRobbie 1991) have speculated that this kind of academic work may exemplify 'secondary deviance', i.e. a species of romanticism which allows its authors to identify with, and vicariously participate in, proscribed practices. It is, however, the possible effect upon readers, rather than the motives that may be imputed to authors, which is of more immediate relevance. The prospect is that although it is morality which is (vicariously) celebrated, it is expediency which is (effectively) reinforced. In this way the literature on whistleblowing induces a contradictory positioning of the reader which has affinities with the Prisoner's Dilemma as it appears in textbooks on decision theory and modern logic. The irony is that at the level of textual organization, these whistleblowing studies tend to replicate, rather than to interrogate, the kind of difficulties which whistleblowers find themselves confronting at the level of social practice.

Whistleblowing as 'structural signal' and as social practice: towards a theory

These difficulties are the place to start. Engaging with such problems requires a different orientation, one that breaks with the existing literature's dependence upon (tacitly metaphysical claims about) the qualities of those who initiate or suppress such conduct. And one that seeks to contextualize the associated prioritizing of those verities which whistleblowers serve to make manifest.

The bases of such a perspective are prefigured by Weisband and Franck's (1976) comparative study of resignations 'in protest' by senior political executives between the years 1900 and 1970. Their methodology is exemplarily cautious but it nevertheless exposes a clear contrast between the British and American patterns. Of the seventy-eight British resigners, forty-two (53.8 per cent) left office in a public declaration of protest against a government policy. Of the 389 American officials who resigned during this period, 355 (91.3 per cent) did so without any trace of public protest. Weisband and Frank observe that 'in the United States, the rules insist that the resignation statement must trivialize the reasons for leaving; but in Britain the rules require that the reasons must be significant ones. A trivial resignation is *de rigeur* in America but inexcusable in Britain' (1976: 112).

This contrast is interpreted through a discussion of the discrete characteristics of the two political systems and the social backgrounds and career patterns of their senior personnel. The analysis presupposes that political systems enjoy substantial autonomy and it is framed by the assumptions of political pluralism. The American pattern is thus found wanting when judged against the constitutional premise of checks and balances, with the major problem being seen as that undue accretion of presidential power which was dramatized by Watergate.

Weisband and Franck (1976: 170–1) go on to suggest that the intermittent disclosures from within the middle and lower levels of state bureaucracies, and their amplification and dissemination by media interests, represent a partial, counter-systemic response to this failure of senior level functionaries to speak out. Such whistleblowing is seen as an important, but less than satisfactory palliative, as an incipient and imperfect functional alternative to a normatively given standard of successful system functioning. This has the merit of firmly locating whistleblowing episodes within a wider social context, but it subordinates their specificity to the requirements of a pre-existing theoretical imperative. The effect of such premature closure is that whistleblowing is not so much explained as explained away. In avoiding the undue voluntarism which is characteristic of much of the literature on whistleblowing, it is effectively reductionism which is embraced. What is required is a more theoretically indeterminate emphasis on the contradictory character of the whistleblowing process, combined with a foregrounding of the discursive, institutional and structural forces whose operations are displayed in and through such episodes.

An interpretation of whistleblowing as a historically determined, institutionally shaped, culturally mediated social practice offers just such an alternative approach. It is less epistemologically secure, in the sense of being less willing to assume, or attempt to legislate for, a single transcendental conception of reality. Read from such a standpoint, whistleblowing incidents are explicable not as the manifestation of prior ontological certainties or universal truths, but as constituted in and through the social order that generates them, the discourses that articulate them and the subject positions which realize them.

Whistleblowing is by no means exclusive to America (compare, for example

Adams 1984; Lampert 1984; Lennane 1993). The volume and predominance of American literature on the topic is, however, an indicator that it is in America where it most nearly approaches something like an institutionalized form. Watergate and *The Pentagon Papers* had provided the leitmotif for the initial flurry of documentation in the early 1970s. By the end of the 1980s the practice had acquired its own unofficial archivist, William Bush, who had assembled a database of some 1600 cases (Glazer and Glazer 1989: 258). There had also been a growth in the number of advisory clearing houses and support agencies (of which the Government Accountability Project is probably the oldest and best known).

Whistleblowing's entry into the language and on to the agenda of American public debate has been shaped by such particularities of time and place. What makes the practice of more general and theoretic interest, however, is that the very notion of whistleblowing is highly symptomatic of, and sensitive to, emergent features of social structure and political process. This is a characteristic it shares with its obverse, the concept of white-collar crime (cf. Aubert 1952; Carson 1980) so that the meaning and significance of both notions is contested. Thus in America whistleblowing is partially protected by law but it is none the less likely to be penalized with impunity. Conversely white-collar crime is formally subject to legal sanction, but prosecutions are so infrequent as to have prompted doubts as to whether the term 'crime' can meaningfully be ascribed to such conduct. The point to note is that the situation is not static with respect to either of these concepts. Thus there have been incremental improvements in the legal position of whistleblowers (Glazer and Glazer 1989)[2] and an enhanced awareness of, and some initiatives against, white-collar crime.

This pattern of contestation and dispute is not restricted to technical questions of legal and academic definition. And the struggles in and around the practice are not limited to its generation, but extend to include the terms of its initial reception and subsequent path through various cultural sites. Thus whistleblowing is celebrated in both popular and high culture, from American television series (*Serpico*) and Hollywood films (*Silkwood*, *Serpico* again) to classic European drama such as Ibsen's *An Enemy of the People*. It is also institutionalized in such influential newspapers as the *New York Times* and the *Washington Post*. Yet such actions have as often been censured and condemned, not only by partisans but by the public(s) in whose name they are exercised.

There is an order to this disorder. The discontinuities which seem integral to whistleblowing are instructive in something other than the arts of dissimulation. My argument is that the ambiguous status of whistleblowing and the contradictory responses associated with instances of such behaviour are an indicator of the uneasy coexistence of competing discourses and contrasting social imperatives, each of which carries its own kind of necessity.

It is therefore precisely *because* of the concept's anomalous character that whistleblowing is of special interest. To think of it only as an isolated, idiosyncratic or aberrant form of conduct is unwarranted, not least because the very language to be employed in characterizing such activity is itself in question. What is implicit within the existing literature is that to replicate the language of only one of the parties, i.e. 'to be realistic', is both theoretically and morally asymmetrical – but the literature's own counter emphasis is on the motivation and morality of those who speak out. My alternate interpretation of whistleblowing practices as tracers of shifts and realignments within and between discursive and institutional structures is both more explicitly contextual and less axiomatically heroic. From such a perspective: the psychology of the whistleblower is seen as less pertinent than the social construction and imputation of motives; the foundationalist emphasis on the consciences of individuals gives way to a focus on how individuals are positioned within discourses; and the statistical (in)frequency of such behaviour is viewed as less salient than the extent and intensity of the controversy it promotes.

The production of whistleblowing: regimes of truth and the politics of lying

The case material indicates that the characteristic trajectory of whistleblowers' careers (after they have gone public) is, with few exceptions, a downward spiral. There is the further prospect that this will be linked to a blame-the-victim strategy, i.e. that the associated psychological deterioration may be cited as a vindication of the imposition of sanctions in the first place. Whistleblowing might therefore well be classified as a form of occupational suicide – or perhaps as accidental career death. But, as with Durkheim's (1952) classic study of bodily suicide, there is no need to presume that this most individual of acts is only to be understood by seeking to grasp its meaning for individuals. The interpretation of whistleblowing as a signal of the state of social organization depends less upon investigating the purported (ir)rationality of particular individual perpetrators, than upon probing the social explicability of the practice. Moreover, just as for Durkheim there were different kinds of suicide, corresponding to different patterns of social integration, so too there are different kinds of whistleblowing, each grounded in the different 'regimes of truth' represented by the law, ethics, science and technology and their corresponding discursive and institutional characteristics.

The term 'regimes of truth' derives from Foucault (1980) and is an acknowledgement that truth is generated only as a result of multiple constraints. The threefold classification of such regimes likewise nods towards those domains of governmentality, the self and rationality which are characteristic of Foucault's historical writings (Dean 1994). This chapter does not however lay claim to being Foucauldian in method and it also has a limited focus on just one of these regimes, that associated with science and technology. But before turning to such details, something needs to be said about a more general dilemma; a dilemma which is a concomitant of the institutionalization and development of any and all such regimes.

Truth and falsehood are correlative concepts. A notion of truth requires a conception of falsehood and it is by defining the limits of truth that falsehood invests truth with meaning. But the possibility of falsehood is not just a purely formal requirement of a regime of truth. Falsehood also generates its own possibilities, and the social and political implications of those possibilities are both consequential and contradictory. Thus although there is a symbiotic relationship between the generation of specialized knowledge and the effectiveness of political control there is also the prospect of an opposition between the claims of truth and the practice of politics. There is no paradox here; in so far as knowledge gives power then deception can effect the distribution of power. Indeed, the presumption that deception is integral to politics links the noble lie of Platonists with the wor(l)d w(e)ariness of Machiavellians; it has a history that is almost as long as the history of political thought itself.

Put bluntly, those who lie get more and those who are lied to get less. Even in modern democratic states the institutional proscriptions against political lying are less than categorical and the social controls against it are rudimentary in their operation and limited in their effects. The recourse to lies means that objectives and alternatives may be eliminated or obscured, estimates of costs and benefits affected and degrees of (un)certainty amended (Bok 1978: 20–31). More generally, however, what Bok demonstrates is that even in the case of 'high', rational politics, truth cannot be an absolute political value, and that the notion of 'responsible lying' is not axiomatically an oxymoron.

Lies, secrets and silence are neither wholly equivalent nor wholly discontinuous terms. Rather they form a continuum (cf. Rich 1979). Maintaining silence and keeping secrets are more pervasive and more passive forms of deception which may none the less have similar implications and effects to the overt telling of lies. Whether singly or in combination, both the said and the unsaid may therefore contribute to the production of deception. Deception also shades off into that process of dissembling which Edelman (1977) has described as the distinction between words which succeed and policies which fail (and with it the contrast between those who are symbolically reassured and those who materially benefit from a given policy). Moreover, since it is often not events themselves, but language about events (or should one say a language event) which is experienced, the resulting reality is, phenomenologically speaking, no different from any other reality.

The efficiency of all of these procedures does, however, depend upon a clear notion of the truth that the deceiver/dissembler wishes to hide (Arendt 1972: 31), and upon the practice of deception remaining selective in use and unperceived (Bok 1978: 142; Wise 1973: 25). Without the first there is the prospect of the deceiver's self-deception; without the second there is the self-defeating emergence of cynicism amongst the deceived. Whether this is viewed in terms of the substantive rationality of the larger system, or interpreted from the purely tactical standpoint of powerful actors, lying therefore has its limits. There may be lying in politics, lying may be integral, even indispensable, to politics, but politics cannot be reduced to lying. For should the self-deception of deceivers and the cynicism of the deceived become endemic then both the integrity of the political process and the interests of the powerful themselves are threatened.

It is clear that 'events' and 'facts' can be eliminated or ignored in current debate and excluded from histories, even from history. But to the extent to which such events or facts signal the neglect of a consequential reality other than the prevailing symbolic one then it is also clear that they (or 'similar' facts or events) can exhibit an irritating intractability. Such resilience may be made manifest within any of the regimes of truth identified earlier, namely, science and technology, the law, and ethics. The extant literature on whistleblowing does, however, draw heavily upon discourses associated with 'the law' and 'ethics' rather than 'science and technology'. Furthermore, all of these discourses tend to be taken as simply given (here again, Bok's subtleties provide an important exception), rather than being subject to any interrogation of their terms, let alone the kind of all purpose subversiveness of a Foucauldian approach.

Whistleblowing clearly does raise legal and ethical issues, issues which Bok has helped to clarify and which would further benefit from an engagement with the concerns expressed by, for example, MacIntyre (1981) with respect to the practice of management (cf. Horton and Mendus 1994; Mangham 1995). Yet what seems neglected in the commentaries on whistleblowing is that many of the examples discussed, including the book-length case study by Anderson and his colleagues (Anderson *et al.* 1980), actually involve scientists and technologists who see themselves as acting primarily in (accordance with) their *technical* capacity – as servants, if you will, of instrumental reason. Moreover the aforementioned criterion of 'irritating intractability' assumes particular significance with respect to that reliable knowledge of the physical world which is generated by science and technology. The extent to which established legal rules and ethical standards can be broken and evaded depends upon the state of the social organization in which they are implicated. This is *not* to say that the physical laws upon which the cognitive achievements of science and technology depend are immutable. But a necessary condition of such efficacy is the formal abstract domain of mathematics and computation in which Woolley (1992) argues that reality resides – and which, moreover, is what also makes hyperreal simulations possible.

The production of whistleblowing: science, technology and the rationale of the corporate system[3]

A consideration of the full range of those episodes which media institutions recruit to the common category of 'whistleblowing' invites a book. This chapter has a limited and modest focus on that version of whistleblowing which derives its impetus from scientific and technical notions of rationality and the associated regime of truth. A study of, for example, the act of going public on sexual harassment would require the mapping of a very different balance of forces and discursive practices than that which is attempted here with respect to purported violations of technical imperatives or scientific truths. What I would nevertheless want to suggest is the wider applicability of this mode of theorizing to other regimes of truth and other versions of blowing the whistle.

What constitutes reliable scientific or technical knowledge may sometimes be a consequence as well as a condition of the exercise of power, and not all such knowledge may assume (or be granted) political relevance. The crucial point, however, is that it is not always possible to provide such a substitute for reliable knowledge. Michel Callon (1986) has demonstrated just how and why the production of opinion and ideology cannot simply be translated into the production of knowledge, no matter how forcefully such a stratagem may be pursued. Callon shows how the social and material conditions of successful translation are at once contingent *and* far too exacting for them to be overridden in such a cavalier fashion.

A historically specific version of this general dilemma of the truth/politics relation thus emerges from the interaction between science and technology (or what Latour (1987) calls 'technoscience') and 'the rationale of the corporate system', to use Burns' (1974) term. A brief exploration of the changing relation between these institutional orders is therefore a precondition to understanding the structural and discursive bases of scientific and technical whistleblowing. For the discoveries of science and technology, together with the institutionalized pursuit of theoretical and technical knowledge upon which they depend, are integral to modernity and modernization. They are the main productive resource upon which continuing economic growth, expanding systems of surveillance and the enhanced military capabilities of nation states now rest (Bell 1973; but cf. Kumar 1976, 1978: 185–230). It is because science and technology are cognitively powerful that they are strategically important to the preservation and extension of economic and state power. Yet at the same time science and technology are continually and routinely invoked as transcendent and unchallengeable values for ratifying the existing power structure and promoting depoliticization. It is this double function which underpins Habermas' (1970b: 81–122) argument that the expansion of rationality has become the basic exploitative strategy of capitalist society. As he puts it:

> What is singular about the 'rationality' of science and technology is that it characterises the growing potential of self-surpassing productive forces which continually threaten the productive framework – *and at the same time* sets the standard of legitimation for the production relations that restrict this potential.
>
> (Habermas 1970b: 89 italics in original)

Habermas argues that inasmuch as science and technology tell us what the world is like and how to control it, then they are authoritative in ways that are independent of their use by specific interests. But with the expansion of the large firms and state agencies which are the major actors within the corporate system

(Burns 1974) then it is in the name of science and technology that those interests are disguised. The associated scientization of political discourse is a manifestation of depoliticization, an index of the accelerating decline in the functional significance of the public realm.

Yet despite such blurrings of the boundaries between science and modern politics, their ordering principles and institutional logics do remain stubbornly discrete. The practice of science and the potentialities of technology are not reducible or equivalent to the ideology of scientism and the technocratic conception of politics. What defines the idea of politics is the conviction that there is always an alternative; its voluntaristic premise is that social life can be other than it is. The clash of interests, opinion, debate, and compromise is the very 'stuff' of political practice. Invoking science and technology as a means of restricting debate and advancing interests has thus proved to be double-edged. Political and public controversy in and around purportedly scientific and technical matters has become more, rather than less commonplace (Nelkin 1979), albeit cast in the form of cognitive disputes and political struggles between competing experts. The expansion of such scientized forms of political discourse has thus been accompanied by a more evidently partisan (because now more explicitly public) form of the politics of scientific practice, thereby further eroding faith in the idea of a transcendent cognitive authority.

As for the institution of science, then as Mendelsohn and his colleagues observe, its continuing distinctiveness does not presuppose either an essentialist definition of truth or any assumption that its pursuit is asocial or disinterested. 'It simply means that people belonging to the system act on the assumption that it is possible to differentiate between truth and, say ideology or power. That assumption structures their activities, their communication and their institutional arrangements' (Mendelsohn *et al.* 1988: xv).

Science as an institution is not beyond the reach of politics, but nor is it a manifestation of 'politics as usual'. Latour's (1987) provocative claim that science is 'politics by other means' is thus only explicable (let alone acceptable) if the full specificity and distinctiveness of that 'other' is acknowledged. Political decisions have been consequential in determining the pace and overall direction of scientific activity (cf. Greenberg 1967; Dickson 1986) notably in supporting its dramatic expansion during the Second World War and the decades which followed. Moreover, scientific practitioners are necessarily mindful of the micropolitics of their own practice.

But if science is not and cannot be outside such social processes, nevertheless its institutional development took place under conditions which allowed it to remain remarkably insulated from external appraisal of its methods, and therefore its most distinctive structural characteristics. Within the shared limits accompanying a given level of social development, science and politics can be said to embody contrasting tendencies of action, rival principles of organization, disparate linguistic conventions, opposed structures of communication and different patterns of incentives. And since the cognitive efficacy and power of science has historically been predicated upon such relative autonomy, then this latter constitutes a problem for decision makers seeking to circumscribe the use and implications of scientific findings.

For integral to such a relatively autonomous science were three features which both helped to account for its accomplishments and problematized its subordination to powers external to it. First, the traditional incentive system, operating through the publication of scientific results, strongly supported adherence to cognitive and technical norms (otherwise known as 'truth-telling') (Mulkay 1972: 23–30). Science is not, and was not immune to fraud (Bridgstock 1982; Broad and Wade 1983) but the social controls against lying are much more effective within scientific communities than they are outside them. What is crucially at work is not the developed consciences of individuals, but a refined institutional mechanism. Second, successful scientific communication operates in and through networks constructed on the basis of shared cognitive interests rather than current institutional affiliations, organizational boundaries or national frontiers (Crane 1972). Third, scientific communities have evolved a distinctive solution to the political problem of organization, by constructing their practices around the allegiance to and extension of exemplary instances of cognitive work. Consensually validated scientific rules and procedures thereby exert a unique authority over the way a given group of scientific practitioners produce their results (Kuhn 1970).

The ordering principle of science as an institution is whether something (an explanation) is or is not true. Its counterpart with respect to technology is given by the related criterion of whether something (a material or social artifact) will or will not work. Yet by comparison with the relative autonomy of scientific communities and the distinctiveness of their forms of organization, there has been a tendency for technology to have evolved in close conformity with the requirements of its main sponsors. Compare, for example, Noble's (1977) history of professional engineering in America. He argues that engineering and management were linked together from the outset, so that by around 1930 technical progress and the development of corporate capitalism had not merely been rendered compatible but were intimately interwoven. In emphasizing the novel institutional connections, social initiatives and ideological programme on which this achievement rested, Noble was concerned to uncover and identify those particular social relations which the doctrine of an autonomous technical necessity obscures, and to explain the failure of engineers to conform with the expectations of Veblen and of Marx before him.

Innovation networks and the logic of institutional blurring

Both this relative subordination of technics to business, and the relative autonomy of science from the state, may be threatened by the novelty which they are mandated to produce. Each is to be seen as a contingent and problematic accomplishment rather than as a trans-historical characteristic. Moreover, with the expansion of the corporate system, business and the state have moved into new relationships, not only with the forms of instrumental rationality which they sponsor, but also with each other. In like fashion it is now widely recognized that the traditional distinction between 'pure' science and 'applied' technology has become untenable. One of the effects of these inter-institutional blurrings and boundary crossings (and the associated realignments in control and legitimation) has been to create pressure points and the prospect of fissures in the technical/scientific stratum's pattern of compliance.

The main arena in which scientific findings and politically defined needs are brought into contact is provided by the elaboration and extension of contractual agreements and consulting agencies (Habermas 1970b: 70–4). As a mediating institution the contracting/consulting system provides for a double interchange between the two realms. In any given instance the initiative may flow from scientific findings to possible application(s), or from a vaguely defined need to its formulation in scientifically relevant terms and eventual implementation. The efficacy of this process is crucially dependent upon sustained contact and information exchange between users, researchers and designers, right up until the point at which a specific technology or strategy has been developed.

In America this general pattern evolved out of the distinctive management system that was developed for the building of the atomic bomb. Burns and Stalker's (1966: 37–42) brief account of the development of radar in Britain is, however, no less prototypical – so much so that the remainder of their book is an analysis of efforts to replicate the innovatory potential of such a system in the changed post-war context of the commercial market for electronic equipment. Burns (1974: 153–4) later went on to point to the dense network of contacts within which the Route 128 firms in the Boston area operate as a more contemporary exemplar of such a pattern. It is a densely textured, inter-organizational but none the less closed, milieu marked by a web of acquaintances and connections between the world of Boston institutional finance, the area's major universities, Washington and the large corporations, operating against the background of the (at that time) assured 'big R and D spend' of the defence ministries.

What this illustrates is the post-war emergence of a pattern of institutional development which retains the explanatory and innovative potential of science and technology but reconciles it with the prevailing structure of political and economic interests. *Ad hoc* contacts between the once discrete realms of science and politics are routinized and consolidated via the contracting and consulting system. Business and financial groupings coalesce around the latter, plugging into the institutional infrastructure whenever and wherever there is the prospect of commercial benefit. Conversely, the availability of consultancy, contracts and careers allows for differential levels of scientific involvement and for variations in involvement over time. This ranges from the university professor who occasionally gives advice in Washington to the scientist or technologist working full time in an industrial firm.

The cognitive integrity of the scientific process depends upon communication.

The restrictions on publication that may be associated with the forms of involvement outlined above do not, in themselves, necessarily threaten the integrity of the scientific process or the interests of individual scientists. Publication (i.e. 'going public') is *not* the primary mode of scientific communication but its end product. Its main significance lies in the material and symbolic rewards that it confers (Mulkay 1972: 29). Scientific activity is, in principle, perfectly compatible with the alternative or supplementary structure of incentives represented by consultancy, contracts and careers. The underlying structural problem reveals itself not through this changed pattern of rewards but through the correlative change in the system of control. For there is a disjunction between the construction of scientific communication networks on the basis of shared cognitive interests and the restriction of information flow for the purpose of establishing or maintaining political or commercial advantage.

This clash of contrasting principles of structuration was perhaps most clearly demonstrated by the struggle to reconcile security with innovation in the making of the first atomic bomb (Jungk 1958: 105–23), where it was dramatized by the competing approaches to organization associated with Los Alamos director J. Robert Oppenheimer and his immediate military superior General Groves (Davis 1969: 178–87, 203–10). In a commercial context it has been best illustrated by the origins and development of the microprocessor industry, where the efforts by individual firms to control their intellectual resources, clashed with very high rates of inter-company mobility and densely organized informal linkages amongst the scientifically and technologically talented (Rogers and Larsen 1984). Both are examples of situations in which the strategic significance of scientific and technical expertise takes its most developed and visible form. The structural dilemma they represent is here displayed, regulated and *managed* rather than resolved. This takes place on several fronts, namely, the content of the information to be communicated; the channel or channels to be employed; the communicants to be involved. With respect to any given episode any, or all, of these may be at issue, but what is invariably at stake is the system of communication control.

The limits to the exercise of such control derive from the fact that there comes a point at which modifications to the structure of incentives, the pattern of communication and the rules of research communities turns counter-productive. The more central the requirement for innovation the greater the incentive to preserve the principles of organization that are characteristic of science; the more science-like the social organization the greater the problem of achieving the selective appropriation of results.

The proliferation of such innovation systems and networks, initiated and sponsored by the major political and economic actors, are working solutions to this dilemma, with the 'open channel' of publication replaced by other rewards (cf. Cringeley 1993; Rogers and Larsen 1984). The underlying problem of communication control which is, in Burns' (1974: 174) phrase, 'both the basis and the overt expression of power within the corporate system' becomes a background assumption. Within these systems there is the occasionally explicit requirement, but usually implicit presumption, that confidentiality will be maintained. It is this presumption, and the organizational resources available for ensuring compliance, which increasingly regulates the relation between knowledge and its public expression, particularly the relation between the authoritative discourse of science and the public discourse of authority. Communication control is a functionally indispensable means for uncoupling the conditions which govern the production of conduct and policy within the system from the rhetoric of justification. With the expansion of the large firms and government departments that are the core of the corporate system, such uncoupling becomes progressively more important and those who learn to practice it increase in number.

Specialists between technical reason and corporate rationale

These uncoupling practices are thus the locations at which organizational forms, the career interests of specialists, institutional realignments and structural transformations must somehow be made compatible. In like fashion the innovation networks which Burns and others have described represent nothing less than particularly developed instances and limiting cases of a more general social process. Both the construction of such networks and the practice of uncoupling have as their corollary the effort by specialized and specialist occupational groups to combine, and reconcile, their knowledge of the material world with an interpretation of their material interests, to merge technical reason and corporate rationale. From the standpoint of such groups what can be said to distinguish such networks is the organizational centrality of the innovation function, the cognitive power and facticity of scientific findings and technical processes, and the (relatively) privileged pattern of employment and market position of scientific and technical personnel. This maps the limits of the professional project under corporate capitalism.

Professionalism as a social project is directed towards the monopolizing of control over a given set of skills in order to acquire material and social rewards for its practitioners (Johnson 1972; Larson 1977). The organizational device of uncoupling external rhetoric from internal conduct rests upon the exercise of discretion; this is facilitated by the claims to a monopoly of competence and tendencies to social closure that are associated with professionalism. Monopolies of competence and monopolies of control are not, however, equivalent terms. For organizational professionals the latter is an aspiration rather than an accomplishment. The associated struggle is clearly not to be explained as the clash between professional and bureaucratic principles of organization, but as a conflict between the structure of institutional and organizational power and the occupational ideology and work preferences of some of its members (Perrow 1972: 50–5; Larson 1977: 219). The dilemma which such practitioners characteristically face is how to reconcile the perceived cognitive and technical necessities of their tasks with the social and political imperatives associated with their organizational positions. Moreover, the communication control that is characteristic of the inter-organizational networks of the corporate system is reinforced and made that much more effective by the asymmetrical structure of the employment relationship.

In America such strategies of communication control can now be seen to have begun to gather momentum during the 1950s, and were thus contemporaneous with the intellectual dominance of end of ideology assumptions. The associated emergence of managerialist doctrine was for public consumption; for insiders acquainted with the precariousness of its logic, it was protected by a supplementary system of belief, a loyalty code which sanctioned that social selectivity in communication which Johnston (1979) refers to as structural silence.

At the time, this development attracted attention, and oblique recognition, in works of cultural criticism. Whyte's (1956) organization man, Reisman's (1950) other directed man and Wright Mills' cheerful robot (1951) were widely discussed accounts of changes in the moral sentiments and social types associated with the rise of the corporate system. Such convergence was all the more marked in that the works in which these notions were expressed were grounded in very different political perspectives. Subsequent critical commentary suggested that the polemical thrust of these works had led their authors to construct an idealized conception of the past and a discounting of the social and psychological resources available to, and employed by, the growing number of middle-level employees in large organizations. For Rosenberg (1970: 232–44) it was an 'orgamerican fantasy'; an unwitting but instructive commentary on the changing social role of intellectuals rather than the nominal subjects of their inquiries; for Mailer (1961: 180–93) it was the inversion of a platitude. Dalton's (1959) empirically based critique argued that what Whyte saw as the triumph of the social ethic was no more than the adaptive camouflage of the ambitious in their traditional struggle for influence and advancement.

Neither Dalton's no change individualistic imagery of the 'rat race' on the one hand, or the purported conversion to social conformity and 'team player' on the other, conveyed a sense of process or tension, of the dynamics of coexistence and interaction between these themes. It was, above all the cool sardonic style and theatrical metaphors of Goffman (1959) and, to a lesser extent, a concept such as Maccoby's (1976) gamesman which were suggestive of the interpersonal initiatives through which these competing action tendencies were handled (cf. Gouldner 1971: 378–90). What Goffman's work also posited, and probed at, was the precariousness of such patterns of accommodation, the secular anxieties and sense of threat which are their intra-psychic correlates (cf. Goffman 1971).

Organization, rationality and ritual

A remark of Wolin's hints at how the changing social psychology associated with this putative transformation might be seen as grounded less in the emergent moral sentiments of individual agents than in the transformation of corporate discourses and organizational structures. His description of Selznick's organizational sociology as 'Leninism clothed in the language of Burke' (Wolin 1961: 427) is provocatively misleading in its identification of intellectual antecedents (Perry 1979: 265–9) but substantively correct in locating a basic dualism between the legitimatory principles and operational practices of large-scale organization.

Gaining and sustaining such legitimacy is no mere epiphenomenon. Given the density and interconnectedness of those networks of communication and exchange that have become characteristic of the wider corporate system, then the perceived legitimacy of a given organization within the system is often crucial to its acquisition of resources and the maintenance of its stability. This is the basis of Meyer and Rowan's (1977: 341) argument that the formal structures of such organizations 'dramatically reflect the myths of their institutional environments instead of the demands of their work activities'.

Meyer and Rowan go on to suggest that organizations may thus be located on a continuum in accordance with the relative importance to their survival of cere-monial conformity or productive output. At one end are organizations which celebrate, and are congruent with, rationalized institutional rules, at the other end are organizations which are dominated by performance criteria and consider-ations of technical efficiency. In between are those organizations which have such institutionalized rules enshrined in their formal structures and which direct considerable efforts towards building and maintaining gaps between those struc-tures and the practices which govern output. Such 'gaps' are the locations in which 'scientism' is reconciled with science (and 'legalism' with social practice). Scientism (like legalism) is an aspect of that expansion of 'rationalized institu-tional rules' through which attempts to translate social and political problems into technical and administrative ones is undertaken. Scientism remains, however, stubbornly discrete from those scientific and technological practices upon which productive efficiency depends.

The contrast to which Meyer and Rowan draw attention has a close family resemblance to Bagehot's (1963) classic formulation of the opposition between the 'dignified' and the 'efficient' principles of a political system. It might also be interpreted as a permutation on the contradiction between the imperatives of accumulation and legitimation. Their distinction between an externally orien-tated ceremonial conformity and a productivist emphasis on output does, however, tend to blur the boundaries between specifically organizationally gener-ated contradictions and those which derive from contrasting institutional imperatives. Meyer and Rowan draw attention to one class of secrets, those which are generated by and through the differences between an organization's mythic public face and its technically-based operational practices. But as Weber recog-nized, secrets also arise out of the very process of coordinating and appropriating the abstract generality of technical competencies for localized and specific purposes. Not only may such purposes have nothing to do with *either* external legitimation *or* formal criteria of productive effectiveness, they may indeed be quite at odds with both. In an influential and much quoted observation Weber (1947: 339) had insisted that 'Bureaucratic administration means fundamentally

116

the exercise of control on the basis of knowledge. This is the feature of it which makes it specifically rational'. But this was only a part of the story that he wished to tell. For he goes on to point out that:

> This (knowledge) consists on the one hand in technical knowledge which, by itself, is sufficient to ensure it a position of extraordinary power. But in addition to this, bureaucratic organizations, or the holders of power who make use of them, have the tendency to increase their power still further by the knowledge growing out of experience in the service. For they acquire through the conduct of office a special knowledge of facts and have available a store of documentary material peculiar to themselves. While not peculiar to bureaucratic organizations, the concept of 'official secrets' is certainly typical of them. It stands in relation to technical knowledge in somewhat the same position as commercial secrets do to technological training.
>
> (Weber 1947: 339)

The continued uneasy coexistence of formal structures with both effective practices and such localized and specific interests thus depends upon a variety of decoupling devices (cf. Weick 1976). For example, inspections are ceremonialized and effective evaluation is avoided. Goals are made ambiguous or vacuous. Since coordination is both important and likely to be in violation of the rules, informal interpersonal competences are highly valued. Anomalies are ignored and discretionary behaviour tolerated or encouraged. These and related devices are typically well known to the incumbents of high discretion roles, but their public discussion is tabooed (cf. Bailey 1977), and the development of such roles hedged around with rituals of confidence and good faith (cf. Fox 1974: 31–6). The responsibility for 'laundering' organizational knowledge in this way rests with the technical specialists and professionals who occupy such high discretion roles.

Thus although these developments are driven by what Habermas understood as the exploitative expansion of rationality, their effect is to give rise to whole new areas of ceremonial and ritual activity. Viewed one way, they lead to the social selecting out of a utilitarian sensibility and a consolidation of the interests associated with it. Viewed another, they suggest that the rain dance of the econometrician, the cargo cultism of the stock market analyst, the management consultant as exorcist are not mere whimsies, but plausible working hypotheses (cf. Cleverley 1971; Jarvie 1964: xiii–xvi; Devons and Gluckman 1964: 259; Turner 1977).

There is thus a *double* movement involved, only one side of which is grasped by Hampshire's account of the error of the optimistic utilitarian:

> He carries the deritualisation of transactions between men to a point at which men not only can, but ought to, use and exploit each other as they use and exploit any other natural objects, as far as this is compatible with

general happiness . . . [there is] no theoretical barrier against social surgery of all kinds. Not only is there no such barrier in theory; but more important, the non-existence of the barriers is explicitly recognised. The draining of moral significance from ceremonies, rituals, manners and observances, which imaginatively express moral attitudes and prohibitions, leaves morality incorporated only in a set of propositions and computations.

(Hampshire 1978: 18)

Hampshire's account attends to the consequences of a utilitarian habit of mind. But it needs to be supplemented by asking how it is that such a habit has been rendered both habitual and consequential. This directs attention towards the development of whole new areas of ceremonial and ritual activity. The erosion of those particular rituals in which, for Hampshire, meaning and significance reside, does not mean the end of ritual *per se*. What Meyer and Rowan demonstrate is that ritual has not disappeared, but it has moved house, and is now to be found in the hyperreal formal structures of the expanding corporate system. Meyer and Rowan view these attributes somewhat sardonically. It is, however, important to recognize that an understanding of such developments depends upon the recovery of their logical and practical necessity, their reason and their *raison d'être* (Bourdieu 1977: 116). The practical accomplishment of ritual and ceremony lies in just such a fusion of knowledge and power. Its social meaning lies not so much in the products of such activity as in the practices which routinize their production. It is through such practices that the symbolic and social orders are connected. Whatever may be the disputed epistemological status of witchcraft and magic amongst the Azande[4] or econometrics amongst Treasury officials, the moral and social significance of each such case simply cannot be understood *only* by inspecting goat entrails or computer printout.

From Luther to Ellsberg and beyond, the insider who speaks out in violation of such practices is thus not merely deviant but heretical, i.e. a challenge to the prevailing symbolic order and through it to the social order itself. The unclothed emperor may be deviant, but it is heretical to say as much in public (cf. Harshbarger 1973: 25). For what this may bring into question is not just the propriety of specific actions but the legitimacy and status of the code which sanctions them.

The point is that every established order tends to produce what Bourdieu (1977: 164) calls 'the naturalisation of its own arbitrariness'. The decisive mechanism for this symbolic achievement is that articulation of structures of opportunity with the aspiration of agents (cf. White 1970) which is called 'the sense of reality'. It is 'what everybody knows' and is the force (and appeal) of the injunction to 'be realistic' (cf. Golding 1980). Indeed what could be more hyperreal, more real than real, than this taken for granted milieu of the corporate system? After all, the scale and complexity of organizational action, and the 'limited liability' structure of organizational roles, characteristically provides the necessary self-justification for compliance (cf. however, Nagel 1978). Furthermore, this language of legitimation quickly shades into the identification of sanctions should the communication of individual misgivings not remain severely circumscribed in its circulation. But what such ordinary language also conveys is a hint of inertia or resistance, a residual tension, the capacity to imagine alternate courses of action. 'Be realistic' is therefore an injunction to compute personal costs, rather than being an invitation to attend to truth content.

Faced with such a situation there is no reason to assume that the professional stratum of scientists, technologists and experts of various kinds are any the less concerned with the preservation and expansion of their skills, their knowledge *and* their privileges (Gouldner 1979) than are other 'new class' members. But there are times when this kind of advice contradicts the epistemological grounding of their occupation, so that the resulting qualms and frustrations are experienced as not only moral but cognitive. This is demonstrated by, for example, the Vandivier (1972) case, in which the brake assembly for a new aircraft persistently failed all tests (due to a design fault) but the company responsible for the project insisted that the engineers responsible for administering the tests falsified the relevant reports. Despite some ingenious and ingenuous attempts at data massage, it became apparent that what was at stake was not *whether* there would be an exposé, but *when* (i.e. before or after actual flight trials). It was not, or at least not only, the claims of conscience, but rather the inevitability of discovery which provided the incentive to blow the whistle. For the most part (and for most participants) the attempt to manoeuvre along just such a socially constructed cusp between truth and power will remain tactical, expressed in and through reservations to close colleagues, in-house debates, anonymous leaks to third parties and the like. With the act of publicly blowing the whistle, however, the demarcation line between the tactical and the existential is perforce breached.

Whistleblowing texts, speech acts and media discourse

This dramatization of the practice is not confounded by the matter-of-fact emphasis which some whistleblowers place on the content rather than the consequences of their utterances. Those such as Jacqueline Verrett of the US Food and Drug Administration, A. Ernest Fitzgerald (formerly) of the US Department of Defence and William Steiglitz (formerly) of the US Department of Commerce were reluctant to regard themselves as whistleblowers at all, but simply as truth tellers (see Nader *et al.* 1972: 38–55, 89–109; Peters and Branch 1972: 190–206). But Fitzgerald's sardonic suggestion that he 'committed truth' makes it clear that the meaning of truth telling is transformed with the entry into the public realm. And what is characteristic of political situations is that the consequences as well as the content of speech acts be considered (Searle 1971: 133) – that is precisely what makes them political. What emerges from the case study by Anderson *et al.* 1980: 140 *et seq.*) and Peters and Branch's (1972: 16) ironic stylization of a series of cases, is that even if the content of the whistleblower's message is not contested, its significance may be challenged, the motives of the messenger impugned, complexities invoked.

A characteristic control strategy is thus the insistence that the status of whistle-blowers' propositions is context dependent, that they do not have access to the whole story. Against this, the associations of an expression like 'truth telling' may seem to belong to the mythology of an earlier era. The implication is of an author-itative and unambiguous message which 'speaks for itself', the existence of a clear line between right and wrong and its evident transgression. Whatever the *content* of the whistleblower's message, this is precisely the implication which its *form* conveys. The result is that the truth claim which the whistleblower's message advances is always not just cognitive (its content) but moral (its form). Whistleblowing is a speech act in which the act itself speaks.

But it necessarily speaks in context, and what it therefore speaks *to* are the narrative conventions, codes and dramatic categories which the media routinely produce. There is therefore nothing random or accidental about the presence of whistleblowing reports in the media or about the patterning of a given report. The pressure to suppress (from powerful interests) the pressure to publish (from the competitive struggle for readers) and the way the message is encoded (jour-nalistic conventions and interests) are all systematically structured (cf. Gouldner 1976: 107–10). Both the properties of the medium and the structure of social relationships through which the message is disseminated therefore serve to delimit the range of possible meanings. The social meaning of the whistleblower's text cannot be understood independent of this context. It becomes 'dissent' through this process of media definition, irrespective of the intentions of whistle-blowers themselves.

Conflicts within this circumscribed public realm are stylized as contests and performances. The result is not so much the appearance of pluralism as a pluralism of appearances, an indirect, refracted and formulaic representation of competing interests and contradictory demands. That the whistleblowers' challenge to the structural ceremonies of their employing organizations becomes a resource in the mythologizing function of the media, is perhaps an ironic achievement. But if this is patently not (yet) the enlightened public discourse of classical democratic theory, nor is it (yet) the critically functionless rhetoric bemoaned by the gloomier critics of postmodernism.

Lyotard (1984) is both sceptical about the former and affirmative about the latter. Thus, *contra* Habermas, he eschews the possibility and the desirability of generating consensus through any 'ideal speech' variant of democratic dialogue, and he also rejects any interpretation of postmodernism as axiomatically retro-grade. His own particular permutation on the truth/politics relation is accomplished by drawing up a contrast between the denotative language game of scientific knowledge and the narrative language game through which social bonds are developed and legitimation achieved. Both the contrast itself and the stability of its constitutive parts are seen as eroded by the expansion of the performativity criterion and that process of delegitimation which, in a now famous phrase, consists of a widespread 'incredulity towards metanarratives' (Lyotard 1984: xxiv).[5] Whistleblowing episodes can be read as tracers of this transformation, which Lyotard (1984: 3) sees as having been under way since 'at least the end of the 1950s'. Moreover, the foregrounding of language games and the rules which govern them provides a way into probing public responses to the act of blowing the whistle.

Characterizing the response: whistleblowing as 'inform and dissent'

This is because the ambiguities associated with whistleblowing practices are not limited to the social conditions under which they are generated or their subsequent positioning within media narratives. For the resulting texts are, in their turn, subject to further contestation and interpretation at their multiple points of reception. A more diffuse struggle over meaning thus takes place which is beyond both the immediate partisanship associated with a given whistleblowing episode and the narrative conventions through which such episodes come to be represented. Social reactions to whistleblowing are often ambivalent, and one way to probe into such responses, and the competing social characterizations of whistleblowers which accompany them, is by investigating the immediate language of appraisal. But, as Quentin Skinner (1980) points out, such an analysis of the vocabulary of public debate advances our understanding only to the extent to which it indicates the role played by particular words (such as 'blowing the whistle') in supporting some *concept* and some conception of public life. Conceptual change is therefore signalled by the emergence of new meanings for old terms and by additions and deletions to the language in use. When, or if, a term changes its meaning, it also changes its relation to the meaning system in which it is, or was, incorporated. Kuhn's account of scientific change is, one might say the paradigm case, but the point has general application.

This bears directly on the ambivalent patterns of response. My suggestion is that these responses are to be understood not only by reference to the differing implications such acts have for immediately identifiable interests, but also by reference to their impact upon taken for granted assumptions about what is politically virtuous. More specifically, *whistleblowing is an activity in which informing and dissenting are merged*.

This definition consciously inverts and exploits the expression 'advise and consent', that constitutional euphemism for the passage of a Bill through the US Congress. As employed in the well-known novel (and film) of that title by Allen Drury (1960), *Advise and Consent* is seen as an expression whose effect is to mask the normality of backroom politics. One effect of interpreting whistleblowing as a combination of 'inform and dissent' is precisely to foreground the distinctively *public* character of its politics.

It is, of course, a tautological definition. For it to be an instructive one depends upon an acknowledgement of two claims and a demonstration of how they interact. First of all, it presupposes a recognition that 'the informer' and 'the dissenter' occupy contrasting positions in the normative vocabulary and cultural inheritance that is the Western liberal tradition. Within that discourse informer is a term of disapproval, whereas dissent and the dissenter are celebrated. Second, there is a presumption that where this pre-existing language of evaluation is at odds with the emergent practices of control agencies then they will engage in efforts to reconcile the language with the practice. The development of the distinction between informer and informant, and the equation of dissent with resistance, are typical of such moves. The ambiguous and ambivalent response to whistleblowing is due to its location at the point at which these contrasting and contested vocabularies of evaluation intersect.

Let me briefly develop this. 'Informer' and 'informant' have a common etymology but divergent social meanings, the latter word largely lacks the moral freight characteristic of the former. This is made clear by the way in which the semantic authority of Webster's dictionary and the linguistic policing of the former head of the FBI are combined in J. Edgar Hoover's observation that, 'An "informant" is one who gives information of whatever sort; an "informer" is one who informs against another by way of accusation or complaint. Informer is often, informant never, a term of opprobrium' (quoted in Navasky 1981: xviii). Despite rather more leakage than Hoover acknowledged, the distinction still holds good. 'Informant' remains relatively free of contamination by its near neighbour in the lexicon, and the systematic effort to improve the status of the term 'informer' during the heyday of McCarthyism (Navasky 1981: 11–12, 15–19) has proved to be abortive.

In contrast, 'dissent' and 'dissidence' are etymologically discrete terms that are increasingly interchangeable in linguistic practice; Webster's defines dissidence as dissent or disagreement. The shared prefix 'dis' (Latin) means apart, but dissent descends from the Latin verb *sentire* (to feel, to think) whereas dissidence is rooted in *sidere* (to sit). It is not that what was originally a way of distinguishing 'thinking differently' from 'behaving differently' are now combined in conventional usage. It is rather that the modal act of dissent combines thinking and doing so as to become a member of that class of actions which, after Searle (1969), have come to be called speech acts. Individuals who, figuratively speaking, are at odds only with themselves are not dissenters. At a minimum dissent presupposes oral or written disagreement. It is a quintessentially political phenomenon, both behaviourally and in the sense of having a privileged status in the liberal democratic tradition.

But if Edgar Hoover spoke for 'informers' then Hannah Arendt might be said to have spoken for 'dissenters' in suggesting that in contemporary America dissent has come to be defined as resistance (Arendt 1972: 102). This claim, made against the background of the Vietnam War, marks an identifiable tendency rather than an established outcome. Indeed it depends for its effect upon what it seeks to deny, namely that the meaning of dissent is in dispute. The term's prescriptive force remains intact, what is found wanting is the presumption of institutional support for its traditional meaning. It is none the less clear that dissent continues to enjoy a special place in the realm of cultural production, in that a dominant theme of mass media output is that of the individual (or the people) against authority. Conversely informers, almost without exception, are depicted unsympathetically.

It is this contingent relation between the origins of words and their present or emergent functions within the discourse of public life which helps to make the response to whistleblowing cases more explicable. This can be illustrated by a cursory comparison of the Otepka and Ellsberg cases. As Peters and Branch's (1972) discussion makes clear, there are formal similarities between the conduct of Otto Otepka and Daniel Ellsberg, and yet the pattern of public comment shows that those newspapers and politicians who supported one of these cases tended to oppose the other. Otepka, like Ellsberg, violated national security, in his case by passing classified documents to the US Senate Internal Security Subcommittee. Like Ellsberg he had his telephone tapped, was subject to surveillance and harassment and was eventually fired from the State Department in 1963. Ideologically, however, and hence in the allegiances which they inspired and the constituencies to which they appealed, the two cases were quite distinct. Otepka's commitment was to the pursuit and extirpation of what he claimed was communist influence in the executive branch, whereas Ellsberg's action exposed organized government lying about the Vietnam War and was intended as a contribution to stopping that war. As Peters and Branch's account reveals (1972: 222–46) those in the public realm who found Otepka's conduct commendable were inclined to find Ellsberg's deplorable, and vice versa. Those who invoked 'orderly procedure' and 'subversive behaviour' in one case switched to the 'right to know' and 'freedom' in the other, both groups moving back and forth across the line between suppression and expression, between the denigration of informers and the celebration of dissenters. US State Department officials were more consistent – they disapproved of both cases.

It has, however, been the argument of this chapter that the contradictions associated with the notion of whistleblowing are more instructive than the consistencies. Such contradictions are at work in how such episodes are produced, in how they are encoded and distributed by media institutions and in how they are interpreted by publics. They are experienced as intra-psychic dilemmas but they are the product of inter-institutional realignments and discursive shifts as mediated through organizational forms. They are historically specific permutations on a more general opposition between the truth as politically transcendent and the political as an absolute imperative. They are expressive of the clash between technoscientific realism and hyperreal organization structures. The former is thus placed under a powerful compulsion to be at once cognitively effective and politically reflexive, whereas the drive to naturalize the textualities of formal organizations is threatened by the very realism that they strive to simulate. Such contradictions suggest that these 'indecent exposures' should take up a place alongside 'normal accidents' (Perrow 1984) as both symptom and signal of the structural imperatives and changing dynamics of the corporate system itself.

7

DEAD MEN AND NEW SHOES

Of This Time, Of That Place is a much-anthologized short story/novella by Lionel Trilling (1978). First published in the 1940s, it can be read as a fictionalized exploration of the cultural meaning of American higher education, as manifested in and through a particular teacher–student relationship (Trilling himself was a longtime Columbia University professor and distinguished literary critic who died in 1975). His story charts the plurality of determining forces that ripple across and around that relationship as it develops during the course of an academic year. The student in question is strange enough to be certifiable (which is what is destined to happen to him). He is also presented as gifted, as having not just grasped what (literary high) culture 'really' means but as exemplifying what that culture is for. Trilling's fictional teacher recognizes the presence of these qualities, but is effectively complicit with bureaucratic authority, cultural vulgarity, social ambition and a utilitarian ethos in having the student declared insane.

The basis of the novella has been rumoured to derive from Trilling's experience of having the then unknown Allen Ginsberg attend one of his classes. The very idea of such an encounter – between one of America's most influential cultural critics and the beat generation's leading poet – seems made for literary mythologizing. After all, Ginsberg had been expelled from Columbia in 1945 for having made some unflattering remarks about the university's president and for scrawling a skull and crossbones and some allegedly anti-Semitic slogans on to a university window. This latter incident was subsequently enshrined in *Howl* (1956), the poem for which he is best known, as an instance of just how 'I saw the best minds of my generation destroyed by madness . . . expelled from the academies for crazy and publishing obscene odes on the windows of the skull'. And in 1959, Lionel's spouse Diana, herself an accomplished critic, was to publish a memoir that seems permeated by an implicit regard for Ginsberg, in which his (a)social talent for excess is seen as gainsaid by his qualities as a student and as a poet (Trilling 1959).

It is, however, primarily as an *enfant terrible* – or, more nearly, as an ageing bad boy – that 'Allen Ginsberg' entered into legend; the icon of a particular subculture who, in and through the manner of his resistance to such a definition, had by the time of his death become the model of what 'poet' means to the dominant

American media. Inasmuch as *Of this Time, Of that Place* now trails in the wake of this larger system, it has become a tiny ripple in those very currents which the story had originally set itself against.

More generally, however, with the passage of some fifty years, *Of This Time* is manifestly and immutably not of our time. And notwithstanding the higher education setting of *That Place*, it does not shade easily and seamlessly into the here and now of a contemporary academic readership. A story which can be read as having as its subject matter the relation between the familiar and the strange, has itself now acquired a (modest) measure of strangeness. It therefore requires a different order of imaginative effort for today's reader to approach the story as redolent of, and thus pertinent to, teacher/student interaction wherever it occurs. For in that process of crossing between then and now which is involved in reading it in the 1990s, it must perforce pass through those filters which temporal distance and subsequent cultural transformations have put in place. If 'we' read the story at all, then we are inclined to read it within the parameters which are tacitly enforced by the coeval presence of a very different cultural milieu. The result is that a sympathetic contemporary reading which is orientated towards recovering its original meaning gravitates towards nostalgia, whereas a critical reading which points to the manner of its supplanting tends to edge towards condescension.

My intention is not, however, churlishly to construe these as axiomatically *mis*readings, but rather to signal their enabling and limiting role (and 'our' own implication in it) in setting the story's present conditions of legibility. I want only to foreground that my reading of the story interprets it as signalling that contemporary crisis of cultural authority which provides the forage for this book. It is therefore a reading which knowingly and explicitly attempts to recruit the story to and for the here-and-now, whilst yet remaining mindful of that sense of cultural loss to which the narrative originally gestured, a loss for which the story itself has, in its turn, now come to serve as a further testimonial.

The title hints at that contradiction which the story straddles. The same words reappear within the narrative as having been written by Ferdinand Tertan, Trilling's fictional student. They form a small part of an extemporaneous assignment that has been set on the first day of a new class taught by Joseph Howe. What Trilling's teacher had intended and expected was a standard exercise in autobiography, but what he elicits from Tertan is a swollen but not quite inchoate river of rhetoric. Amongst the phrases which ride easily within and upon this torrent are, 'Tertan I am, but what is Tertan? Of this time, of that place, of some parentage, what does it matter?' (Trilling 1978: 78). Yet within the story's own terms time and place are made to matter. And to matter precisely in that an (eventual) effect of Tertan's flood of words is that it at once opens up closures and reveals connections between claims for an autonomous world of ideas and the exigencies of academic organization, and breaks down and threatens to dissolve those boundaries which are used to separate cognitive fields and their fruits from the social practices which sustain them.

In a story constructed across the distinction between materialism and idealism, Tertan is thus the custodian of the latter but becomes the victim of the former. His fate is therefore wholly consistent with the cultural pessimism that is characteristic of literary modernism. It is also in accord with the romanticism of Dostoevsky's remark (in *A Raw Youth*) that 'The nobler type of people are all mentally ill nowadays', long before such a claim was invested with the kind of theoretical support that it has now acquired from Deleuze and Guattari, Foucault and Kristeva. But as between the fact of cultural diversity and the idea of universal culture, between culture understood as historically contingent and spatially delimited, and culture as a manifestation of a more general truth, Tertan speaks for and to the second set of terms with a confidence that contemporary theory can no longer muster.

The student's narrative function is, however, to reveal the compromises and contradictions of his teacher's position, and it is Trilling's engagement with those contradictions which is my justification for resurrecting a dead man's story and for exploring the conception of culture that it enacts. In *Of This Time* the very details of cultural expression are presented both as evidence of an ineluctable grounding *and* as the indispensable accomplices of a claim to transcendence. The story proclaims its universality through an insistence upon the irreducibility of Tertan's individual difference. Roland Barthes' (1973) now classic analysis of myth is both an explanation and a subversion of the process by which such a union is routinely accomplished, and how 'blissful clarity' is thereby established. It would, however, be an unwarranted foreclosure on Trilling's sense of a problem to regard it as having been displaced by such developments in semiotics. It is precisely his equivocation and the associated awareness of difficulty that I want to recover and to preserve, not least because that difficulty bears a family resemblance to Barthes' (1977a: 190–215) own distinctive and inimitably Gallic inflection of the paradoxical demands of teaching, writing and intellectual work. For Barthes, 'writing', which was the most valued term in his very considerable lexicon, was understood as an act of transgression that was to be set over and against the authority-serving legality of 'speech'. Intellectuals, defined as persons who print and publish their speech, thus lay between. One hint of, and a way into Trilling's version of such a dilemma is signalled in the opening pages of his *The Liberal Imagination*, where he offered his own definition of culture:

> A culture is not a flow nor even a confluence; the form of its existence is struggle, or at least debate, it is nothing if not a dialectic. And in any culture there are likely to be certain artists who contain a large part of the dialectic within themselves; their meaning and their power lying in their contradictions . . . .
>
> (Trilling 1950: 9)

That such a maxim is immanent in Trilling's own story emerges more clearly when it is compared with Stewart Ewen's account of a much briefer academic encounter. Ewen too is a New York-based university teacher, but the episode that he records is both more obviously of this time and reads as more nearly exemplary of that place – and of this one – as each of them now occupy 'our' imaginations in our own particular here-and-nows.

Almost fifty years after the appearance of Trilling's novella, Ewen introduced his *All Consuming Images: The Politics of Style in Contemporary Culture* (1989) with 'Shoes for Thought'. Ewen's is a concise, factual and altogether more matter-of-fact anecdote about a fleeting exchange between professor and student. By contrast with the Trilling story the ambience is hurried, urban, contemporary. The academic discipline is not English literature but 'media studies'; the informing theoretical stance is not liberal humanism but cultural Marxism. And whereas Trilling's local subtext was diffusely influenced by the anti-Stalinist stance of the New York intellectuals who had gathered around *Partisan Review*, Ewen's representation of resistance to consumer culture seems a response that is less obviously mediated through any such communal micropolitics. Moreover, as a text written in the shadow of the Gordon Gekko years of the Reagan presidency, Ewen's book is perhaps even more clearly beleaguered in tone than the Trilling novella. Ewen tells his story not as a fictional exploration of the moral meaning of the teacher–student relation, but as an empirical illustration of the cultural form that the relation takes under modern conditions.

Having concluded a review session for a forthcoming final exam in media studies, he heads for his office, but becomes aware of being pursued by one of the students from the class. Ewen writes:

> I stopped at the third floor landing and waited for him to reach me. Out of breath and with the familiar look of final exam jitters in his eyes, he approached me. 'Professor Ewen, Professor Ewen', he gasped. 'Can I ask you one more question?' 'Sure', I responded, attempting to soothe his nerves. 'One more question', he repeated, and then, in dead seriousness, he continued. 'Professor Ewen, where did you get your shoes?'
>
> I had just spent the better part of two hours reviewing course materials with students in the class, and my *shoes* were – for this young man – of utmost importance. My first reaction, hopelessly professorial, was 'why bother?' On reflection, however, I took heart. This kid with ingenuous clarity, had absorbed the essence of the course. In the contemporary world where the mass media serve as increasingly powerful arbiters of *reality* the primacy of style over substance has become the normative consciousness. My shoes *were* after all, what the course was all about. On some level, they are what this book is all about.
>
> (Ewen 1989: 1–2 italics in original)

Both stories thus rest upon, and acquire their force from, a teacher-perpetrated error and its recognition. It is this, in turn, which allows the reader to infer the theoretical stances (and conceptions of what is real) that underpin them. At the same time the stories can provide a way into investigating the kind of repair work that is characteristically undertaken in attempts to bridge the gap between received academic approaches to contemporary culture and the world(s) which students are perceived to inhabit.

(Knowing readers will of course see through this transparent attempt to ensure that a dead author's work of fiction will now be haunted by the ghostly facts of Ewen's more obviously contemporary encounter. But let it stand. It is no more than an imperfect proxy for that which I am unable to see but can at least dimly sense, i.e. the material specificities of whatever cultural position you understand yourself to occupy. To be sure, in the best loved fairy story the shoe fits *exactly*. But for even the most eager and compliant readers to put themselves into Cinderella's (shoeless) place still requires an imaginative engagement with the narrative. The invitation for you to step into someone else's shoes is therefore not so much an attempt to encourage cultural cross-dressing or even cognitive tourism, as it is an incentive to reflect upon just how that (other) place might relate to your own. For this purpose the notion of an 'essential' teacher/student difference is a tactical assumption which I will eventually problematize.)

The challenge which Tertan, as Trilling's fictional student, poses for Joseph Howe, as his teacher, is presented as one which shrugs off the latter's initial attempts to give it a name. To name would be to permit its annexation; to open it up to those processes of closure and categorization through which potentially dislocative effects might safely be both acknowledged and regulated. Against this, the narrative invests the student's written work and his forms of talk with a defining elusiveness and a categorical indeterminacy. On the one hand his words seem to be predicated upon, and purport to enact, assumptions of an affinity between teacher and taught. The invocation and appeal is to a secure, settled and shared conception of culture; a discourse in common. Yet Tertan's words also seem to derive from, and give expression to, a strongly and strangely attenuated angle of vision. The result is that received meanings, although not actually confounded, nevertheless become so charged and fissured that they continually threaten to buckle. Tertan's speech is thus mannered yet mobile and intense, and his otherwise ornate and florid writing is shot through with such aphorisms as 'existence without alloy', which Howe experiences as disconcertingly astute. The effect is not one of a loss of meaning but rather of its refraction; not of language breaking up but rather of language breaking out; of the discourse of high culture changing shape as it passes through and along the flaws and fractures of a self which that discourse can only imperfectly construct. The result is, that whether they are written or spoken, Tertan's words become allusive and elliptical, as if matter-of-factly drawn towards the boundaries of (another) sense.

For Howe, a salient but unintended effect of Tertan's unfamiliar articulation of a familiar discourse is to focus his attention not only on the manner of its construction but on the conditions of its persistence. Within the terms of the story this is highlighted by the contrast between Tertan and a student politician called Blackburn. Whereas the correlate of Tertan's lack of worldliness is his sternly disciplined respect for an unnamable and unsayable reality beyond appearance, for Blackburn the present exigencies of time and place set the parameters of appropriate conduct and self-definition. Blackburn is thus wholly single-minded in his careerism and wholly pragmatic as to the means of its accomplishment. He is recognizably a variant on a social type which was made familiar by American fiction and cultural commentary in the late 1940s and 1950s, i.e. the conformingly competitive, Goffmanesque organization man in whom the rat-race and other-directedness are made to meet. Blackburn is mindful of appearances because he is eager for influence, attuned to the ways in which institutional imperatives might be reconciled with personal advancement.

Blackburn's interest in 'literature' is thus limited to its possible contribution to a desired image of well-roundedness. Its purpose is to provide more-or-less useful, more-or-less exotic embellishments upon what really matters, cultural fig leaves which both draw attention to, and coyly cover up, his otherwise very ordinary ambition. Moreover, what is transparently expressed by Blackburn's perception of Howe is the absence of a perceived warrant for the authority that Howe exercises, other than that which derives from his institutional position. That authority is seen as in no way dependent upon that literary conception of intellect for which Howe sees himself as standing. On the contrary, a crucial feature of Blackburn's challenge to Howe is his calculatingly cavalier play with that positive sanctioning of feeling and opinion that is (or rather was) characteristic of the rhetoric of literary criticism. More generally, Blackburn is a student who does not just lack an understanding of Howe's conception of culture, but who clearly embodies the notion that it simply does not matter. What therefore comes to disturb Howe is that Blackburn is nevertheless able to do more than just get by, but to actually flourish within the academy. It is therefore not only dislike, but fear, which leads Howe to give a bare pass mark to a Blackburn paper that he regards as a clear failure. But he cannot avoid confronting his own expediency when Blackburn comes to him to complain about his grade. Blackburn threatens to go over his head to the Dean. As evidence of Howe's shortcomings, he plans to present a bizarre misreading of a critic's response to Howe's poetry ('self-intoxicated' is interpreted as 'drunk') together with the teacher's endorsement of Tertan's application to membership of the college literary society. Howe changes the grade to an unequivocal fail. Faced with the prospect of course failure, Blackburn is prompted into a display of compliance which is so extraordinarily obsequious, 'that Howe, whose head had become icy clear in the nonsensical drama, thought, "The boy is mad" and began to speculate fantastically whether something in himself attracted or developed aberration' (Trilling 1978: 109).

This episode plays in counterpoint to an earlier sequence when, in a moment of exasperation, Howe had fallen back on to 'madness' as a shorthand way of naming/controlling (for) Tertan's disturbing resistance to categorization. But notwithstanding an inner conviction that he must not let the matter out of his own hands, Howe had none the less raised Tertan's case with the Dean. Thus:

He alone could keep alive – not forever but for a somehow important time – the question, 'What is Tertan?' He alone could keep it still a question. Some sure instinct told him that he must not surrender the question to a clean official desk in a clear official light to be dealt with, settled and closed.

He heard himself saying 'Is the Dean busy at the moment? I'd like to see him'.

It was frequently to be with fear and never without a certainty of its meaning in his own knowledge of himself that he would recall this simple routine request and the feeling of shame and freedom it gave him as he sent everything down the official chute. In the end of course, no matter what he did to 'protect' Tertan, he would have had to make the same request and lay the matter on the Dean's clean desk. But it would always be a landmark of his life that, at the very moment when he was rejecting the official way, he had been, without will or intention, so gladly drawn to it.

(Trilling 1978: 94)

Trilling presents a traditional conception of cultural authority in and through the character of Howe. The text is thus suffused with images of authority and respect; from 'the lawful seizure of power' and 'the scrawl (which) confirmed his authority', on the story's second page (1978: 73); through to the exchanges characteristic of a settled classroom routine marked by 'respectful curiosity' (1978: 88), 'this mark of respect' (1978: 89); the 'vaguely respectful surprise of the other students' (1978: 90) and 'a coma of respect for words' (1978: 91); deviating briefly to quickly and successfully rebut a 'certain insolence' (1978: 89); before moving on to the first encounter with Blackburn's 'eager deference' (1978: 96), and 'slightly impudent play with hierarchy' (1978: 96) that foreshadows his eventual challenge to Howe.

The legitimacy of Howe's authority is, however, dependent upon a distinctive fusion of institutional position and cognitive assertion. It is Howe's growing realization of the tensions associated with such a combination which gives the story its dynamic. It first surfaces in Howe's recognition that 'his literary contempt for Frederic Woolley meant nothing, for he suddenly understood how he respected Woolley in the ways of the world' (1978: 80) (Woolley is the editor of a well-known journal who proves to be critical of Howe's poetry). It is the implications of this contradictory combination for Howe's conduct which Blackburn and Tertan (unwittingly) conspire to reveal. The contrasting assumptions and rival action tendencies across which this conception of authority has been constructed are highlighted by the contrast between the two students. Blackburn so prioritizes the workings of the institution, that legitimacy is not just rendered coextensive with the fact of consent, but effectively reduced to it. Against this, Tertan's understanding of, and allegiance to, the traditional cultural mission of a liberal education affords him no protection against the workings of those secular formalities and day to day routines by which he is to be excluded from the campus.

Blackburn does more than exemplify an emergent student type; he is a manifestation of a more general cultural tendency and evidence of a wider social change. The associated threat to a literary-derived conception of culture is also clearly signalled by the way in which the story opens and closes with – and is therefore literally framed by – the taking of photographs. To begin with, this alternate technology of representation is presented as if it were quite incidental, no more than a background image in which the camera itself is being handled with something less than assurance by its young custodian (the Dean's niece). But by the time of the graduation day with which the story ends, her rudimentary box camera has been replaced by an altogether more elaborate device which, together with tripod and light meter, its owner has learned to use decisively and with confidence, so that:

> In its compact efficiency the camera almost had a life of its own, but Hilda treated it with easy familiarity, looked into its eye, glanced casually at its gauges. Then from a pocket she took still another leather case and drew from it a small instrument through which she looked first at Howe, who began to feel inanimate and lost, and then at the sky. She made some adjustment on the instrument, then some adjustment on the camera. She swept the scene with her eye, found a spot and pointed the camera in its direction. She walked to the spot, stood on it and beckoned to Howe. With each new leather case, with each new instrument and with each new adjustment she had grown in ease and now she said, 'Joe, will you stand here?'
>
> Obediently Howe stood where he was bidden. She had yet another instrument . . . .
>
> (1978: 112)

This sets the scene for an encounter in which the Dean links arms with (a reluctant) Howe and Blackburn, and offers Blackburn not just his congratulations but indicates his approval:

> 'Isn't that good?' the Dean said. Still Howe did not answer and the Dean, puzzled and put out, turned to Hilda. 'That's a very fine looking camera, Hilda'. She touched it with affectionate pride.
>
> 'Instruments of precision' said a voice. 'Instruments of precision'. Of the three with joined arms, Howe was the nearest to Tertan, whose gaze took in all the scene except the smile and the nod which Howe gave him . . . .
>
> 'Instruments of precision' said Tertan for the last time, addressing no one, making a casual comment to the universe. And it occurred to Howe that Tertan might not be referring to Hilda's equipment. The

131

sense of the thrice woven circle of the boy's loneliness smote him fiercely.

(1978: 114–15)

Earlier in the story, however, in the discursive setting of the official records which contain Tertan's file, it is the small identifying photograph of the student which unsettles the disciplinary ordering of a system that is otherwise reliant upon the printed word. The effect is to open up the file(s) to an interpretation which foregrounds the(ir) governing principles of selectivity and their limits; the kind of reading systematized in Garfinkel's (1967: 186–207) classic account of 'good' organizational reasons for 'bad' clinic records. For at the moment of exposure (telling phrase), Tertan had turned his eyes upwards and away from the camera and, 'His mouth, as though conscious of the trick played upon the photographer, had the sly superior look that Howe knew' (1978: 93). The result is an image which the Dean's secretary finds 'fascinating'. For Howe, however, seeking reassurance that Tertan is not insane, it is precisely such evidence of resistance which is disturbing. Whereas the printed records had suggested only sadness rather than madness, the photograph with the 'absurd piety of the eyes and the conscious slyness of the mouth' provided 'little enough comfort'.

If this passage is read with a sense of the range and variety of discourses that are described therein, then it reads as indeterminate and subversive of settled meanings. Within the photographic image the organs of vision and of voice are presented as offering a contradictory message; within the file the photographic image contradicts the written text; and within Howe's literary humanist discourse it is the disturbing contradictions of the file which accelerate that movement towards closure which impels him to send 'everything down the official chute'.

Yet within the overall movement of the narrative it is photography which acts as a metonym for those forces which threaten (literary high) culture, forces understood as *external* to it. The general effect is therefore to forge a link between the practice of photography and the extension of control over, and undermining of, that humanistic conception of the subject and individual rights which provides Trilling's story with its moral ground.

At this level then, the story serves to protect both its own discursive foundations and its own technology of representation by aligning and implicating an alternate, image-producing technology with those social changes which threaten humanist, literary discourse. But at another level, the discernible disturbances in the text can be seen to derive from the external projection of problems that are internal to such a discourse. Those disturbances reveal, for example, that it is only in so far as it is an indicator of respect for literary culture that Tertan's waywardness is positively sanctioned. The narrative may grant a privileged place to the combination of humanist subject and transgression, but even within the story's own limits that place is confined to the *printed* page. Tertan's photograph signals difference without deference, resistance without respect. It is therefore understood as unfamiliar rather than universal, as other rather than as the same, and as a consequence it offers 'little enough comfort'.

On the one hand therefore, Trilling's story is made possible by, and constructed across, his understanding of culture as contradictory and tension-filled. On the other, that tension is not extended to the production of images, or to the relation between words and images. Thus 'photography' here seems designed to serve only as a primitive term; it is (made) undialectical, understood only as a disciplinary technology and not as a mode of representation; it *means* control. But if the story is read against (or perhaps that should be with?) the grain, then 'photography' does more than simply signal the closure characteristic of the dominant culture of the time. It exposes the story's own guiding discourse and *its* limits, opening up that place in which the text's own movement towards closure and control is most evident.

Of this Time, Of that Place predates both television and the transistor. It is located at what can now be seen as no more than the threshold of media expansion and the associated proliferation of new forms of cultural discourse. The concern it displays about photography as an iconic form of representation could be said to anticipate the subsequent anxiety of literary intellectuals about the hyperreal. Yet at the same time it is a text permeated by the kind of cultural fears about 'mass society' which had their origins in the nineteenth century but which were much amplified by the impact of Hollywood. That the narrative makes a young woman the agent of these changes dovetails with Huyssen's (1986b) suggestion that with the development of the mass culture thesis fear of the masses and fear of the feminine became linked. If, for Trilling, these waves had begun to lap dangerously close to the once secure ground of high culture, then for Ewen they clearly now constitute a sea in which (shoes and all) he is obliged to swim. His 'Shoes for Thought' anecdote therefore has a more obviously contemporary cultural resonance as well as being filtered through a different theoretical allegiance. It none the less shares an underlying continuity with the Trilling story, not least by the kind of confidence it displays in the correctness of its own assumptions and authority. That Ewen proves to be mistaken about the 'familiar look of final exam jitters in his (students) eyes' is what helps to give his anecdote its force. That he might be mistaken about the cultural import and meaning of the student's words is not considered. It is this which links his 'hopelessly professorial' initial reaction of 'why bother', and his subsequent taking heart that 'This kid, with ingenuous clarity, had absorbed the essence of the course'. For neither of these responses poses a threat either to his pre-existing theoretical dispositions or to the associated presumption of cultural authority. Yet in *All Consuming Images* Ewen writes of his coming to recognize that 'style' is both an elusive and an important notion. And in setting his students an assignment on 'What style means to me' he edges towards an awareness that his own settled and secure meanings may not be wholly adequate to the question. He begins, that is, if not to learn from his students ('these kids'), then at least to recognize their allegiance to discrete protocols and foundations for cultural authority and to alternate configurations of resentment, resistance and pleasure. Amongst the extracts from student essays which Ewen reproduces, there is one written by a young woman who had been caught up in the Beirut war zone. Her remarkable narrative moves matter-of-factly between designer clothes, bombed-out buildings, domestic minutiae and death. Its juxtapositions offer a chastening counterpoint, not just to Ewen's initial condescension, but also to Benetton's advertisements and to Baudrillard's accounts of the (Gulf) war which did not take place.

There is, by comparison, something endearingly loopy about the apocalyptic account of rock music in general and Mick Jagger in particular which appears in Allan Bloom's *The Closing of the American Mind* (1987: 74–81).[1] It is an interpretation filtered through Nietzsche and sanctioned by Plato but the basic premise is the presence of folk devils and the controlling sentiments are fear and loathing. In a somewhat more subdued fashion, Bloom approaches Woody Allen's *Zelig* through Heidegger and finds it badly wanting, and 'never nearly as funny as was Kafka' (1987: 146). There is no sense that the film might be of philosophical (or pedagogical, or artistic, or commercial) interest because of its attempt to use and extend a popular medium in a distinctively *cinematic* way. The problem is not that Bloom seems ignorant of (Woody Allen's commanding knowledge of) the language of film or (Mick Jagger's modestly talented dependence upon) the tradition of the blues. The problem is his (anti-Socratic) conviction that such ignorance does not matter, that it does not materially affect either his ability to pass such judgements or their quality. The determining tone of Bloom's book thus derives as much from his own temporally and socially specific experience of deskilling as it does from an epistemological allegiance to unchanging Platonic forms; as much from its methodological limitations and pedagogical conceits as from its cultural conservatism. In short, inasmuch as Bloom's book is an example of what Nietzsche once called 'philosophizing with a hammer', it is thereby subject to that methodological maxim which Kaplan refers to as 'the law of the instrument', i.e. if you give a small boy such a bludgeon, then he will hit everything in sight.

Bloom exemplifies the conservative wing of a more general tendency. His familiar and formulaic combination of resentment of, anxiety about, and condescension towards the mass media has its counterpart on the left in the ambiguous legacy of the Frankfurt School. They share a profound antipathy towards media culture and its presumed consequences, but differ in what they take to be the locus of determinacy. The lines of fault are variously seen as grounded within the industries which produce such debased forms of culture, and/or with the texts which realize them, and/or with the audiences which recognize them. An awareness of the limitations of such responses has, in effect, been institutionalized within academic populism (as, for example, by John Fiske), but such scepticism reaches beyond the ranks of this latter, and is now associated with a range of positions and takes a variety of forms. For example, the shortcomings of 'the-media-as-wicked' thesis have been exposed to (and by) Umberto Eco's (1987: 151) concise wit and Jim Collins (1989: 7–27) has sardonically documented the (popular) representation of the selfsame thesis within some of the most popular products of this purportedly irredeemable system. The specifics of Bloom's own closed-mindedness can be highlighted by substituting (whether as whimsy or as heresy) 'popular culture' for 'Plato' in the following passage. The effect is that his roundly rhetorical remarks about his students' exasperation come to serve as an ironic commentary on his own stance:

> The very fact of their fury shows how much Plato threatens what is dear and intimate to them . . . . Yet if a student can – and this is most difficult and unusual – draw back, get a critical distance on what he clings to, come to doubt the ultimate value of what he loves, he has taken the first and most valuable step towards the philosophic conversion. Indignation is the soul's defence against the wound of doubt about its own; it reorders the cosmos to support the justice of its cause . . . . Recognising indignation for what it is constitutes knowledge of the soul.
>
> (Bloom 1987: 71)

What leads me to select these particular authors and the issues of reality and representation with which they are concerned? The specific permutations on liberalism (Trilling), marxism (Ewen) and conservatism (Bloom) which inform these texts are each understood as formally sanctioned by cultural authority, but also as effectively threatened by social marginality. Taken together they offer the opportunity: to observe how the custodians of received but embattled ideas and practices accommodate disturbances which derive from alternative discourses as refracted through and by their students; to see just how they strive to bridge the gap between modes of cultural understanding recognized as phenomenologically discrete from their own; to locate just where and when a purportedly pedagogical problem begins to blur into a theoretical difficulty. And they also provide a first cut into the cultural circumstances under which a concern with demarcating between reality and hyperreality comes to be experienced as pressing.

The intention is *not* to reduce these informed and informing theories to being no more than reflections of their institutional location. *Or* to axiomatically adjudicate in favour of their students as more attuned to the present and more inventive about future possibilities (whether because they are understood as individually gifted, subculturally discrete, or socially typical). But I do want to resist understanding the disturbances that they introduce as at best nothing more than aids to lower level manoeuvring, as just so much (more or less inert) ballast which must be jettisoned in moving onwards and upwards.

What I therefore share with Ewen's student is an altogether more pedestrian concern; that of trying to slow down such fast-moving intellectual machinery. In the first instance, this is in order to indulge in nothing more demanding than the joys of just looking, and of taking delight in the kind of metaphorical mixing that such an activity both makes possible and necessitates. In its turn, however, this random browsing through classic hits and new releases serves as a preamble to the more obviously analytic pleasures of blurring and reordering their principles of categorization.

Such 'botanizing on the texts' (cf. Smith 1990: 166–7; Du Plessis 1992: 1–2) bears a family resemblance to Benjamin's (1973: 36) classic description of Baudelaire as *flâneur*, as the poet/observer of the flux of modernity through his practice of 'botanising on the asphalt'. It is also related to Buck-Morss' (1986) remarks on the practice of station or channel hopping on radio and television; to Smart's (1994) discussion of contemporary eating and dining as 'botanising with the palate'; and to that 200-year-old encounter with irrepressible profusion and 'savagery' whilst 'botanising in a pleasant wood'[2] which, for Raban (1990: 154), is still the quintessential distillation of America as seen through European eyes. More generally, it is an indispensable adjunct to a pragmatic interest in the possibilities of bricolage. By this is meant an unprincipled probing of, and borrowing from, the workings and settings of such theories before they can take wing and begin their long philosophic flight into that higher, purer and more rarefied atmosphere of academic professionalism in and on which they thrive.

This is to redefine the disturbances in these texts as neither encumbrances (at best) nor threats (at worst), not even as side effects or symptoms, but as endemic, as constitutive of a cultural condition that is distinguished both by the enhanced density and layering of its component features and by the enhanced permeability of its categories. The teacher/taught relation provides a floating marker for this accelerating leakage across proliferating boundaries; a still privileged, but no longer insulated site. On the one hand, it can still function as the enabling position from which to explore the impure pluralities and sustaining inequalities of a hybridized, globalized, localized, polyglot cultural milieu understood as the object of inquiry. On the other hand, however, specific mediations of that milieu also impact upon such a critical practice – in the form of institutional realignments, disciplinary developments and concomitant attempts to facilitate, regulate, constrain and control the general features of professionalized intellectual work. The teacher/taught relation is here understood not as a residual outcome of such institutional and discursive determinations but as the appropriate location from which to begin probing the limits and possibilities of this overall pattern. This serves as an ongoing reminder that whereas (as Trilling's story recognizes) 'professionalized intellectual' is an oxymoron, 'specific intellectual' (in Foucault's sense of that term) need not be. By using the tensions and pluralities of the teacher/taught couplet as an aid to keeping 'professionalized' away from the temptations of closure, and 'intellectual' away from the conceit of free floating, they may also create a space within (and against) which Foucault's notion can begin to assert itself.

Which is why the American academy, with its sheer institutional density, its huge number of participating organizations, its graduate schools as the locus of both professional closure and competitive struggle, seemed a good place to start. For one of the correlates of such a system is that the modal conception of social and cultural research and scholarship is one whose products and practices are more nearly isomorphic with other forms of large scale organization than is typical of the British pattern of 'academic as artisan' (cf. Perry 1992). But before crossing the Atlantic to see how they do such things in Britain, there are some counterfactual hints discernible in the critical writing of Robert Warshow (and in Trilling's response to it). From his studies of American popular culture there is a pedagogical lesson to be drawn, a methodological point to be made, and a cultural connection to be claimed, and for that composite purpose it is Warshow's wedge (rather than Bloom's hammer) which can provide the necessary leverage.

Warshow belonged to a later generation of critics than Trilling but at age 37 he was dead. Almost everything he published was brought together in *The Immediate Experience: Movies, Comics, Theatre and Other Aspects of Popular Culture* (1962), a posthumous collection for which Trilling wrote the introduction. Warshow was effectively a solo father (his wife was incurably ill), a journal editor (rather than a career academic), and a lover of movies *as* movies (i.e. not just as a hunting ground for 'art', 'sociology', or any other extraneous theoretical predisposition). The reading of his work by commentators such as Christopher Brookeman (1984: 59–66) and Andrew Ross (1989: 30–34) makes it clear that Warshow was other things as well, not least a highly politicized interpreter and product of his time rather than ours. Their emphasis on placing him politically leads them to foreground his antipathy to what he saw as the banality of Julius and Ethel Rosenberg and the over-inflated claims made for Arthur Miller's *The Crucible* as a play.

By contrast, my own interest is not so much in documenting the genealogy of what Warshow was against, as in exploring the present significance of what he was for. His writing is not, of course, reducible to his roles as a father, as a non-academic intellectual and as a fan of popular culture. These roles do, however, impact upon and instructively reinforce both its plurality and its power, and it is their pedagogic and methodological import which leads me to foreground those occasions in his work which are discernibly informed by a distinctive configuration of paternal affection, critical scepticism and a pluralist('s) cultural respect.

Consider, for example, the claims he made for the gangster film, long before the classics of the genre were culturally upgraded by the development of *auteur* theory and the creation and valorization of film noir as a category. For Warshow, 'the gangster is the "no" to that great American "yes" which is stamped so big over our official culture' (1962: 90). In a society officially 'committed to a cheerful view of life' (1962: 83) the gangster movie has, 'From its beginnings . . . been a consistent and astonishingly complete presentation of the modern sense of tragedy' (1962: 84–5). The gangster is both driven to succeed and condemned to be punished; to both assert himself as an individual and to die because of it. But what dies in a gangster movie is a cultural meaning and a style of life, not 'the undifferentiated *man*, but the individual with a name, the gangster, the success; even to himself he is a creature of the imagination' (1962: 88, italics in original). Warshow thus sees the form of the genre as depending upon a contradictory (de)construction of (American) individualism – that one must not fail and that one cannot succeed. This Mertonian[3] dilemma is at once dramatically displayed and (aesthetically) resolved by the gangster's death.

Half a century later Mike Davis' book *City of Quartz* (1990) employs just such a basic antinomy as a point of entry for his analysis of Los Angeles. Davis inflects and refracts it through film noir, grimly and powerfully bringing it up to date, first by recording the amplification and acceleration of its political subtext into dystopian myth, and then by revealing how its radical potential is now subject to *post-noir* multiple fracturing along a bleakly apocalyptic/romantic oppositional axis. Underpinned and disciplined by the depth of Davis' historical understanding of class and ethnic divisions in Los Angeles, this then becomes a synoptic grid with which he both orders and deconstructs that city as a place and as an idea.

So although Warshow's claims for the gangster film (and for the western) were innovative at the time of writing, there is a clear sense in which his essays now appear as dated. Given their emphasis on form, they can only be said to have successfully weathered that time's passing at the cost of being assimilated into nostalgic myth. As such, they are vulnerable not just to more-or-less-obviously cynical appropriations and to more-or-less-obviously misanthropic send-ups. They are also open to displacement by such second order satires as Pynchon's *Vineland* (1991), a work whose targets include both such appropriations and their satirical offspring.

What I none the less hope to at least hint at, if not to demonstrate, is that aspects of Warshow's method do remain fresh (cf. Martin 1993). This is seen in his subsequent interpretation of the western, which is filtered through and constructed against his reading of the gangster film. The (classic) western may now be a moribund form, but what Warshow does is to enshrine that cultural moment when the western offered a serious orientation to the problem of violence that was otherwise unavailable in American culture. It also represented a popular art form which depended upon and explored the concept of honour. Honour is understood as a matter of personal bearing, 'a style, concerned as much with harmonious appearances as with desirable consequences' (Warshow 1962: 94). It is above all the purity of his own image that the gunfighter is concerned to defend, so that no matter what he has done:

(H)e *looks* right, . . . he has judged his own failure and assimilated it . . . he can do nothing but play out the drama of the gunfight . . . . What 'redeems' him is that he no longer believes in this drama and neverthe-less will continue to play his role perfectly; the pattern is all . . . .

The gun tells us that he lives in a world of violence and even that he 'believes in violence'. But the drama is one of self-restraint; the moment of violence must come in its own time and according to its special laws, or else it is valueless . . . . Really it is not violence at all which is the 'point' of the Western movie, but a certain image of man, a style, which expresses itself most clearly in violence. Watch a child with his toy guns and you will see: what interests him is not (as we so much fear) the fantasy of hurting others, but to work out how a man might look when he shoots or is shot.

(Warshow 1962: 98–105, italics in original)

It is because Warshow never repudiated a boyhood passion for the movies that his child with a toy gun behaves so differently from Kaplan's small boy with a hammer. It is the boy in the man who looks for the man in the boy, bringing his cultural understanding to bear with generosity and affection – with style, if you will – employing it not as an all purpose weapon but as a selective visual aid.

This selectivity is shaped by a cerebral sentiment that is as much moral as it is cognitive, one which allows the writing to tread a line between mere sentimentality and critical detachment. It is this sentiment which makes Warshow's filial essay, 'An Old Man Gone', not just possible, but recognizably intertextual with the others in the collection. It is above all at work in Warshow's account of the running argument between his 11-year-old son and himself with respect to horror comics, where it survives those contrasts in mood and register that derive from the essay's explicitly parental inflection. 'Paul, the Horror Comics, and Dr Wertham' thus exemplifies that willingness to implicate himself in what he wrote about which Trilling sees as crucial to Warshow's achievements as a critic.

The point then is that Warshow was always already complicit with popular culture, willing from the beginning to acknowledge it as *his* culture, of having been constituted by it, and hence capable not just of thinking about it but of thinking *with* it. Yet he responded to it not as some kind of fair weather populist, but as a fully paid-up intellectual mindful of its pleasures, its limitations and its possibilities and what they might teach him about his society – and about himself. He therefore made the (sometimes/often) congruent relation between the movies' fantasies and his own integral to his criticism rather than an incidental or accidental feature of it.

Read one way, *The Immediate Experience* is a title which serves to signal both the distinctiveness of popular culture and Warshow's involvement with it. But in the moment of embracing the present, it also alters relations with the past and orientations to the future, and thereby hints at a larger discontinuity. Writing at the end of the 1960s Leslie Fiedler (1972: 73) refers to it as the specifically American tendency 'to *imagine* a destiny rather than to inherit one' (italics in original). But then for Fiedler we can all be imaginary Americans, 'decadent children playing Indians', and he suggests that what comes with this is the predisposition to inhabit myth rather than history. The child that Warshow observed was neither quite that innocent nor quite that decadent, and the confident absolutism of Fiedler's oppositions is at odds with Warshow's recognition of their interdependencies. It is precisely Warshow's awareness of both some shared legacy of origins and the inevitability of present difference (as, for example, this is mediated through his son/father/(grand)son subtext) which makes him so antipathetic to such evasions as 'We'll go on forever, Pa. We're the people' in the closing frames of John Ford's film of *The Grapes of Wrath*. But Warshow does not just knowingly write from within a changing culture; he writes in order to change the terms by which it has conventionally been interpreted. The tone is sometimes sombre but not melancholy, so that Warshow's writing moves at the edge of that sensibility and that sense of possibility which prompted Raymond Chandler to insist that:

> Shakespeare would have done well in any generation because he would have refused to die in a corner; he would have taken the false gods and made them over; he would have taken the current formulae and forced them into something lesser men thought them incapable of . . . . Instead of saying 'This medium is not good', he would have used it and made it good. If some people called some of his work cheap (which some of it is) he wouldn't have cared a rap . . . .
>
> (Chandler 1962 : 82)

Greil Marcus (1975: 97) approvingly cites this same statement as an indication of how Chandler completely 'understood what it means to be an American artist', even as he was failing to come to terms with screenwriting in Hollywood. Marcus goes on to say that, 'The momentum of democracy (of equality) (of conformity) that powers American life does not, as Tocqueville thought it might, bleed all the life out of culture: it has created a wholly new kind, with all sorts of risks and possibilities'. This is a thesis demonstrated by Marcus' own classic text (*Mystery Train*), both through the cumulative plausibility of its general thesis (that rock 'n roll is not just youth culture or counter culture, but quite simply *American* culture), and through the splendid waywardness of its detailed claims (e.g. that 'there was a lot of Harmonica Frank in Lyndon B. Johnson . . . that the dreams of Huck and Ahab are not always very far apart' (1975: 14–15)).

Marcus' words move in a different register than do Warshow's. Their tone was not so much made possible by the 1960s as it was powerfully sanctioned by that time. Nevertheless Warshow on the movies and Marcus on Elvis can – and should – be read together. Warshow wrote that he had, 'not brought Henry James to the movies or the movies to Henry James, but . . . the man who goes to the movies is the same as the man who reads James' (1962: xxviii). Given that *The Age of Innocence* (a novel by James' friend Edith Wharton) has been successfully filmed by the director of *Taxi Driver* and *Raging Bull*, then Warshow's enthusiasm for both Edward G. Robinson and *The Bostonians* no longer seems unusual. In fact, his words no longer seem in any way challenging, but rather as curiously tentative and excessively circumspect. Conversely, when Marcus observes that he cannot mull 'over Elvis without thinking of Herman Melville', he can now be interpreted as tacitly drawn towards the very refinements of which he was then so overtly suspicious. In short, when Warshow and Marcus are brought to bear on each other they can now productively be read for their convergences, notwithstanding the contrasts in idiom, in mood and in subject matter.

One incidental effect of such a reading is to make plausible the idea that

Edward G.'s Rico and Melville's Ahab might comfortably share the same sentence. That leaves Presley and Henry James bereft of their original textual partners. But if director Martin Scorsese can discern traces of prizefighter Jake La Motta's volcanic furies in his subsequent representation of the sedimented rigidities of turn-of-the-century New York's upper strata, then perhaps some future critic might find common ground between the rock of Elvis and Henry's hard place. The pedagogical significance of both Warshow and Marcus (and the cultural significance of Scorsese) is that rather than taking such distinctions as given, they encourage us to look at and across them, because they recognize that that is where culture itself moves.

That Warshow took a child's play seriously was of a piece with his continuing commitment to taking 'all that [popular] nonsense seriously' as Trilling (1962: xx) effectively recognized in his introduction to Warshow's *The Immediate Experience*. Trilling explicitly invokes Warshow's understanding of fatherhood and documents the younger man's conduct and advice with respect to his own son. This not only provided a point of social contact through which the two men's critical differences and disagreements could filtrate. It signalled a recognition of what Raymond Williams called the ordinariness of culture, as it is enacted in, for example, the day to day details and routine patterning of parent/child negotiations. Williams' preferred term for grasping what is at stake in the way such cultural work gets done was 'structures of feeling'. But Thompson's (1971) notion of 'tensions in consciousness', with its invocation of stress and latency as between the established, the excluded and the yet-to-come, has the advantage of gathering in both Trilling's dialectical definition of culture, and Williams' (1977: 121–7) own contrast between the dominant, the residual and the emergent. It is just such an understanding of culture which links Warshow's carefully constructed insights into the westerner's conception of honour with Warshow's off-the-cuff suggestion to Trilling that maybe his young son's haircut could be allowed to wait. And it (does so because it?) also anticipates those criticisms of the very *forms* taken by social and cultural theorizing that would subsequently be voiced from within second wave feminism, i.e. objections to those conceptions of cultural praxis which systematically neglect to ask 'who gets to do the washing up?' and 'who gets to mind the kids?' Brought up to date, it is that sentiment which connects the astuteness of Andreas Huyssen's (1986a) collection of essays on the high/popular culture relation with his willingness not just to record, but to *recognize* (on the collection's acknowledgements page) his son's enthusiasm for McDonald's restaurants and his own ambivalent reaction to it.

What Warshow's gangster essay first put into play gathered momentum in his response to the western. The forms through which these movies are realized and the audience which recognizes them are bridged by the notion of style. The status and meaning of this term shifts as between Warshow's criticisms of the Rosenbergs and middlebrow culture and his affirmative essays on popular cinema. Andrew Ross (1989: 30–8) has noted how Warshow's critiques of the former rely upon the familiar tropes of surface/depth and derived/authentic. But by simply ignoring Warshow's essays on the movies, Ross misleadingly presents him as at odds with popular culture *tout court*, as distinct from that partisan (re)view of it to which Ross subscribes. For Warshow, popular culture meant not only his political vexation with John Steinbeck and Arthur Miller, but also his critical respect for Gary Cooper and Edward G. Robinson.

In his writing on popular film Warshow's valorization of fantasy is therefore both knowing and selective and it is achieved through an affirmation of style. Style is understood as neither an Althusserian's 'imaginary relation to the real conditions of existence' (irony intended), nor as axiomatically on the wrong side of a binary contrast with substance. Rather style here becomes constitutive, a play with meaning that is also a making of it, an engagement with artifice which weds it to the very experiences that it helps to articulate. The notion of culture as organic/natural/authentic – a triplet molly-coddled both by romanticism and by liberal humanism – here begins to unravel. What moves in to replace it is style conceived of as a celebration of cerebrated pleasure; pleasure in which promiscuous fantasy persistently presses up against an otherwise austere allegiance to pattern. This is congruent with a conception of cultures as made and of culture as making it. But the resulting liberation of what would now be called desire jostles with, and is set off against, the no less cultural but much more traditional imperatives of parenthood, and the mysterious intensities of domestic political disputation amongst American intellectuals during the Cold War period.

Pleasure; parenthood; politics. Immediately experienced; reflexively understood; theoretically positioned. Textual properties; processes of reception; conditions of production. Waywardly dispersed; responsibly integrated; resolutely committed. Warshow's writing is constructed across these notions of discursive practice, their associated grid of antinomies and the discrete conceptions of the subject to which they give rise. In his essay on horror comics, for example, Warshow is pulled towards an ethnography of pre-adolescence by parental affection, towards an aesthetic of the comic book form by its appeal to his son's tastes, and towards a political economy of production and a cultural politics of reception by how he sees the encounter between the comic book industry and the excesses of its most apocalyptic critic.

The conceit that Warshow's work insinuates and the cultural condition to which it aspires thus resists being drawn into that circling flurry of binaries which gather around the interpretation of popular culture, i.e. as either felicific or calculating, as either sign or commodity, as either desire or politics, as either folk sentiment or culture industry. Rather it reproduces, at the level of critical commentary what Roland Barthes found so appealing about Chaplin's films,

[the] looping together [of] several tastes, several languages . . . [thus] afford[ing] the image of a culture that is at once differential and collective: plural. This image then functions as a third term, the subversive term of the opposition in which we are imprisoned: mass culture *or* high culture.

(Barthes 1977b: 54)

My warrant for attempting to draw a lesson for contemporary pedagogy from a long dead critic who did not teach is precisely that he literally 'comes from somewhere else'. As such he was exposed to different pressures, modalities and opportunities than those characteristic of the institutional and occupational context of the mainstream American academy. His ordering of cultural hierarchies could not, of course, be read off from his social location but it was instructively different as a consequence of it. If, however, this employment of Warshow as a counterfactual wedge is not to seem either wilfully perverse or hopelessly idealist, then it needs to be tempered by a comparison with how the teacher/taught relation has been represented in academic settings outside of America. But as in David Lodge's (1975) fictional precedent, the act of 'changing places' can offer no guarantee of transcendence or of coming to occupy some purportedly more correct location. Its (modest) purpose is rather to engineer the production of (limited) difference. This latter is not to be understood as some new kind of hegemonic principle. It is instead a rhetorical tactic for better exposing those procedural justifications whereby the privileging of privileged locations is achieved and the dislocative effects of extrapolating from their particular social contingencies are presumptively normalized.

If Warshow's uses of childhood can be said to have a British counterpart then Richard Hoggart's account of the scholarship boy in *The Uses of Literacy* (1957) would be a candidate. So too would be the way in which Raymond Williams (1973: 1–8) made links between the complexities of the country/city relation and the historical trajectory and immediate minutiae of his own life. In the methodological importance that they are seen to confer upon 'experience', such paradigmatic works have come to be understood as foundational of British cultural studies. Experience in this sense is to be understood not as some irreducibly primitive term or some Archimedean point but as an aspect of a distinctive rhetorical strategy, at once mediated and constituted through discourse. In other words, the category of 'experience' is to be read not just for what it purportedly is but also for what it effectively does. It becomes efficacious when it names. Only then does it cease to be either an irritatingly opaque black box that purports to be outside of theory, or an implausibly transparent naturalism that is nominally subversive of theory but actually the prisoner of it. The way to salvage the referential function of this notion of experience is therefore to explicitly acknowledge it as that struggle to construct a place within that which it could never hope to leave, i.e. within language. That is where it can act to provide a methodological control on both received and emergent categories and work as a theoretical labourer for the notions of agency and active, knowing and changing subjects.

The early writings of Hoggart and Williams (along with E.P. Thompson's work) were to prove consequential for the development of British cultural studies (Hall 1986). With the latter's transition from such isolated achievements to institutionalized orthodoxy, it should not be forgotten that it was initially the discrete imperatives of extra-mural teaching which provided a sustaining impulse and an enabling institutional matrix. These founding texts were constructed at a tangent to traditional conceptions of a legitimate subject matter and to received disciplinary boundaries. What they thereby signalled was a distinctive refraction of both the general institutional form of the (now tacit, now explicit) contract between teacher and taught and of its more proximate determinants.

Yet then as now, the associated conception of cultural pedagogy, the concern to rescue ordinary lives from what Thompson (1968: 13) called 'the enormous condescension of posterity', continues to gesture beyond its own temporal and relational specificities. Thompson's memorable phrase weds recovery of the past to a critique of the present; it links the neglect of historical continuities to contemporary impediments to change. And it nods towards a defining tension of such a methodology, i.e. how to prioritize the concept of experience whilst yet privileging the interrogation of its content.

It is by bringing such divergent strands together that this tau(gh)t line of descent/dissent acquires its strength. If it is allowed to slacken, then the resulting loss of tension makes it neither quite as efficacious nor quite as durable. Thus Hoggart's presentation of working-class life has proved vulnerable to the criticism that it was filtered through a nostalgia for those aspects of popular culture which were already passing. In fact, some of what Hoggart had viewed with hostility or suspicion, such as Butlin's holiday camps, have become, in their turn, the object of nostalgia as they too passed into history.

The methodological lesson and continuing legacy of these writings is further suggested by the range of readings and reworkings that they provoked amongst a subsequent generation of writers (and their subjects) for whom media images and consumer culture were more obviously formative. Thus read with an eye to empirical continuities, such a conception of experience prefigured and gave way to a melancholic bleakness, as in Jeremy Seabrook's (1983: 192–4) observations[4] on the use of pornographic videos by unemployed men in Bolton. Read for its internal divisions, it lead to an acerbic romanticism of resistance, as in Paul Willis' (1977) study of schooling. Willis not only recorded the hostility of his 'lads' to would-be scholarship boys but signalled a vicarious understanding of their stance that tacked between phenomenological assent and political ambivalence. Read for novel forms of cultural representation, both as a refraction of structural changes and as constitutive of a kind of political code, as in Hebdige (1979), it implied that such new modes of display indicated the persistence of popular forms of resistance. Read for its neglect of gender, it prompted that countervailing pattern which links the writings of Carolyn Steedman (1986) and Angela McRobbie (1991). Thus Steedman made use of her own childhood and her mother's biography, affirmatively recording the latter's pleasure in the very idea of a new dress as a counterfoil to Hoggart's antipathy to an expanding consumer culture (cf. Williams 1989: 30–5). McRobbie's (1991) critical response to the work of Willis and Hebdige offered an altogether less complicit reading than theirs of the male subcultures of (and for) which they wrote. Both Steedman and McRobbie thus drew attention to a kind of tacit compact between observer and observed which had led to the cultures of girls and women being ignored or devalued and entire forms of pleasure being either overlooked or proscribed.

This is a sparse, severely compressed glossing of a densely textured tradition of inquiry. It is a tradition which is inimical to such peremptory treatment precisely because of its guiding respect for the details of cultural practice. My justification for such a move is that it facilitates a foregrounding of the relation between the character of the tradition's methodologies, the legacy of its founding pedagogy and the presumptive permeability of its knowledge-constitutive practices. Bob Connell suggests one way into such an approach in his essay on the (late 1970s) Birmingham Centre for Contemporary Cultural Studies (CCCS). What Connell (1983: 222–30) emphasized was the Birmingham Centre's distinctive combination of a punishing Althusserian theoricity and a selectively 'ethnographic' methodology. Connell saw the associated contrast and tension between structural determination and cultural creativity as characteristically mediated through a depth/surface metaphor and with it a concomitant privileging of the first term in each couplet.

Drafted in 1980, Connell's (Orwell-indebted) essay was written at – and unequivocally against – that high tide of Anglo-Althusserian sentiment which threatened to swamp unbelievers. With that prospect having long since receded, so too has the kind of conceptual absolutism into which these Birmingham studies threatened to dissolve. In reading such works now it is therefore that much easier to read them for their openness rather than for their closure; for the productive instabilities induced by their improbable combination of influences, rather than for their reductionist tendencies; for their acknowledgement of the resilience of the experiential as much as for their recognition of the intractability of material life.

Connell argues that a crucial subtext of such studies is their all-too-familiar presumption of the privileged epistemological position of radical intellectuals vis-à-vis the working class, and with it a misleading and immobilizing conception of the relation between them. Read another way, however, this seems less a product of academic arrogance than a textually mediated response to the precarious institutional position of the CCCS at that time. The struggle to establish the CCCS had, after all, taken postgraduate training and research as its focus rather than undergraduate or extra-mural teaching. With the benefit of hindsight, it seems to me that those biographically- and pedagogically-derived concerns which had been so characteristic of the founding texts of English cultural studies were muted rather than erased during the subsequent development of the Birmingham Centre. Hence the linking of 'experience' and pedagogy – and with it a more clearly interpretative rather than a legislative stance (cf. Bauman 1987) – reasserts itself in Dick Hebdige's (1988: 159–76) reflections on the appeal of *The Face* magazine for his graphics students, in Judith Williamson's (1981) remarks on the problems of teaching representations of gender to day release students and in Angela McRobbie's (1993) response to her teenage daughter's excursions/immersions within rave culture. It is not just that there is in each case

145

the sense of an encounter with meanings and social practices that are themselves emergent. It is that these encounters are recognized as sustained by a plurality of determinations and hence there is an attempt to avoid falling back upon categorizing those meanings, and the subjects who enact them, as either already known or as axiomatically alien. This is another way of saying that they read more like Warshow than they read like either Ewen or like Bloom. Their dramatization of questions about the locus and legitimacy of a specifically cultural authority – which had emerged only from the disturbing effects of an out of the ordinary individual in Trilling's story – is here more diffusely and matter of factly distributed across social categories and cultural differences as such. The movement is not just away from a print culture to media cultures. It is from the pedagogic challenge posed by the possibility of individual genius to that posed by the typicality of a social mosaic that is cross cut by social divisions and competing discourses.

This same template can be used to trace a pattern across another kind of map. For the path from dead men to new shoes also cuts across that terrain which Fredric Jameson has marked out as going from high modernism to postmodernism. Jameson's (1991: 6–10) sign post for the first of these locations is Vincent Van Gogh's painting of *A Pair of Boots*, his post sign for the latter is Andy Warhol's *Diamond Dust Shoes*. He finds in the canonical high modernism of the former just what Trilling's teacher had found in Tertan, namely 'radical isolation and solitude, anomie, private revolt, Van Gogh-type madness' (Jameson 1991:14) and like Tertan's work, the painting is seen as powerfully gesturing to a transcendence of those dislocations that its content records. Against this he interprets the Warhol painting as evidence of 'the emergence of a new kind of flatness or depthlessness, a new kind of superficiality in the most literal sense' (Jameson 1991: 9). Jameson goes on to say that:

> we must surely come to terms with the role of photography and the photographic negative in contemporary art of this kind; and it is this, indeed which confers its deathly quality to the Warhol image . . . [indicating a] fundamental mutation both in the object world itself – now become a set of texts or simulacra – and in the disposition of the subject.

To this echo of Trilling's anxieties about the culture of the image,[5] Jameson further adds that there is about Warhol's painting 'a strange compensatory decorative exhilaration . . . the glitter of gold dust, the spangling of gilt sand that seals the surface of the painting'.

It is just such caveats and qualifying afterthoughts to his theoretically ordained critical judgements and principles of selection which makes Jameson so interesting a critic – particularly when they draw him into a tactical use of poststructuralist methodology which is formally at odds with his theoretical commitments. In this case, however, that caveat is promptly qualified so that the painting's overlay becomes an instance of 'gratuitous frivolity'. It is the imperiousness of this kind of move which prompted an exasperated and irritated John Docker (1994: 115–28) to accuse Jameson of writing a complacent 'Modernist Prim'. The tone in which Docker responds may be misconceived, but what is justified is both that critical impulse in which his reaction is grounded and his suggestion that Jameson is drawn towards a too obviously asymmetric and precarious theoretical closure. Jameson claims that his own emphasis is on readings which recover the realm of material life in which works are produced and received. Yet what he refers to as that 'strange compensatory decorative exhilaration' in the image of women's shoes conjures up a very different set of associations if it is read against the significance which Carolyn Steedman (1986) gives to her mother's pleasure in contemplating a new dress. Placed in the context of her striving for a better life and the attempt to secure an affirmation of her integrity as a subject, then neither 'gratuitous frivolity' nor 'compensatory' can do justice to what that dress came to mean. The point about Warhol's painting is that it seems as readily available for a reading informed by such sentiments as it is for that no less partisan reading which Jameson proffers. For what Jameson identifies as its 'flatness' – a flatness that is also discernible in Warhol's electric chair or traffic accident series – is precisely the flatness of a mirror. What is 'layered' here is the range of possible readings. Hence Jameson's perspective on Warhol's shoes invests them – and the postmodern for which they stand – with those same familiar modernist tropes (decorative, frivolous, seductive) which Huyssen (1986b) had identified as characteristic of modernism's response to the emergence of mass culture, namely, its status as other and as 'woman'. In other words there is here yet another incidental revisiting of Trilling's anxieties, together with an echo of Ewen's uneasy bemusement.

The methodological difficulty which besets Jameson can be dramatized by an allegory which draws on 'Black Shiny FBI Shoes', the opening chapter of Tom Wolfe's *The Electric Kool-Aid Acid Test* (1969: 1–14). Wolfe's account of the clothing preferences of a band of LSD freaks called the Merry Pranksters reads:

> The cops now knew the whole scene, even the costumes, the jesuschrist strung-out hair, Indian beads, Indian headbands, donkey beads, temple bells, amulets, mandalas, god's-eyes, fluorescent vests, unicorn horns, Errol Flynn dueling shirts – but they still don't know about the shoes. The heads have a thing about shoes. The worst are shiny black shoes with shoe laces in them. The hierarchy ascends from there, although practically all lowcut shoes are unhip, from there on up to the boots the heads like, light fanciful boots, English boots of the mod variety if that is all they can get, but better something like hand-tooled Mexican boots with Caliente Triple A toes on them. So see the FBI-black-shiny-laced-up-FBI shoes – when the FBI finally grabbed Kesey.
>
> (Wolfe 1969: 2)

Jameson is likewise too much the cultural policeman and too little the anthropologist to know about the shoes. He is too committed to recruiting such artifacts to a preordained schema and too reluctant to acknowledge their specificity within the orders in which they circulate. What such reportage or 'ethnography' (or its various 'proxies' in the form of child rearing, or unconvinced undergraduates, or sceptical publics) can offer is a thoroughly pragmatic and characteristically materialist methodological corrective to the consequences for theory of a tendency towards social closure amongst its practitioners. For such closure, and the distancing which it permits, seems to be at once a prerequisite of contemporary theoretical work, an incentive for such work to become excessively textualist, and a tracer of the decline in the very idea of the public intellectual. Mary Douglas offers a (textually mediated) instance of such a methodological corrective in her recognition and reprinting of a somewhat longer version of this Tom Wolfe extract. In her collection of readings on the moral order and the knowledge which sustains it Douglas is as concerned to elucidate the fundamentals of social organization as is Jameson. She draws attention to two points about the Pranksters' dress code (Douglas 1973: 208); first, that there is a logical contrast between soft hued high boots and shiny black low cut shoes; and second, that amongst its members no mistake was possible about how that social world was constructed. It is a world whose specific contents seem phenomenologically remote from that which Jameson constructs, but note the connection between the structure of binary oppositions and the closure of the attendant discourse. Read one way Jameson may resemble the FBI, but read another he is akin to the Merry Pranksters. 'If the shoe fits . . . .'

Yet the proliferation and elaboration of binary oppositions *can* generate new possibilities. For in recruiting Jameson to the task of elucidating the link between dead men and new shoes, I have noted that although he drew attention to old boots he left out young women. The not quite formal symmetry of including the latter provides a matrix from which to generate an updated instance of Warshow's methodology – and with it a homily that nods towards Hebdige, McRobbie, Steedman and Williamson.

Warshow's son was 11 years-old when he entered the debate with his father over horror comics. Our elder daughter was 13 when she first put down a serious marker for a pair of bright purple Doc Martens. Her mother's reservations were primarily aesthetic, her father's were primarily economic; but both of us were wary of the idea of obtaining an expensive pair of boots by mail order from a supplier who was over 12,000 miles away. It is elevating whimsy too much and stretching credulity too far to note that 'Martens' is not quite an anagram of Tertan's. For in context those purple boots were not particularly strange and certainly not mad. They offered both a logical contrast with (no longer quite so) shiny black school shoes and an explicitly indeterminate location on that axis whose end points are given by men's work boots and women's diamond dust shoes respectively. To this semiotic interrogation of the traditional authority of school and the received oppositions of gender can be added the material engagement with parental authority ('I'm old enough'), the negotiation of access to resources ('You can save at least $NZ80 by buying them this way instead of in a shop downtown'), an individuated implication in peer group discourse, and the achievement of a provisional closure of sense within the entropic disorderliness of adolescence.

Such an initiative might then be tracked against the transformation of Doc Martens from specialized work boot to its position as the icon of a spectacular male subculture in Britain, through the further reworking of its meaning by boot girls, on to its subsequently more diffuse and androgynous amplification within youth culture as a whole, to its eventual globalization and canonization as a design classic. This is unequivocally capitalism at work, following a trajectory whose basic outline has been made familiar by denim's passage from cheap fabric to designer label (Fiske 1989: 1–21; Scheuring 1989). Nevertheless the task of probing the reasons for such efficacy would seem to require some rather more delicate procedures than those associated with such blunt instruments as 'commodity fetishism' or 'consumer sovereignty'. Some six or seven years on, our elder daughter's Docs are still wearable and still worn, intermittently reconfigured within the evolving pattern of a young woman's tastes, which move across the full range of image cultures and along the full width of that axis from new diamond dust shoes to old boots. Playing across the enactment of that pattern are discursive shifts and the effects of structural realignments; within the pattern there are judgements to be made, criticisms to be voiced, values to be expressed, priorities and rankings to be asserted, street credibility to be claimed.

There is a difficulty with theorizing which *axiomatically* locates itself outside the culture of the image and against such commodities as new shoes. It is not that it may (more or less knowingly) forsake that version of phenomenological adequacy which goes under the label of street credibility. It is perfectly possible to claim that this latter criterion is not necessary, or not sufficient, or not desirable. Rather the difficulty is a procedural one. The very effect of such theoretical closure is that such details as a boy's haircut, a pair of shoes, specks of gilt sand on a picture, are seen as theoretically random or trivial. Yet theorizing which claims to be efficacious must do its work down amongst those details, especially if its aims are to transcend, transform or otherwise displace whatever combination of aesthetic, cognitive and political concerns those details serve to express. This is what Trilling learned from Warshow, what Ewen seemed on the edge of learning from his students, and what Tom Wolfe (and Mary Douglas) can teach Fredric Jameson.

8

TRAVELLING
THEORY/NOMADIC
THEORIZING

The notion of 'hamburger as text' sounds suspiciously like an academic joke. It could perhaps be a permutation on Jonathon Miller's memorable description of airline meals as 'printed food' – thereby identifying a paradigm case of hyperreality before the latter had found a name. Then again, it could possibly be a parodic extension of Marvin Harris' (1979: 188–90) waspish critique of Lévi-Strauss' structuralism as 'the raw, the cooked, and the half-baked'. Or maybe a postscript to Andreas Huyssen's (1984: 32) sardonic characterization of European social theory as 'frankfurters and french fries'. Aphorisms of this kind are a part of the academic's stock-in-trade, the *lingua franca* of faculty gossip. As (ideologically) sound bites, they are the secular signs of an occupational communion.

Given this acerbic pattern of conduct, the very idea of a Big Mac seems to be an invitation, an opportunity to over-indulge in such linguistic games. The symbolic possibilities of fast food are not, however, limited to, or by, the cultural idiosyncrasies of academic taste. And with around 19,000 outlets in more than seventy countries, McDonald's is manifestly no joke. It has become a metaphor of organization and an icon of globalization. The franchiser (and its products) might now be said to signal not just the continuities between these two complex terms, but to serve as a rhetorical symbol of their integration. Whenever and wherever a McDonald's retail outlet is established, the marketing of the product (right down to the carefully orchestrated impression of an abundance of french fries) is designed into the Fordist-style assembly line system. Under McDonald's familiar yellow arches, the demands of customers thus articulate directly with an overarching system of technological control and its attendant low level of employee discretion and highly formalized training of store managers (Levitt 1972). Standardized products and standardized methods are wedded to a modal conception of the experience of consumption and are represented through a distinctive advertising style (Boas and Chain 1976). With the development of what Ritzer (1991) has called the McDonaldization of society, these processes are understood as exemplifying the organizing principles of the wider social order. More generally, McDonald's has come to be seen as an expression of the combination of a fully routinized and invariant production system with the expanding uniformities of a global culture.

In practice, such an interpretation serves as no more than a first cut, or perhaps a limiting case, for what is at once a more general theoretical tendency and its more nuanced empirical application. For to trace the trajectory of McDonald's growth is also to document its links to the emergence and development of franchizing as a business system, and franchising in its turn was closely connected to developments in travel and transportation. Beginning with American automobile dealerships in the 1890s, the franchise system extended from them to service stations and subsequently to fast-food outlets, a process which was powerfully reinforced by the construction of the US Interstate highway network in the 1950s and 1960s (Patton 1986: 187–206). Read one way, therefore, the context within which 'fast food' evolved was unabashedly Fordist, a pattern in which assembly line principles of production and marketing were applied to the service sector. Read another way, however, franchising is exemplary of a distinctive form of capital formation; one which permits flexible accumulation but eschews flexible specialization. For the franchisee it offers entrepreneurship in a package, ambition-by-numbers, capitalism in kit form; for the franchiser it gives access to capital without ceding control, reconciles integrated administration with entrepreneurial motivation.

Or read yet another way, as, for example, by Zukin, the meaning of McDonald's is filtered through her account of the transformation of urban centres. In her more general framework, McDonald's forms part of an emergent 'landscape of power' in which such landscapes are understood as the symbolical and material mediation of 'market' (with its implication of the socio-spatial differentiation of capital) and 'place' (which suggests the socio-spatial homogeneity of labour). This theme is set and developed through her contrast between Detroit and Disneyworld. McDonald's is seen as closer to the postmodernist latter than to the modernist former, whilst yet epitomizing the connections between an international urban form, globalized production and consumption and a concomitant displacement of localized craft production (Zukin 1991: 43).

Yet despite the refinements which come with elaboration, what sustains even the most developed manifestations of such theorizing is a kind of axiomatic reflex. By this is meant the predisposition to see cultural phenomena, whether in the form of beliefs, practices or objects, as more or less determined by social or economic relations (cf. Wolff 1991). With varying degrees of ingenuity and sophistication, i.e. by the deployment of varying levels of relative autonomy, the realm of culture is allowed some space in which to play, albeit within the limits provided by these structural constraints. As applied to the McDonald's example, this is one way to preserve the continuities between the received organizational meaning and the positions that the resulting products occupy within the development of processes of globalization. It seems all too obvious that McDonald's is a clear cut case of such institutional and structural determination – hence the expression McWorld (cf. *Business Week* 1986; Barber 1992).

On this view the presumption that cultural meaning can be subsumed under or subordinated to such factors needs little or no further justification. It is in this vein that Turim gloomily refers to a recent McDonald's television commercial in which 'Mack the Knife', Bertolt Brecht and Kurt Weill's theme from *The Threepenny Opera* becomes 'Its Mac Tonight' complete with an animation of a floating moon singer (Ray Charles). 'In one short clip much of modernist culture is reincarnated as an emblem that effaces any other purpose to or history of modernism except as style of the urbane' (Turim 1991: 185). Oppositional structures are thereby incorporated into a single culture of commercialism by 'using the tropes and structures of artistic resistance outside of their contexts and without the notions of contestatory textuality that marked their earlier use' (Turim 1991: 185).

The (reassuring?) familiarity of this kind of analysis is not without plausibility. Yet such an apocalyptic tone has come to seem wearily formulaic, since the text in question was (in line with Weill's own subsequent embrace of commercial values) long ago assimilated to the realm of musak (by entertainers who are themselves now dead, such as Bobby Darin and Louis Armstrong). It is, therefore, important to insist on the tactical merit of approaching the cultural/economic/social relation from another side, one which does not take the meaning of commodification in general, and fast food in particular, as a theoretical given. If, under the sign of global culture, we conceive of 'hamburger as text', then this avoids subsuming cultural meaning under, or at best inferring it from, its commodity status. Considered only as a methodological corrective (rather than a methodological alternative) to the dominant form of interpretation, this involves the recognition of a Big Mac as both a product and a sign. The concomitant emphasis on the notion of cultural representation (and thus on culture as constitutive) has the effect of foregrounding, rather than subduing, the contrasts between organizational uniformity and cultural difference, between standardized commodity and promiscuous signifier. The methodological pertinence of such an approach thus rests upon a procedural assumption that cultural phenomena only achieve their meanings through their interpretation. Whether they are read with, or against, the grain of the encoded meaning(s), it is through recourse to the notion of text that a given cultural artifact and the processes of its recognition are combined.

'Hamburger as text' may therefore be a whimsy, but it is a whimsy with analytic possibilities. That an artifact that is purportedly emblematic of 'organization' and 'globalization' is available for interpretation in this way, provides a way into the analysis of other (rather more obviously linguistically elaborated and cognitively orientated) texts which aspire to universal import. Put another way, if (even) a globally standardized and presumptively culturally uniform (aka culture free) 'Big Mac' can be shown to yield food for (different forms of) thought, then the problematizing of meaning associated with such a demonstration assumes a wider relevance. In serving as an allegory on how theories of formal organization and models of the working of markets are read, when they too are launched around the globe, it can also serve as a methodological preamble to a way of reading such theories that reflexively foregrounds the complex effects and interdependencies of globalization and indigenization.

One route into this territory is suggested by *The Economist*'s (1993) demonstration of the theory of purchasing power parity (PPP) through its use of the Big Mac as a currency index. The theory posits (a) that the exchange rate between a given two currencies is in equilibrium when the prices of the same bundles of traded goods and services in those countries are equalized, and (b) that there is a long run tendency for currencies to move towards such parity. First introduced in 1986, the index is premised upon the Big Mac, as 'the perfect universal commodity', thereby serving as a proxy for that wider bundle of commodities from which such measures are usually constructed. Using a four city US average to establish the base line price, the 1993 index effects a comparison across twenty-four countries. Whether a currency is under- or over-valued (against the US dollar) is then determined by whether the actual exchange rate is above or below the rate indicated by the PPP as calculated from the price of a Big Mac. The results of this exercise are identified as 'strikingly consistent' with those obtained using more sophisticated techniques. In 1993 the Japanese yen and most of the EEC currencies were seen as overvalued against the dollar; the rouble and the Chinese yuan as undervalued. By extension, the pound sterling was seen as slightly undervalued against the German mark, whereas the surviving members of the European Exchange Rate Mechanism were somewhat overvalued against it; and so on (see Table 8.1).

What is of interest is how this lighthearted, but nevertheless academically sanctioned (and Ph.D.-inspiring), use of the Big Mac as a benchmark for a rudimentary modelling of the operation of markets (cf. *The Economist* 1996), forms part of a discourse which can be seen to imply the conditions for its own elaboration. Even the most casual interpretation of the results depends upon the mobilization of supplementary knowledge and additional variables (mention is made of farm subsidies and interest rates as sources of variance). What remains intact, however, is the notion that there is, in principle, an *in*variate universal commodity (bundle) to which the Big Mac approximates. What underpins the subsequent probing of variation is the theme that a Big Mac is everywhere the same. This predictability and standardization is emphasized in many accounts of the development and appeal of fast food, whether by the industry's own apologists or by its most gloomy and apocalyptic critics (cf. Kroker *et al.* 1989: 119).

Note, however, that it is not the actual product which gets to travel, but the *concept* of it, and with it a model of that system of formal organization through which that concept is realized and the meal is actually produced. Hence the general form of interpretation which sustains *The Economist*'s index can be read as akin to that which sustained that version of organization theory known as contingency theory. The development of contingency theory was informed by a positivistic reworking of the Weberian-influenced analysis of bureaucracy. It involved the construction of operational measures of formal organization and the use of survey techniques and the effect was to dethrone the notion of an ideal organization structure understood as a particular configuration of administrative attributes. The concept of an optimal organizational form was none the less retained as an informing theoretical principle by construing it as that structure which is most efficiently adjusted to the cluster of contingencies characteristic of its milieu. For contingency theorists, variations in the structural attributes of organizations were therefore functionally analogous to the role played by variations in price in the theory of purchasing power parity. Money is, to be sure, the measure *nonpareil*. It thereby attracts a consensus which the scaling techniques associated with contingency theory could not hope to match, even with respect to such apparently common-sensical yet deceptively wayward and theoretically crucial characteristics as organizational size (cf. Kimberley 1976). Despite such differences in performativity, technical complexity and concomitant levels of cognitive integration, a formal parallel between these instruments is nevertheless evident. It is as a conceptual approximation of the perfect commodity that a Big Mac becomes part of a theory which not only travels but is global in its reach. It was as a method of determining efficient organization structure that contingency theory got to do the same (cf. Donaldson, 1985; 1987). What *The Economist*'s Big Mac thus routinely accomplishes is the kind of methodological task which for (this and related versions of) organization theory remains an aspiration.

If, however, emphasis is placed upon a Big Mac as an indeterminate and complex sign rather than a perfect(ly) simple commodity, then it is not standardization and uniformity which assumes priority but variation and difference. From such a perspective the price of a Big Mac is merely one aspect of what it signifies; and what it signifies slides promiscuously along and across the disparate (geographical, cultural, social, and discursive) locations from which it is read. On this view, when it comes to hamburgers, the word itself is made fresh even as the world is made flesh. For example, Barry Smart's (1994) analysis of the Moscow McDonald's provides a schematic, but very different, account of the meaning of a Big Mac and its relation to putative developments and continuities in Russian economic organization. The 700 seat McDonald's restaurant in Pushkin Square is interpreted as a place of pilgrimage, in which the disjunction between the utopian future promised by Western capitalism and its grim implications for the present is briefly bridged, so that:

> For Muscovites a McDonald's Big Mac is now a luxury item: it has 'become a souvenir, taken back in its wrapper to show off to admiring friends in distant Siberian villages. "We had to come", says Yuri Tishunin, a postal worker from the Yemal Peninsula in the remote far north, "just to see if its real" (Moynihan 1992: 13) .... Lenin, preserved in his black marble mausoleum, icon for a fast fading socialism, to which people can now gain ready access by queuing for a mere 40 minutes or so, has evidently been displaced by the Big Mac, preserved as a souvenir in its red box, an icon of fast feeding American capitalism, for which, ironically, it seems people are prepared to queue for hours (Macdonald 1990). It is the paradox of slow fast food that has allowed the hamburger hawkers to offer their services as surrogates in the queue

Table 8.1 The *Economist*'s 1993 'Big Mac' currency index

Country	Price of 'Big Mac' in Local Currency	Price of 'Big Mac' in US Dollars	Implied PPP of US Dollar*	Local Currency under- or over-valuation (%)
USA	US$2.28	2.28	——	——
Argentina	Peso3.60	3.60	1.58	+58
Australia	A$2.45	1.76	1.07	–23
Belgium	Bfr109	3.36	47.81	+47
Brazil	Cr77,000	2.80	37,772	+23
Britain	Pound1.79	2.79	1.27	–23
Canada	C$2.76	2.19	1.21	–4
China	Yuan8.50	1.50	3.73	–34
Denmark	D.Kr25.75	4.25	11.29	+86
France	F.Fr18.50	3.46	8.11	+52
Germany	DM4.60	2.91	2.02	+28
Holland	Fl5.45	3.07	2.39	+35
Hong Kong	HK$9.00	1.16	3.95	–49
Hungary	Forint157	1.78	68.86	–22
Ireland	Ipound1.48	2.29	1.54**	0
Italy	Lire4,500	2.95	1,974	+30
Japan	Yen391	3.45	171	+51
Malaysia	Ringgit335	1.30	1.47	–43
Mexico	Peso7.09	2.29	3.11	0
Russia	Rouble780	1.14	342	–50
S.Korea	Won2,300	2.89	1,009	+27
Spain	Ptas325	2.85	143	+25
Sweden	Skr25.50	3.43	11.18	+50
Switzerland	SwFr5.70	3.94	2.50	+72
Thailand	Baht48	1.91	21.05	–16

Source: *The Economist*, 17 April 1993: 83

Notes: *Based on exchange rates as at 13 April 1993. ** Dollars per pound.

for wealthier diners prepared to pay 200 roubles for the delivery of orders to their cars. And around the hawkers who are able to earn ten times the average monthly salary, hierarchies of minders and their bosses have gathered to collect their cut.

(Smart 1994: 27)

Both these specific social practices and the general freedom to record their presence are novel. But when such conduct is read against the record of the past, then notwithstanding the manifest unevenness of the relevant sociological archive, it is a pattern which comes to seem both familiar and expected. This is illustrated by Berliner's (1957) observations on how the very goals and incentives enjoined upon the centralized official system of Soviet factory organization and economic planning gave rise to the elaboration of extra-legal forms of intra- and inter-organizational linkages through which resources were (re)allocated. The name given to these illicit processes for the transfer of goods and services was 'blat' and an individual who specialized in the development of such connections came to be called a 'tolkach' (the latter being the term for a supplementary loco-motive which was located and employed on those stretches of the railway system where the gradient was too steep for the underpowered main engine to keep the wagons on the move). The institutionalization of these tendencies was obliquely expressed by the folk maxim that 'blat is higher than Stalin'. If, by the 1990s, a Big Mac had become more revered than Lenin, then this hints at secular conti-nuity as well as at religious difference. The economic activity around Pushkin Square seems rather more explicit, but no less organized, than its illegal and subterranean precursor in the command economy. It is a past and future image of the present; at once a signal of the determinate effects of an officially sanctioned transformation in Russian economic organization and a pointer to the material and prospectively consequential continuities in its underlife. Berliner had under-stood 'blat' as a rudimentary manifestation of market mechanisms, an undeveloped and imperfect functional equivalent to the allocation processes of a market economy. Now it is the market which is officially sanctified. Yet the para-criminal hierarchies which cluster around its new icon hint at the rather different prospect of particularistic and pre- or non-modern patterns of organization playing more than a merely residual role in shaping the future of the Russian economy.

Note that the very approach which encourages my indulgence in this kind of large and speculative interpretative leap is also one whose empirical application would serve to discipline it. The relevant theme is institutional embeddedness, i.e. the presumption that organized economic activity is not to be understood as a series of approximations to a formal model, but as always grounded in a distinc-tive configuration of generic social forces and processes through which its present functioning and probable trajectory come to be constituted. Perrow's (1972) now classic account of the institutional school could be said to have first sketched the antecedents of this approach. Since then it has given rise to a line of inquiry whose paradigmatic formulation by Granovetter (1985) has been developed by Hamilton and Biggart (1988), Clegg (1990) and Whitley (1990, 1991, 1992) with respect to the 'puzzle' (for earlier approaches) of explaining Asian business organization. For present purposes, therefore, the significance of the specific details of the Russian case is that they serve to highlight a general methodological principle of respect for anomalies. These are not seen as residual features awaiting elimination by the unfolding logic of the long run. Rather they are understood as resilient and constitutive elements within a discrete, boundary blurring matrix of inter-institutional relations. As such they are resistant to demarcation by operationalist modes of definition. But it is important to note that not only is such an institutionalist perspective still grounded firmly within the modern, but that its accomplishment is to ground the modern more firmly.

Both *The Economist*'s and Smart's study move at the intersection between burgernomics and burgerology. But they also move across each other and thereby point to a more general contrast. The salient distinction is not, however, between comparative analysis and case study. Smart's essay is consciously comparative, and *The Economist* invokes either the teleological 'long run' or the residual *ad hoc* in its explanation of how individual cases deviate from the general model. What is dramatized by the juxtaposition of the two studies is therefore not different levels of inquiry, but contrasting conceptions of theory. The opposition to which they call attention is between a theory which is firmly wedded to differentiation and theorizing which is loosely coupled to *différance*.

Permutations on the differentiation/*différance* couplet have become a critical marker in modern/postmodern and related debates. A characteristic example is its employment by Martin Jay (1988) to argue that Habermas' acknowledged allegiance to differentiation/modernity is nuanced, refined and defensible. *Différance* is, of course, a no-longer-new neologism coined by Jacques Derrida. Each of these terms now bears the weight of an enormous amount of cultural freight. Each has therefore proved to be both awkward to handle and yet reassuringly robust. So if awkwardness as a characteristic points to the difficulty of recognizing just 'which way is up?' (cf. Connell 1983), then robustness as a property suggests the resilience of this odd couple(t) when subject to the kind of *bricoleur* tactics and peremptory handling that they receive in this chapter.

This kind of unprincipled scavenging amongst the detritus of high theory is how this book began. In this chapter it is a brief but necessary detour which points towards the book's conclusion whilst purportedly journeying away from it. Thus Derrida's formulation of differentiation does not just apply to *The Economist*'s Big Mac index and contingency theory, but also to the more nuanced analysis associated with the notion of institutional embeddedness – thereby serving to interrupt its otherwise confident forward progress within this narrative. Differentiation, argues Derrida,

> suggests some organic unity, some primordial and homogeneous unity, that would eventually come to be divided up and take on difference as

an event. Above all formed on the verb 'to differentiate' this word would annul the economic signification of detour, temporalizing delay, deferring.

(Derrida 1973: 143)

Set off against such differentiation is the all purpose subversiveness, fluidity, heterogeneity, lack of direction and irreducibility of *différance*, understood as that systematic play of differences, spacing of elements and traces of a radical otherness (Derrida 1981: 38–9) which the homogeneity of economic indices, measures of organizational structure and concepts of institutional ordering all s(w)erve to efface.

Does this subvert the very possibility of theory? E.V. Walter (1988: 18) notes that the word 'theory' is from the Greek *theoria* – to see the sights or to see something for yourself. He goes on to suggest that the first theorists were 'tourists' for whom *theoria* implied a complex mode of active observation – a perceptual system that included asking questions, listening to stories and local myths – and seeing the sights. From such a perspective the epithet that the cognitive basis of anthropology is 'mere' travellers' tales (Louch 1966) begins to lose its opprobrium. Yet in our time it is not only tourists but theory itself which travels, routinely cast free from its geographical point of origin and inflected and refracted through and by its adherents. In the process theory's readers and writers construct their own fictionalized territory in a fashion analogous to the imagined communities described by Anderson (1983: 39–40) as characteristic of modern nationalism. Yet the texts which provide the occasion for such practices are unable to control for the manner of their reception and use. To anticipate, then – what arises from this globally/locally-induced further permutation on the differentiation /*différance* couplet is the distinction between travelling theory and nomadic theorizing.

We have seen that for those travellers who are most at home with traditional theory there could hardly be a better indicator that they are not just on the right track, but also on familiar ground than the sight of McDonald's yellow arches and the prospect of a Big Mac. Yet even here, on terrain that is so conducive to the claims of such theory, there are persistent anomalies and signs of disturbance. Traditional theory, with its officially approved and organized routes for visitors, both contrasts with and criss-crosses (the acquisition of) that tacit knowledge of unmarked pathways upon which nomadic theorizing depends. I have hinted at some of the tensions and interdependencies between these approaches by showing how their adherents may (sometimes) share the same well worn tracks but not the same journey. Tourists in the land of theory may (sometimes) see the same reassuring and familiar signs but none the less read them very differently, no matter whether they are interested in the dubiously demotic Big Mac, the arcane prose of French cultural theory,[1] or the more conventionally academic texts of organizational analysis.

It is nevertheless evident that some kinds of theory are efficacious on a global scale. Such theories are not only able to travel across spatial, political and cultural frontiers, but to do so without much in the way of impediment or amendment – just like such typical examples of their material manifestation as 747s and satellite signals. Yet even these instances of performativity are reliant upon the development both of particular institutional preconditions and of highly specific forms of tacit knowledge (cf. Collins 1982). My interest in this chapter is in investigating forms of theoretical activity whose history is studded with aspirations to this kind of global-wide efficacy, but whose present achievements are rather more circumscribed, and in which confidence in the future possibility of such accomplishments has become altogether more muted. The contemporary mosaic that is social and cultural theory is manifestly disparate and pluralistic rather than socially integrated and cognitively unified (cf. Whitley 1984), such that the exhortations of custodians of 'the' theory of society or of 'the' theory of organizations cannot be made to work. Theories and theorizing continue to flourish, but whether as grammar, as narrative, or as text, the idea of 'the' theory has become, in every sense, an indefinite article.

For any theory to travel successfully, it must be in accordance with the tacit and emergent rules of the associated community of practitioners, practitioners who are at once geographically dispersed, discursively interdependent and intermittently nomadic. What then would a tourist in the land of theory look for and what would a tourist guide to theory look like? What are the implicit principles of structural selection and the preferred modes of cognitive practice within and around which such practitioners organize themselves? What aspects of theory get to travel legitimately, what gets smuggled through and what gets left out? Under conditions of globalization what are the characteristic forms of slippage between the circumstances which produce theories, the objects of theoretical inquiries, the texts which realize those theories and the readers who recognize them?

The development of the contrasts and contacts between travelling theory and nomadic theorizing is one way into such questions. As employed here it is more nearly an analytic distinction than an empirical one. Amongst the major guides to exploring this terrain are Edward Said, Gayatri Spivak, Clifford Geertz and Dorinne Kondo.

Theory not only travels to unexpected destinations; it may also be put to unexpected uses. This is not to say that the patterns of reading and interpretation are to be understood as random or idiosyncratic. On the contrary, the specific ways in which theory collides and/or colludes with the meanings which circulate in the milieux that it enters are thoroughly social and highly structured processes. Martin Albrow's (1970) study of the concept of bureaucracy, a concept which has sometimes doubled as a synonym for organization, can be read as just such a recording of shifts in the meaning of a favoured and familiar term (cf. also Kamenka and Krygier 1979). What Edward Said (1981) highlights is the theme that whenever theory travels its movement from one place and time to another is never unimpeded; both its mode of representation and its pattern of institutionalization are different from those characteristic of its point of origin. This is shown,

159

for example, by the way in which recent French theory both signifies and commodifies differently as between America (cf. Lamont 1987) and Australia (cf. Murray 1992).

Said's own account is a sketch of the trajectory and transmutation of 'reification-and-totality' as a theoretical idea and form of critical consciousness. He begins with its particular formulation by Georg Lukács in Budapest in 1919, going on to chart its post-Second World War migration to Paris via Lucien Goldmann, and its eventual appearance in Cambridge, England, in the 1970s through Raymond Williams' response to Goldmann. The result is a metamorphosis from Lukács' adversarial act of political insurgency 'in language bristling with . . . metaphysics and abstractions' (Said 1981: 233), to Goldmann's muted and accommodating tragic vision, to Williams' cordial, but coolly distanced awareness of the theory's tactical uses and systemic limitations. The substantive shifts in meaning thus correspond to formal changes in use, namely: theory as politically committed and insurrectionary; theory as the scholarly means of fusing detail and *Weltanschauung*; and a measured borrowing from, but resistance to, theory as closure. Said's own text can, in turn, be read as the attempt to keep each of these three conceptions, and the tensions between them, continuously in play.

He therefore challenges the presumption that such transformations are just instances of misinterpretation and misreading. For the purposes of evaluation this is much too blunt a critical instrument. There are wholly discrete pressures and limits attendant upon politically engaged writing in and for Budapest in 1919, an expatriate's historical scholarship in and for Paris in 1955, and reflective cultural criticism in and against Cambridge in 1970. Just as Albrow's exploration of the definitions of bureaucracy is explicable as a cautionary tale against attempts to establish *the* definition, so too can Said be said to eschew any notion of *the* interpretation. For what tends to accompany any such movement towards closure is either a regression into the cognitive conceit that it is somehow outside of culture and history, or an expansion of the political condescension that it is the only culture and history that counts. This is most manifest in theory which is tacitly or explicitly supportive of the totalizing forces of globalization. But what Said can be understood as emphasizing is that a purportedly critical theoretical tendency which is reluctant to theorize its own situation, may thereby also become complicit with the very forces to which it is otherwise substantively opposed.

Said himself is therefore effectively a practitioner of what can be called nomadic theorizing, a mobile, process-orientated practice which does not just consciously foreground the social location from which it speaks, but just as consciously employs such awareness for theoretical purposes. It *matters* that he is at once a Palestinian intellectual, a distinguished professor of comparative literature, based at an elite university and located in the heart of New York; a named star in a star system. The associated contradictions are what allow him to be fully responsive to Lukács and Goldmann and Williams and to the differences between them. They provide the context out of which he writes, but it is important to insist that neither he nor what he writes can be reduced to them. It does, however, sensitize him to the presumptions and the presumption of theory understood as a kind of universal template or a form of global cartography. This latter form of theory seeks, as in Barthes' (1973) pithy summation of the role of mythologies, to 'establish blissful clarity'. It does so by requiring the subjects of its inquiry to lie still (and think not of England, but only of the mode of production, or multiple regression), albeit after those same subjects have (like England before them) been suitably organized through and within categories whose conventionality has been naturalized and whose origins have been effaced through the recourse to abstraction. Given this kind of perspective on theory, then 'local variations' can both be acknowledged and rendered residual, fixed by/in/difference, since they, unlike abstraction, do not travel. For such theory prejudgement is the very condition of its elaboration; it is neither consciously designed nor culturally equipped for understanding that *terra incognita* which its own expansion nevertheless requires it to map (So that, by contrast with the prioritizing of mobility which is characteristic of the nomadic mode of theorizing, this form of theory might be said to put the cartography before the horse). Yet because such theory is constituted as universal and abstract, as against local and particular, its form at once facilitates its circulation amongst (spatially dispersed but discursively interdependent) co-practitioners and exemplifies its claim to cognitive efficacy.

Against this, Said can be understood as arguing for the cognitive necessity of acknowledging or uncovering the institutional embeddedness of theoretical practice itself. There is thus a double movement involved; a recognition of the effect of context not just on the object(s) of theoretical inquiry but on the site(s) from which investigation proceeds. The overall effect of such a move is to deconstruct the universal/local and abstract/particular oppositions and the associated privileging of the first terms in these and related couplets. Theory always comes from a somewhere, a somewhere understood not as an actual place but as a complexly mediated social location and an enabling discursive positioning. Theory which presents itself as if coming from nowhere/anywhere is not so much concerned to escape its origin as at pains to essentialize it; and thereby to defend and disguise itself against what is understood as the threat of dispersal, fragmentation and plurality.

By contrast, and precisely because he is both positioned by and scattered across disparate discursive and social locations, Said uses theory in order to articulate the processes of such positioning rather than to elide them. This latter mode of theorizing is impelled to 'travel' between a plurality of sites by the conditions of its practice. As such it is equipped both to reveal the parochialism of a cosmopolitanism which effectively depended upon a door-shutting contrast with the local, and to resist being marginalized as 'merely' local knowledge. And by making the foregrounding of its own practice a general precondition for the interrogation of others, it is also resistant to being marginalized as 'merely' subjective knowledge.

Furthermore one of the ways in which theory has traditionally sought to signal its efficacy has been by way of the conceptual elimination of the theorist (albeit only from the body of the text, and not, of course, from its head). The writing of

(a different conception of) the theorist into theory therefore involves the obliga-
tion to rewrite theory itself. Against the essentializing demands of theory's
categorizing imperative, dispersal is re-evaluated as enabling. It becomes a 'place'
from which to mount a critique of the conceit of theory which does not (care to)
know its (own) place (cf. Perry 1992) at a time when this latter is itself under-
going change under the impact of globalization. This provides the conditions for
theorizing as a process that is both mindful of its own contingency yet responsive
to its own provisional possibilities; a privileging of theorizing (now elevated to
strategy) over theory (now understood as tactic), a practice thus attuned to, and
critical of, attempts to naturalize the arbitrariness of concepts.

This goes beyond the kind of critique which the historian E.P. Thompson
(1965, 1978) made of Althusserian theory, but it rescues what is of most value
from that confrontation. In insisting on 'the peculiarities of the English'
Thompson did not just set this against 'the peculiarities of the French', but saw
their contrasting patterns of historical development as vindicating wholly discrete
methodological precepts and modes of cognition. The intention may have been
to reinforce the traditional distinctions between experience and theory, cultur-
alism and structuralism, history and sociology, but the consequence was to draw
attention to their contemporary interdependence. This latter is a theme evident in
anthropologist Clifford Geertz's more recent writing, in which he amplifies
tendencies that were effectively embryonic in his elegant advocacy of the method
of 'thick description' and the pertinence of local knowledge (Geertz 1983).
Geertz's reworking of local knowledge had been constructed across the distinction between the necessity of (a necessarily partisan) translation and the
methodological imperative of (an even handed) conceptual pluralism. His characteristic emphasis was on how to combine a clarification of the (presumptively)
exotic with a problematizing of the thoroughly familiar (often making use of *three*
cases and thereby providing some kind of defence against binary readings). For
Geertz (1988: 147–8) now the pervasiveness of global processes and the pervasiveness of local differences have become so jumbled together as to threaten the
conceptual stability of such terms as 'the English', and the interests and points of
view that those terms are held to imply. The problem becomes one of
constructing an intelligible discourse across the resulting divisions and connections (cf. Robertson 1992: 180–1).

Thus, as Stuart Hall (1991: 59–61) has recently argued, a transgressive film
like Stephen Frears and Hanif Kureishi's *My Beautiful Laundrette* is unmistakably
and peculiarly British, but none the less is concerned to pull out all of the props
which sustain received notions of personal and national identity with respect to
oppressor and oppressed alike. More generally, within contemporary fiction in
English, the best and the brightest (a list which would include Salman Rushdie,
Kazuo Ishiguro, Maxine Hong Kingston and Michael Ondaatje) are commonly
those for whom the principle of dispersal has not just become, but has been made,
enriching rather than inhibiting. Edward Said's writing – and the responses to it –
can be seen as a theoretical and critical expression of this wider tendency. As such,

it both marks the entry to a route along which the practitioners of nomadic theorizing might journey, and it effects a link with some remarkably astute and perceptive fellow travellers.

What is implicit in Said, becomes explicit in Gayatri Spivak. She therefore approvingly singles out Said's response to being commended for his patriotism. Said had replied 'that he was working for the Palestinian state to establish itself so that he could then become its critic' (Spivak 1987: 125). Spivak recognizes the disciplinary privileging, the (three thousand critics') ideology that is at work 'in Said's conviction that the literary critic rather than the other human scientists are the custodians of socio-political interpretation' (Spivak 1987: 126). But what she finds praiseworthy is Said's willingness to interrogate the terms of a choice that is tacitly constructed as being between cosmopolitan and local, between either 'world citizen' or 'indigenous nationalist'. The point is not just that such a construction works to close off the very notion of being both by construing it as a theoretical impossibility, when it is precisely the existential correctness of such a response which is so pressing an imperative for Said. The point is also that this variant on the universal/particular contrast is political through and through, achieving its effects by defining and valuing the first terms by way of contrast with the second.

Having described herself as 'a practical deconstructivist feminist Marxist' (Spivak 1990: 133) and 'the post-colonial diasporic Indian who seeks to decolonise the mind' (Spivak 1990: 67), Spivak knowingly eschews both theoretical purity and political correctness. She chooses rather to make something of the disciplinary predicament into which she has been written by history, deploying it as a resource for writing/answering back. 'My position is generally a reactive one. I am viewed by the Marxists as too codic, by feminists as too male identified, by indigenous theorists as too committed to Western theory. I am uneasily pleased about this' (Spivak 1990: 69–70). Her work thus acquires some of its impetus from her vigilant resistance to categorization. The point is not (or not only) to shrug off all such attempts at definition, but rather to use them so as to open up the links between the theoretical work that such definitions routinely perform and the interests that they actively constitute or tacitly serve. Thus:

> The putative center welcomes selective inhabitants of the margin in order better to exclude the margin. And it is the center which offers the official explanation; or the center is defined and reproduced by the explanation it can express . . . . By pointing attention to a feminist marginality, I have been attempting, not to win the center for ourselves, but to point at the irreducibility of the margin in all explanations. That would not merely reverse but displace the distinction between margin and center. But in effect such pure innocence (pushing all guilt to the margins) is not possible, and paradoxically would put the very law of displacement and the irreducibility of the margin into question. The only way I can hope to suggest how the center itself is marginal is by not

remaining outside on the margin and pointing my accusing finger at the
center. I might do it rather by implicating myself in that center and
sensing what politics make it marginal.

(Spivak 1987: 107)

It is in Dorinne Kondo's (1990) account of a Japanese factory that the themes
and tactics characteristic of such nomadic theorizing are gathered together and
their wider pertinence made most explicit. Both substantively and formally, her
Crafting Selves is an innovative work. It is knowingly informed by a way of writing
which serves to deliberately blur and problematize the boundaries between the
subject(s) that the text investigates, the concepts on which its construction
depends, and the author who reflexively organizes its narrative realization. The
book is based on the empirical investigation of a small, family-owned factory
(rather than a large corporation) and focuses on artisans and women part-time
workers (rather than salary men). The personal and the political are here
combined, not as a tired and tiresome slogan, but in the very choice of subject
and the manner of writing. Thus the text persistently foregrounds complexity,
power, contradiction, discursive production and ambiguity both in its subjects
and in its own ways of telling. The work is explicitly conceived in opposition to
'the insidiously persistent tropes that constitute the phantasm "Japan" in the
contemporary United States: not only Organization Man and automaton, but
submissive subjugated Japanese Woman, domineering sexist Japanese Man,
Japanese despot, or perhaps most basically "the (undifferentiated) Japanese"'
(Kondo 1990: 301). Hence the text refuses, or rather one should say interrupts,
those narrative conventions of fixed identity and essential meaning which sustain
such a discourse. The small firm focus is not designed to support any larger claim,
but rather intended to act as a counterweight to the literature's dominant
emphasis on large corporations (cf. however, Freidman 1988; Weiss 1989).

As a Japanese American woman Kondo brought to the study assumptions
which shaped everyday life in the community in which she grew up. What counts
as experience is therefore recognized as not something apart from theory but
understood as a product of discourse. Conversely what counts as theory is recognized as differentially understood and valued according to subject positioning.
For Kondo the relevant assumptions included 'the eloquence of silence, the
significance of reciprocity, the need to attend closely to nuance, subtlety, ellipsis'
(Kondo 1990: 300). That such orientations were so often at odds with dominant
cultural modes not only spoke to her conviction:

that no account of Japanese Americans could even begin to understand
'us' – this essentialist collective identity itself a strategic assertion and a
site of multiple contested meanings – without lengthy acquaintance and
a sensitive appreciation of the ways 'we' define 'ourselves'.

(Kondo 1990: 301)

It also reinforced, powerfully because experientially, a methodological commitment to appreciate and respect the Japanese subjects of her study.

This is not to say that such a maxim is unusual amongst anthropologists (it was, after all, evidence of Malinowski's deviation from it which made his diaries a *succès de scandale* within the discipline). Rather what gives Kondo's work its edge is that for those selfsame subjects she herself was a conceptual anomaly and a living contradiction. Thus their endeavours to minimize dissonance for themselves by striving to recruit her to their pre-existing cultural and discursive categories had the effect of increasing dissonance for her. Their strategies for consolidation of their identities were predicated upon the fragmentation of her own. This leads her to a conception of identities as constructed oppositionally and relationally, of selves as multiple and shifting, as context bound, rhetorical strategies rather than (more or less) fixed entities. Selves inseparable from context are selves inseparable from power, and this is understood by Kondo in a broadly Foucauldian sense, in which discourses crosscut and contradict one another and dominant idioms such as 'company as family' are differentially mobilized and deployed in ways which undermine their unproblematic operation. Her part-time women workers are both structurally marginal (an economic buffer zone) and discursively crucial (as both the objects and the audience for masculine discourses). Their gender positioning and their links to the home are at once a powerful constraint and the basis for asserting a claim to centrality, such that their enactment of themselves as women is in context both affirmative and yet a reinforcement of their structural subordination. Kondo's attention to the internal differences within the Japanese workplace thus goes beyond Rohlen's (1974) account of a Japanese bank, which had taken as its leitmotif the contradiction between 'harmony and strength' (the bank's own motto). And at the same time her relational conception of selves also goes beyond those constructions of a gendered self and critiques of the whole subject made by Western feminists (which remain wedded to individualism).

Kondo's study thus offers more than a methodological corrective to prevailing Western images of the self and of the Japanese workforce. She employs it as a means of unravelling the theoretical assumptions and narrative conventions which guide such images. The self that writes the text is multivocal, tacking back and forth between vignette and theoricity; the narrative alternately circling around its subjects and back upon itself in a making and remaking of its own rhetorical strategies. By thus doubling and problematizing its own subject what is thereby inscribed into the body of the text is that conception of selves which the text itself describes. These disturbances in the text thus correspond to the disrupting of a bounded, unified concept of self and to a subversion of theoretical categories understood as fixed, stable and culturally invariant. This allows Kondo to stress the constituting of selves as of a piece with the organizing of work, and to construe identity as a process rather than an object (cf. also Knights and Willmott 1989). The nomadic theorist who emerges from this mode of representation is disrespectful of boundaries and resistant to categorization; with the concomitant scattering of theoretical identity, theory is hybridized, mongrelized, customized, made promiscuous, invested with voice; not local, not lost but rather found *elsewhere*, in places where conventional theory does not (and cannot) travel.

For a cognitive tour of theoryland to survive in the contemporary cultural marketplace, it must both recognize and attempt to grapple with the need to cater to a variety of tastes, tastes which are at once flexible and specialized. Kondo's family firm made Japanese confectioneries. Clegg (1990) offers an exemplar of institutional embeddedness by pointing to the persistence of localized, artisanal production of French bread (in France), that staple product which in other modern societies is mass produced by large corporations. This chapter made a quick trip to McDonald's in order to sample their best known product. The first of these commodities remains overwhelmingly local; the second travels, albeit selectively; the third seems to be almost everywhere. Our brief visit to their respective cultural sites strongly suggests that there is no single theory which might embrace the theories which have been constructed around such products, only what Foster (1983: xi) referred to as the 'anything goes' variant of postmodernism and Lyotard's (1984: 76) observation that 'Eclecticism is the degree zero of contemporary general culture, one . . . eats McDonald's food for lunch and local cuisine for dinner, (and) wears Paris perfume in Tokyo'.

Social and organizational analysis may be less exotic than Lyotard's illustration, but it is no less eclectic; a theoretical hypermarket with globally organized brands and regional franchise holders, interspersed with ease-of-access high volume discounters, local craft producers, enthusiastic recyclers, bricoleurs and the hucksters of snake oil remedies. Whitley's (1984) use of the term 'fragmented adhocracy' to characterize these disciplines makes just such a point in a fashion that is at once linguistically more circumspect and analytically more developed.

As with the Big Mac, social theories and their subject matter are everywhere. But as with the Big Mac, they are everywhere complexly mediated, inflected and refracted through and by specific meanings, usages and interests whose full specificity resists standardization and categorization. The Big Mac is, of course, not just a text, and social theories refer to something beyond the texts themselves. But as with the Big Mac in this chapter, this 'something beyond the texts' can only be approached through the texts. The associated dilemmas provide the axis along which nomadic theorizing and travelling theory pitch their respective tents. Somewhere between that radical scepticism towards essentialist and universal concepts to which Kondo gives expression, and the kind of repair work at (and from within) the boundaries of the modernist project represented by Clegg, is where theories and theorizing which claims contemporaneity with globalization must presently move. For although we cannot but essentialize – because of what we are – nevertheless both what 'we' are, and what we 'are', are themselves essentially contested. And this takes place in a world in which we are essentially connected, but a world in which our answers to the question 'what world is this?' (cf. McHale 1992: 146–164) are, in their turn essentially contested. In so far as globalization can be represented at all, it is through the contradictory pluralities of such enforced in-betweenness and the tactics of serious play to which it gives rise. Glimpsed, but not grasped.

More generally, however, what can be glimpsed is how questions about the subject matter of such theoretical inquiries now routinely intersect with questions about the very form which theories should take. What is thereby insinuated is the existence of a third term through which one might knowingly (and hence provisionally) adjudicate on the appropriate relation between travelling theory and nomadic theorizing. For to theorize involves a commitment to something beyond that which is present (cf. Blum 1974: 119). Yet it is just such a commitment which is suppressed by that naturalistic definition of theory as tourism with which this chapter has identified. Associated with a recognition of such commitment is that (examined) presumption of theory as critical which leads Jürgen Habermas to interpret the meaning of the Greek term *theoria* rather differently than does Walter (1988). In his inaugural lecture Habermas observed that 'theory' has a religious etymology, '*Theoros* was the name for the holy representative sent to the public festivals by the Greek cities. In *theoria*, that is in the role of impersonal onlooker, he witnessed the sacred proceedings' (Habermas 1970a: 37). From such beginnings theory came to mean the contemplation of the cosmos *and* the ordering of practical life according to its workings.

This in turn gave way to that bifurcation and enormously complex elaboration of theory into what Habermas identifies as the knowledge constitutive interests which are associated with respectively, the technical control of the empirical analytical sciences and the hermeneutic understanding of the historical interpretative sciences. The former increases technical command through the provision of information, the latter allows for the orientation of action in the light of shared understandings and tradition. Such a distinction does to some extent overlap with that between travelling theory and nomadic theorizing. Yet what defines the works which are of most interest on each side of the travelling theory/nomadic theorizing contrast is precisely that they offer up resistance to being easily recruited to one or the other of the Habermas' categories. It is in so far as they both gravitate towards and problematize his third category of possible knowledge and interest, namely, the critical and emancipatory, that they make claims on our attention.

Habermas argues that:

> Society is not just a system of self-preservation. There is also a restless urge, present as a libido in the individual, which has unharnessed itself from the functions of self-preservation and presses towards Utopian fulfilment . . . the processes of cognition which are inseparable from the creation of society, cannot function only as a means of maintenance and reproduction of life; they serve equally to establish the very definitions of this life.
>
> (1970a: 48–9)

The specific significance of 'travelling' and 'nomadic' as theoretical attributes is that the contrast between them also engages with the foundational status of critique itself. Habermas locates the ground of critique in philosophical anthropology, in the libido of individuals, which subsequently finds expression in discourses which free consciousness from its dependence upon extant material and social controls. The terms travelling and nomadism stand in different relationships to this argument; the former has an origin and a destination as its premise, the latter is premised upon journeying as such. Thus whereas 'travelling' metaphorically and literally invokes a source for that differentiation which is the catalyst of such striving, 'nomadism' posits no such foundational conception and no such sequence, only what Lyotard (1984) would claim as the prospectively subversive play of difference. Inasmuch as such a distinction is a specific version of the now familiar choice between a sociology of the postmodern and a postmodern sociology, then it also, albeit imperfectly, maps on to the contrast between 'travelling in hyperreality' and 'hyperreal travelling'.

In the classical age, says Habermas, *theoria* meant an impersonal witness observing sacred rites. Within the modern, says Benjamin, it became a melancholy angel looking back upon the ruins. This book began its journey from the latter location – but only in order to signal that sea change associated with the metaphor of navigation. In the ocean of signs which is contemporary theory, however, there are neither fixed bearings nor any guarantees as to the reliability of the charts. To navigate under such conditions entails learning to read both the movement of local currents and the present positions of distant stars. It depends upon whatever insights can be gleaned from the passage of flotsam and jetsam and upon inferring the climatic changes signalled by clouds of hot air. It may be refined by the exchange of interpretations and the sharing of anxieties amongst those in the same boat, but it involves choosing between the uncertain efficacy of heading for the main sea lanes and the doubtful strategy of striving for remote landfall. It requires that one gazes abstractedly skywards when pissing over the side.[2] It is the art of waiting and the art of weighting; of judging when to row and when to drift – whilst all the time yearning not so much for an 'ideal speech situation' as for a better cell 'phone.

NOTES

1 ANTIPODEAN CAMP

1 Compare this with a scene which Sloterdijk identifies as emblematic of his thesis. Just before he died, Adorno was prevented from giving a lecture by a group of student demonstrators. Some of the female students who were involved bared their breasts to him in protest. Sloterdijk observes

> It was not naked force that reduced the philosopher to muteness but the force of the naked. Right and wrong, truth and falsity were inextricably mixed in this scene in a way that is quite typical for cynicisms. Cynicism ventures forth with naked truths that, in the way they are presented, contains something false.
>
> (1988: xxxvii–iii)

To which should be added that the critical reason/critical body contrast that is implied is also already gendered – not least in that, according to Gonzales (1984: 208), Adorno was well known for his roving eye. Reason/body is hardly the couplet which the Queen of England and Australian wharfies invoke, but the incident offers a reminder of the elusiveness of the notion of a pure gesture against authority.

2 Both at, and in the build-up to the moment when Ada's husband chops off one of her fingers, *The Piano*'s iconography and *mise-en-scène* nod towards Vincent Ward's earlier feature, *Vigil*.

3 Ward's mother was a German Jew who had fled from Hamburg and the Nazis. Writing of his visit to her country of origin, Ward says:

> The trip to Germany was important to me. I passed through medieval villages and while I was hitch-hiking, tried to cross a seven-lane autobahn. Although I managed to get safely across three lanes of rush hour traffic, the remaining four were impossible to traverse. I was marooned. And as I waited on the median strip it struck me how you would feel if you were dropped from the Middle Ages into the twentieth century and were stranded there like I was. The notion stayed in my mind, and began to expand into the story of *The Navigator*. Expanding the idea from the perspective of my ancestors, I delved into a past that was part invention and part research . . . .
>
> (Ward *et al.* 1990: 83–4)

4 A griffin was a mythical beast with a lion's body and an eagle's head and wings.

169

2 AM I RITE? OR AM I WRITE? OR AM I RIGHT?
READING *THE SINGING DETECTIVE*

1   In an interview with Alan Yentob for BBC2's *Arena* series.

2   Series like *Picket Fences* and *Northern Exposure* also signal how the combination of small-town settings and the concerns of overwhelmingly urban audiences makes for blurred genres and hybridity. In this sense what, for example, could have been more urban, or more urbane, than *Twin Peaks*? Hence what helped make the Coen brothers' film *Fargo* so accomplished and so plausible a spoof was that it undercut conventional representations of both urban low life and mid-West small towns by engineering a collision between the narrative conventions of endearing rural eccentricity and the pulp fiction myth of grittily ruthless criminality.

3   Esslin was unable to recognize that *Hill Street Blues* was not 'just a run of the mill police series'. An émigré Anglophile, well known for authoritative writings on the theatre of the absurd, he worked for BBC drama for many years before becoming a professor in California.

4   QED – *Quod erat demonstrandum*, literally, which was the thing to be proved.

5   After *Double Indemnity* Chandler not only worked in the film capital, but also wrote about it in undisguisedly hostile terms. The contrast with William Faulkner is instructive. Faulkner seemed much more sanguine about the differences between writing for films and writing novels, much better reconciled to the collective and commercial character of popular film making. To judge from his letters, Chandler's opinions on Hollywood (and on television) did eventually mellow a little (see Gardiner and Walker 1962: 115–44).

6   Cook (1995: 270–81) also sees the problems of Potter's subsequent *Blackeyes* as deriving not just from Potter's directorial inexperience, but from the script's reliance upon a literary derived theory of representation. This bears comparison with how some film directors, such as Arthur Penn, have achieved their best work *within* the Hollywood system (so that the still memorable popular achievement which was *Bonnie and Clyde* contrasts with the best forgotten art-movie limitations of *Mickey One*).

3 POST-PICTURES AND EC(H)O EFFECTS

1   'The Family of Man' was the title of a famous photographic exhibition held at The Museum of Modern Art, New York in 1955.

2   *Ways of Seeing* was, in part, explicable as a response to the imperious conceit of Kenneth Clark's earlier BBC series, *Civilization*.

3   Eco must mean The National Gallery rather than the Tate.

4   Compare the American Bill Bryson's encounter with the little-visited remains of a Roman villa near the English town of Winchcombe.

> I cannot tell you how odd it felt to be standing in a forgotten wood . . . looking at a mosaic laid at least 1600 years ago . . . (so that) for the first time it dawned on me in a kind of profound way that all those Roman antiquities I had gazed at over the years weren't created with a view to one day ending up in museums.
>
> (1996: 173)

5 THE EMPORIUM OF SIGNS

1 The reference is to 'We're into chaos, not music' a remark attributed to Johnny Rotten by Dick Hebdige (1979: 109).
2 My thanks to Mike Lloyd for first bringing this phrase to my attention.

6 INDECENT EXPOSURES: THEORIZING WHISTLEBLOWING

1 Sissela Bok (1984: 210–29) explores the limits and limitations of such binary contrasts in her brief but lucid analytic discussion of the ethics of whistleblowing.
2 This Glazer and Glazer (1989) study was cited as influential in a 1994 federal court decision which extended the protection granted to whistleblowers (American Sociological Association 1994: 8).
3 The remainder of this section draws upon Perry (1993: especially 960–2).
4 This example, as described by Evans Pritchard (1937), has become the standard case for discussions as to the rationality of magic and its relation to the rationality of science. See, for example, the collection edited by Wilson (1970).
5 Lyotard's own contestatory 'little narrative' seeks to legitimate a (paralogical, post-modern) science which 'is concerning itself with such things as undecidables, the limits of precise control, conflicts characterized by incomplete information, "*fracta*", catas-trophes and pragmatic paradoxes . . . theorizing its own evolution as discontinuous, catastrophic, nonrectifiable and paradoxical' (Lyotard 1984: 60). Its object is not to reach agreement but to generate difference, thereby facilitating the emergence of new ideas which in turn feed into the heterogeneous language games of the social totality so as to promote new and changing social relations.

7 DEAD MEN AND NEW SHOES

1 These remarks concerning Bloom's book draw upon a more general discussion in my *The Dominion of Signs: Television, advertising and other New Zealand Fictions* (1994: 4–7).
2 Raban's *Hunting Mr Heartbreak* (1990) takes its title and its theme from Hector de Crevecoeur's *Letters from an American Farmer*. For Raban, Crevecouer's image of coming upon the lacerated corpse of a Negro left to die in a cage does not just hang over the entire book. It voices 'a European perception of the United States that has barely altered since his death' (1990: 155). Thus Raban sees that perception as reaching across the centuries so as to inform, for example, Hugh Brogan's account of the civil rights struggles of the 1960s in his *History of the United States*. Peter Mason's *Deconstructing America* (1990) can be read as tracing the earliest roots of such a predisposition.
3 The reference is to Robert Merton's (1968: 185–248) classic analysis of social struc-ture and deviance.
4 'Observations' not in the sense of attempting to elucidate the meaning and use of such practices for their practitioners, but rather as an encapsulated moral homily on and of social disorganization. Compare Ross' (1989) very different reading of pornography and popular culture.
5 In giving his critical attention to cyberpunk science fiction, Jameson (1991: 38) refers to it 'as fully as much an expression of transnational corporate realities as it is of global paranoia itself: William Gibson's representational innovations, indeed, mark his work as an exceptional literary realization within a predominantly visual or aural postmodern

production'. The film of Gibson's *Neuromancer*, a multimillion dollar, Hollywood special effects blockbuster, produced within and by transnational corporate reality might therefore provide Jameson with a test case analogous to that which the film of *Women in Love* provided for F.R. Leavis.

8 TRAVELLING THEORY/NOMADIC THEORIZING

1   In her splendidly scurrilous polemic against French theory and its reception within American literary criticism, Camille Paglia (1992: 220) argues that the resulting 'McDonaldization of the profession means standardized interchangeable outlets, briskly efficient academics who think alike and sound alike'. Lamont's (1987) analysis of this process is altogether more scholarly but rather less entertaining.
2   Habermas (1970a: 37) notes that theory came to mean the combination of contemplation of the cosmos and the ordering of practical life in accordance with its workings – hence my 'gazing skywards and pissing over the side'. The lesson of Diogenes, however, is that in order for theory to become critique then taking *a* piss must become taking *the* piss. Compare the observation of American Anglophile Bill Bryson (1996: 227–8) that there is no equivalent in American speech to Britain's 'dry, ironic taking-the-piss sort of wit . . . [which] is such a fundamental part of daily life that you scarcely notice it'.

BIBLIOGRAPHY

Adams, S. (1984) *Roche versus Adams*, London: Jonathan Cape.

Adorno, T. (1977) 'Commitment' in E. Bloch, G. Lukács, B. Brecht, W. Benjamin and T. Adorno, *Aesthetics and Politics*, London: New Left Books, 177–95.

Albrow, M. (1970) *Bureaucracy*, London: Macmillan.

Allison, A. (1994) *Nightwork: Sexuality, Pleasure and Corporate Masculinity in a Tokyo Hostess Club*, Chicago, IL: University of Chicago Press.

American Sociological Association (1994) *Footnotes*, Summer issue.

Anderson, B. (1983) *Imagined Communities: Reflections on the Origins and Spread of Nationalism*, London: Verso.

Anderson, R. M., R. Perruci, D. E. Schendel and L. E. Trachtman (1980) *Divided Loyalties: Whistleblowing at Bart*, West Lafayette, IN: Purdue University Press.

Appadurai, A. (1990) 'Disjunction and Difference in the Global Cultural Economy', in M. Featherstone (ed.), *Global Culture*, London: Sage, 295–310.

Arendt, H. (1968) 'Truth and Politics', in her *Between Past and Future*, New York: Viking Press, 227–64.

—— (1972) 'Lying in Politics', and 'Civil Disobedience', in her *Crises of the Republic*, New York: Harcourt, Brace, Yovanovich: 1–47, 49–102 respectively.

Armi, C. E. (1988) *The Art of American Car Design*, University Park, PA and London: Pennsylvania State University Press.

Asada, A. (1989) 'Infantile Capitalism and Japan's Postmodernism: A Fairy Tale', in M. Miyoshi and H. D. Harootunian (eds), *Postmodernism and Japan*, Durham, NC: Duke University Press: 273–8.

Aubert, V. (1952) 'White Collar Crime and Social Structure', *American Sociological Review* 58: 263–71; repr. in G. Geiss and R. F. Meier (eds) (1977) *White Collar Crime*, New York: Free Press: 168–79.

Bagehot, W. (1963) *The English Constitution*, Fontana edition, London: Collins.

Bailey, F. G. (1977) *Morality and Expediency: The Folklore of Academic Politics*, Oxford: Blackwell.

Barber, B. R. (1992) 'Jihad vs McWorld', *The Atlantic* 269 (3): 53–63.

Barthes, R. (1973) *Mythologies*, London: Paladin.

—— (1977a) *Image – Music – Text*, London: Fontana.

—— (1977b) *Roland Barthes*, New York: Hill and Wang.

—— (1982) *Empire of Signs*, New York: Hill and Wang.

—— (1984) *Writing Degree Zero*, London: Jonathan Cape.

173

—— (1985) *The Grain of the Voice*, London: Jonathan Cape.

Baudrillard, J. (1981) *For a Critique of the Political Economy of the Sign*, St Louis, MO: Telos Press.

—— (1982) 'The Beaubourg Effect: Implosion and Deterrence', *October* 20: 3–13.

—— (1983a) *In the Shadow of the Silent Majorities*, New York: Semiotext(e).

—— (1983b) *Simulations*, New York: Semiotext(e).

—— (1988) *America*, London: Verso.

—— (1990) *Cool Memories*, London: Verso.

Bauman, Z. (1987) *Legislators and Interpreters*, Cambridge: Polity Press.

Bayley, S. (1985) *The Good Design Guide*, London: Conran Foundation.

—— (1986) *Sex, Drink and Fast Cars*, London: Faber and Faber.

Bell, D. (1973) *The Coming of Post Industrial Society*, New York: Basic Books.

Benjamin, W. (1968) *Illuminations*, London: Jonathan Cape.

—— (1973) *Charles Baudelaire: A Lyric Poet in the Era of High Capitalism*, London: New Left Books.

Berger, J. (1972) *Ways of Seeing*, London: BBC.

Berliner, J. (1957) *Factory and Manager in the USSR*, Cambridge, MA: Harvard University Press.

Bickerton, D. (1995) *Language and Human Behaviour*, Seattle, WA: University of Washington Press.

Blake, K. (1974) *Play, Games and Sport: The Literary Works of Lewis Carroll*, Ithaca, NY and London: Cornell University Press.

Bloom, A. (1987) *The Closing of the American Mind*, New York: Simon and Schuster.

Blum, A. F. (1974) *Theorizing*, London: Heinemann.

BMW (1991a) 'Demographie BMW Fahrer, Triade: USA, Japan, Europa 1988–90', BMW Marktforschung, Munich: BMW AG Public Relations.

—— (1991b) *Kunst am Automobil/Automobile Art*, Munich: BMW AG Public Relations.

Boas, M. and S. Chain (1976) *Big Mac*, New York: Dutton.

Bok, S. (1978) *Lying: Moral Choice in Public and Private Life*, New York, Pantheon Books.

—— (1984) *Secrets: On the Ethics of Concealment and Revelation*, Oxford: Oxford University Press.

Borges, J. L. (1964) 'On Rigor in Science', in *Dreamtigers*, Austin, TX: University of Texas Press: 90.

—— (1965) 'Tlön, Uqbar, Orbis Tertius', in *Fictions*, London: Calder, Jupiter Books: 17–34.

Bourdieu, P. (1977) *Outline of a Theory of Practice*, London: Cambridge University Press.

—— (1984) *Distinction: A Social Critique of the Judgement of Taste*, London: Routledge.

Brabeck, M. (1984) 'Ethical Characteristics of Whistleblowers', *Journal of Research in Personality* 18: 41–53.

Brannen, M. Y. (1992) '"Bwana Mickey": Constructing Cultural Consumption at Tokyo Disneyland', in J. J. Tobin (ed.), *Re-made in Japan*, New Haven, CT and London: Yale University Press, 216–34.

Bridgstock, M. (1982) 'A Sociological Approach to Fraud in Science', *Australian and New Zealand Journal of Sociology* 18: 364–83.

Broad, W. and N. Wade (1983) *Betrayers of the Truth*, London: Century.

Brogan, H. (1986) *The Pelican History of the United States*, Harmondsworth: Penguin.

Brookeman, C. (1984) *American Culture and Society Since the 1930s*, New York: Schocken Books.

Browne, N. (1987) 'The Political Economy of the Television Supertext', in H. Newcomb (ed.), *Television: The Critical View*, 4th edn, New York: Oxford University Press, 585–99.

Bruck, J. and J. Docker (1991) 'Puritanic Rationalism: John Berger's *Ways of Seeing* and Media and Culture Studies', *Theory, Culture and Society* 8: 79–96.

Bryson, B. (1996) *Notes from a Small Island*, London: Black Swan.

Buck Morss, S. (1986) 'The Flaneur, the Sandwichman and the Whore: The Politics of Loitering' *New German Critique* 39: 99–140.

Burns, T. (1974) 'On the Rationale of the Corporate System', in R. Marris (ed.), *The Corporate Society*, London: Macmillan, 121–77.

Burns, T. and G. M. Stalker (1966) *The Management of Innovation*, 2nd edn, London: Tavistock.

Business Week (1986) 'McWorld?', 13 October.

Calder, A. (1987) 'The Pleasures and Politics of Watching *The Sandbaggers*', unpublished lecture, Auckland University Winter Lecture Series.

Callon, M. (1986) 'Some Elements of a Sociology of Translation: Domestication of the Scallops and the Fishermen of St Brieuc Bay', in J. Law (ed.), *Power, Action and Belief*, London: Routledge and Kegan Paul, 196–233.

Carroll, L. (1910) *The Hunting of the Snark*, London: Macmillan.

—— (1929) *Alice in Wonderland; Through the Looking Glass, etc*, London: J. M. Dent.

Carson, W. G. (1980) 'The Institutionalisation of Ambiguity: Early British Factory Acts' in G. Geis and E. Stotland (eds), *White Collar Crime: Theory and Research*, Beverly Hills, CA: Sage, 142–73.

Carter, A. (1982) *Nothing Sacred: Selected Writings*, London: Virago.

Castells, M. (1989) *The Informational City*, Oxford: Blackwell.

Certeau, M. de (1984) *The Practice of Everyday Life*, Berkeley and Los Angeles, CA: University of California Press.

Chandler, R. (1962) *Raymond Chandler Speaking*, ed. D. Gardiner and K. S. Walker London: Hamish Hamilton.

Clammer, J. (1992) 'Aesthetics of the Self: Shopping and Social Being in Contemporary Urban Japan' in R. Shields (ed.) *Lifestyle Shopping: The Subject of Consumption*, London: Routledge, 195–215.

Clegg, S. (1990) *Modern Organizations: Organization Studies in the Postmodern World*, London: Sage.

Cleverley, G. (1971) *Managers and Magic*, London: Longman.

Clifford, J. and G. E. Marcus (eds) (1986) *Writing Culture*, Berkeley, CA: University of California Press.

Cohen, S. (1974) 'Criminology and the Sociology of Deviance in Britain', in P. Rock and M. McIntosh (eds), *Deviance and Social Control*, London: Tavistock, 1–40.

Collins, H. M. (1982) 'Tacit Knowledge and Scientific Networks', in B. Barnes and D. Edge (eds), *Science in Context*, Milton Keynes: Open University Press, 44–64.

Collins, J. (1989) *Uncommon Cultures*, New York and London: Routledge.

Colls, R. and P. Dodd (eds) (1985) *The Idea of Englishness, 1880–1920*, Beckenham: Croom Helm.

Connell, R. W. (1983) *Which Way is Up? Essays on Class, Sex and Culture*, Sydney: Allen and Unwin.

Cook, J. R. (1995) *Dennis Potter: A Life on Screen*, Manchester: Manchester University Press.

Coward, R. (1987) 'Dennis Potter and the Question of the Television Author', *Critical Quarterly* 29 (4): 79–87.

Crane, D. (1972) *Invisible Colleges*, Chicago, IL: University of Chicago Press.

Creighton, M. R. (1991) 'Maintaining Cultural Boundaries in Retailing: How Japanese Department Stores Domesticate "Things Foreign"', *Modern Asia Studies* 25: 675–709.

Crescimbene, S. (1991) *Inside Tokyo*, London: Tiger Books.

Cringeley, R. (1993) *Accidental Empires*, London: Penguin.

Crowley, M. (1970) *The Boys in the Band*, Harmondsworth: Penguin.

Crozier, M. (1964) *The Bureaucratic Phenomenon*, London: Tavistock.

Cumings, B. (1993) 'Archaelogy, Descent, Emergence: Japan in British/American Hegemony', 1900–1950', in M. Miyoshi and H. D. Harootunian (eds), *Japan in the World*, Durham, NC: Duke University Press, 79–111.

Curnow, A. (1962) *A Small Room With Large Windows: Selected Poems*, Oxford: Oxford University Press.

Dale, P. N. (1986) *The Myth of Japanese Uniqueness*, New York: St Martins Press.

Dalton, M. (1959) *Men Who Manage*, New York: John Wiley and Sons.

Davis, M. (1990) *City of Quartz*, London and New York: Verso.

Davis, N. P. (1969) *Lawrence and Oppenheimer*, London: Jonathan Cape.

De Mente, B. and F. T. Perry (1968) *The Japanese as Consumers*, New York and Tokyo: Walker/Weatherhill.

Dean, M. (1994) *Critical and Effective Histories: Foucault's Methods and Historical Sociology*, London: Routledge.

Debord, G. (1994) *The Society of the Spectacle*, New York: Zone Books.

Della Femina, J. (1971) *From Those Wonderful Folks Who Gave You Pearl Harbor: Dispatches from the Advertising War*, London: Pitman.

Derrida, J (1973) 'Differance', in *Speech and Phenomena and other essays on Husserl's Theory of Signs*, Evanston, IL: Northwestern University Press, 129–60.

—— (1981) *Positions*, Chicago, IL: Chicago University Press.

Devons, E. and M. Gluckman (1964) 'Conclusion: Modes and Consequences of Limiting a Field' in M. Gluckman (ed.), *Closed Systems and Open Minds*, Edinburgh: Oliver and Boyd, 158–261.

Dickson, D. (1986) *The New Politics of Science*, New York: Basic Books.

Didion, J. (1979) *The White Album*, New York: Pocket Books.

Docker, J. (1994) *Postmodernism and Popular Culture*, Cambridge: Cambridge University Press.

Donaldson, L. (1985) *In Defence of Organisation Theory*, Cambridge: Cambridge University Press.

—— (1987) 'Strategy, Structural Adjustment to Regain Fit and Performance: In Defence of Contingency Theory', *Journal of Management Studies* 24 (2): 1–24.

Dormer, P. (1990) *The Meanings of Modern Design*, London: Thames and Hudson.

Douglas, M. (ed.) (1973) *Rules and Meanings*, Harmondsworth: Penguin.

Drury, A. (1960) *Advise and Consent*, London: Collins.

Du Plessis, R. (1992) 'Reading Rachel: Dorothy Smith Meets Rachel Hunter', *Sites* 24: 1–8.

During, S. (1983) 'Towards a revision of local critical habits', *AND* 1 : 75–92.

Durkheim, É. (1952) *Suicide*, London: Routledge and Kegan Paul.

Dyer, R. (1992) *Only Entertainment*, London: Routledge.

Dymock, E. (1990) *BMW: A Celebration*, New York: Orion.

Eco, U. (1985) *Reflections on The Name of the Rose*, London: Secker and Warburg.

—— (1987) *Travels in Hyperreality*, London: Picador.

—— (1995) *Apocalypse Postponed*, London: Flamingo.

The Economist (1993) 'Big MacCurrencies', 17 April.

—— (1996) 'McCurrencies: Where's the Beef' 27 April.

Edelman, M. (1977) *Political Language*, New York: Academic Press.

Edwards, W. (1989) *Modern Japan Through Its Weddings*, Stanford, CA: Stanford University Press.

Esslin, M. (1983) *The Age of Television*, San Francisco, CA: Freeman.

Evans-Pritchard, E. E. (1937) *Witchcraft, Oracles and Magic Among the Azande*, Oxford: Oxford University Press.

Ewen, S. (1988) *All Consuming Images: The Politics of Style in Contemporary Culture*, New York: Basic Books.

Eyerman, R. and O. Lofgren (1995) 'Romancing the Road: Road Movies and Images of Mobility', *Theory, Culture and Society* 12 (1): 53–79.

Farnsworth, J. (1992) 'Mainstream or Minority: Ambiguities in State or Market Arrangements for New Zealand Television', in J. Deeks and N. Perry (eds), *Controlling Interests*, Auckland: Auckland University Press, 191–207.

Fiedler, L. (1972) *Cross the Border – Close the Gap*, New York: Stein and Day.

Field, N. (1989) 'Somehow: the Postmodern as Atmosphere', in M. Miyoshi and H. D. Harootunian (eds) *Postmodernism and Japan*, Durham, NC: Duke University Press, 169–88.

—— (1993) *In the Realm of a Dying Emperor: a Portrait of Japan at Century's End*, New York: Vintage.

Fields, G. (1985) *From Bonsai to Levi's*, London: Futura.

Finkelstein, J. (1994) *Slaves of Chic*, Port Melbourne: Minerva Australia.

Fiske, J. (1987) 'Miami Vice, Miami Pleasure', *Cultural Studies* 1: 113–19.

—— (1989) *Understanding Popular Culture*, Boston, MA: Unwin Hyman.

Fiske, J., B. Hodge and G. Turner (1987) *Myths of Oz: Reading Australian Popular Culture*, Sydney: Allen and Unwin.

Foster, H. (1983) 'Postmodernism: A Preface', in H. Foster (ed.), *The Anti-Aesthetic: Essays on Postmodern Culture*, Port Townsend: Bay Press, ix–xvi.

Foucault, M. (1972) *The Archaeology of Knowledge and the Discourse on Language*, New York: Pantheon Books.

—— (1973) *The Order of Things: An Archaeology of the Human Sciences*, New York: Vintage.

—— (1980) 'Truth and Power', in C. Gordon (ed.), *Power/Knowledge*, Brighton: Harvester.

Fox, A. (1974) *Beyond Contract: Work, Power and Trust Relations*, London: Faber and Faber.

Frankovits, A. (ed.) (1984) *Seduced and Abandoned: The Baudrillard Scene*, Sydney: Stonemoss.

French, P. (1977) 'Media Marlowes', in M. Gross (ed.), *The World of Raymond Chandler*, London: Weidenfeld and Nicolson.

Friedberg, A. (1992) *Window Shopping: Cinema and the Postmodern*, Berkeley, CA: University of California Press.

Friedman, D. (1988) *The Misunderstood Miracle*, Ithaca, NY: Cornell University Press.

Fuller, G. (ed.) (1993) *Potter on Potter*, London: Faber and Faber.

Galtung, J. (1981) 'Structure, Culture and Intellectual Style: An Essay Comparing Saxonic, Teutonic, Gallic and Nipponic Approaches', *Social Science Information* 20: 817–56.

Gardiner, D. and K. S. Walker (eds) (1962) *Raymond Chandler Speaking*, London: Hamish Hamilton.

Garfinkel, H. (1967) *Studies in Ethnomethodology*, Englewood Cliffs, NJ: Prentice Hall.

Geertz, C. (1983) *Local Knowledge*, New York: Basic Books.

—— (1988) *Works and Lives: The Anthropologist as Author*, Stanford, CA: Stanford University Press.

Gellner, E. (1970) 'Concepts and Society', in D. Emmet and A. MacIntyre (eds), *Sociological Theory and Philosophical Analysis*, London: Macmillan, 115–49.

Geraghty, C. (1991) *Women and Soap Opera*, Cambridge: Polity Press.

Gilbert, W. S. (1995) *Fight and Kick and Bite: The Life and Work of Dennis Potter*, London: Hodder and Stoughton.

Ginsberg, A. (1956) *Howl and Other Poems*, San Francisco: City Lights Books.

Gitlin, T. (1983) *Inside Prime Time*, New York: Pantheon Books.

Glazer, M. P. and P. M. Glazer (1989) *The Whistleblowers*, New York: Basic Books.

Goffman, E. (1959) *The Presentation of Self in Everyday Life*, New York: Anchor Books.

—— (1971) *Relations in Public*, London: Allen Lane.

—— (1974) *Frame Analysis*, New York: Harper and Row.

Golding, D. (1980) 'Establishing Blissful Clarity in Organisational Life: Managers', *Sociological Review* 28: 763–82.

Goldman, R. and S. Papson (1994) 'Advertising in the Age of Hypersignification', *Theory, Culture and Society* 11: 23–53.

Gonzales, M. (1984) 'Kellner's Critical Theory: A Reassessment', *Telos* 62: 206–9.

Gouldner, A. (1971) *The Coming Crisis of Western Sociology*, London: Heinemann.

—— (1976) *The Dialectics of Ideology and Technology: The Origins, Grammar and Future of Ideology*, London: Macmillan.

—— (1979) *The Future of Intellectuals and the Rise of the New Class*, London: Macmillan.

Graham, J. (1986) 'Principled Organizational Dissent', *Research in Organizational Behavior* 8: 1–52.

Granovetter, M. (1985) 'Economic Action and Social Structure: The Problem of Embeddedness', *American Journal of Sociology* 91: 481–510.

Greenberg, D. S. (1967) *The Politics of Pure Science*, New York: New American Library.

Gross, E. A., T. Threadgold, D. Kelly, A. Cholodenko and E. Colless (eds) (1986) *Futur*Fall: Excursions into Postmodernity*, Sydney: Power Institute.

Habermas, J. (1970a) 'Knowledge and Interest', in D. Emmet and A. MacIntyre (eds), *Sociological Theory and Philosophical Analysis*, London: Macmillan, 36–54.

—— (1970b) *Towards a Rational Society*, Boston, MA: Beacon Press.

Hall, S. (1986) 'Cultural Studies: Two Paradigms', in R. Collins *et al.* (eds) *Media, Culture and Society*, London: Sage, 33–48.

—— (1991) 'Old and New Identities, Old and New Ethnicities', in A. D. King (ed.), *Culture, Globalization and the World System*, London: Macmillan, 41–68.

Hamilton, G. and N. Biggart (1988) 'Market, Culture and Authority: a Comparative Analysis of Management and Organisation in the Far East', *American Journal of Sociology* 94 (supplement): S52–94.

Hampshire, S. (1978) 'Morality and Pessimism' in S. Hampshire (ed.) *Public and Private Morality*, Cambridge: Cambridge University Press, 1–22.

Haraway, D. (1985) 'A Manifesto for Cyborgs: Science, Technology and Socialist Feminism in the 1980s', *Socialist Review*, 80: 65–107.

Harris, M. (1979) *Cultural Materialism*, New York: Random House.

Harshbarger, D. (1973) 'The Individual and the Social Order: Notes on the Management of Heresy and Deviance in Complex Organisations', *Human Relations* 26: 251–69.

Hebdige, D. (1979) *Subculture: The Meaning of Style*, London: Methuen.

—— (1982) 'Towards a Cartography of Taste, 1935–1962' in B. Waites, T. Bennett and G. Martin (eds.) *Popular Culture: Past and Present*, London: Croom Helm, 194–218.

—— (1988) *Hiding in the Light*, London and New York: Comedia.

Hendry, J. (1990) 'Humidity, Hygiene or Ritual: Some Thoughts on Wrapping as a Social Phenomenon', in E. Ben-Ari, B. Moeran and J. Valentine (eds), *Unwrapping Japan*, Manchester: Manchester University Press, 18–35.

—— (1993) *Wrapping Culture*, Oxford: Clarendon Press.

Hirsch, F. (1977) *The Social Limits to Growth*, London: Routledge and Kegan Paul.

Hirshman, A. O. (1979) *Shifting Involvements: Private Interest and Public Action*, Princeton, NJ: Princeton University Press.

Hobson, D. (1982) *Crossroads: The Drama of a Soap Opera*, London: Methuen.

Hoggart, R. (1957) *The Uses of Literacy*, Harmondsworth: Penguin.

Holborn, M. (1991) *Beyond Japan – Photo Theatre*, London: Jonathan Cape.

Horton, J. and S. Mendus (1994) *After MacIntyre: Critical Perspectives on the Work of Alasdair MacIntyre*, Cambridge: Polity Press.

Huyssen, A. (1984) 'Mapping the Postmodern' *New German Critique* 33: 5–52.

—— (1986a) *After The Great Divide*, London: Macmillan.

—— (1986b) 'Mass Culture as Woman: Modernism's Other', in T. Modleski (ed.), *Studies in Entertainment: Critical Approaches to Mass Culture*, Bloomington, IN: Indiana University Press, 188–207.

—— (1988) 'Foreword: The Return of Diogenes as Postmodern Intellectual', in P. Sloterdijk, *Critique of Cynical Reason*, London and New York: Verso, ix–xxv.

Ikegami, Y. (ed.) (1991) *The Empire of Signs: Semiotic Essays on Japanese Culture*, Amsterdam/Philadelphia: John Benjamins.

Irby, J. (1971) 'Borges and the Idea of Utopia', in L. Dunham and I. Ivask (eds), *The Cardinal Points of Borges*, Norman, OK: University of Oklahoma Press, 35–45.

Ivy, M. (1989) 'Critical Texts, Mass Artifacts: The Consumption of Knowledge in Postmodern Japan', in M. Miyoshi and H.D. Harootunian (eds), *Postmodernism and Japan*, Durham, NC and London: Duke University Press, 21–46.

Iyer, P. (1989) *Video Nights in Kathmandu*, London: Black Swan.

James, C. (1977) *Visions Before Midnight*, London: Jonathan Cape.

—— (1982) *From the Land of Shadows*, London: Jonathan Cape.

Jameson, F. (1991) *Postmodernism, or, The Cultural Logic of Late Capitalism*, London and New York: Verso.

Jarvie, I. (1964) *The Revolution in Anthropology*, London: Routledge and Kegan Paul.

Jay, M. (1988) 'Habermas and Postmodernism' in his *Fin-de-Siècle Socialism and Other Essays*, London: Routledge, 137–48.

Jeffrey, I. (1981) *Photography: A Concise History*, London: Thames and Hudson.

Johnson, T. (1972) *Professions and Power*, London: Macmillan.

Johnston, R. (1979) 'Structural Silence in the Conduct of Science, or Why aren't Scientists More Use?', in W. Green (ed.), *Focus on Social Responsibility in Science*, Christchurch: New Zealand Association of Scientists, 165–78.

Jungk, R. (1958) *Brighter Than a Thousand Suns*, New York: Harcourt, Brace and World.

Kamenka, E. and M. Krygier (eds) (1979) *Bureaucracy: The Career of a Concept*, London: Edward Arnold.

Kimberley, J. R. (1976) 'Organizational Size and the Structuralist Perspective: A Review, Critique and Proposal', *Administrative Science Quarterly* 21: 571–97.

Klopfenstein, E. (1984) 'Exclusive Conformity – The Bestseller *Nan to Naku Kurisutara*', in G. Daniels (ed.), *Europe Interprets Japan*, Tenterden, Kent: Paul Norbury, 180–7.

Knights, D. and H. Willmott (1989) 'Power and Subjectivity at Work: From Degradation to Subjugation in Social Relations', *Sociology* 23 (4): 535–58.

Kondo, D. (1990) *Crafting Selves: Power, Gender and Discourses of Identity in a Japanese Workplace*, Chicago, IL: University of Chicago Press.

Krauss, R. (1986) *The Originality of The Avant-garde and Other Modernist Myths*, Cambridge, MA: MIT Press.

Kroker, A. (1989) *Panic Encyclopedia*, Basingstoke: Macmillan.

Kuhn, T. (1970) *The Structure of Scientific Revolutions*, revised edn, Chicago, IL: University of Chicago Press.

Kumar, K (1976) 'Industrialism and Post Industrialism: Reflections on a Putative Transition', *Sociological Review* 24: 439–78.

—— (1978) *Prophecy and Progress*, Harmondsworth: Penguin Books.

Lamont, M. (1987) 'How to Become a Famous French Philosopher: the Case of Jacques Derrida', *American Journal of Sociology* 93: 584–622.

Lampert, N. (1984) *Whistleblowing in the Soviet Union*, London: Macmillan.

Larson, M. S. (1977) *The Rise of Professionalism: A Sociological Analysis*, Berkeley and Los Angeles, CA: University of California Press.

Latour, B. (1987) *Science in Action*, Cambridge, MA: Harvard University Press.

Lefebrve, H. (1971) *Everyday Life in the Modern World*, London: Allen Lane.

Lemert, C. (1981) *French Sociology*, New York: Columbia University Press.

Lennane, K. J. (1993) 'Whistleblowing: A Health Issue', *British Medical Journal* 307: 667–70.

Levitt, T. (1972) 'Production Line Approach to Service', *Harvard Business Review* 50 (5): 41–52.

Lindberg, G. (1982) *The Confidence Man in American Literature*, New York: Oxford University Press.

Lingard, B. (1989) 'Appropriation of Aboriginal Imagery: Tim Johnson and Imants Tillers', in S. Cramer (ed.), *Postmodernism: A Consideration of the Appropriation of Aboriginal Imagery*, Brisbane: Institute of Modern Art, 19–25.

Lodge, D. (1975) *Changing Places: A Tale of Two Campuses*, London: Secker and Warburg.

—— (1984) *Small World*, London: Secker and Warburg.

—— (1988) *Nice Work*, London: Secker and Warburg.

Louch, A. R. (1966) *Explanation and Human Action*, Berkeley, CA: University of California Press.

Lyotard, J-F (1984) *The Postmodern Condition*, Manchester: Manchester University Press.

Maccoby, M. (1976) *The Gamesman*, New York: Simon and Schuster.

MacIntyre, A. (1981) *After Virtue*, London: Duckworth.

Macshane, F. (1976) *The Life of Raymond Chandler*, London: Jonathan Cape.

Mailer, N. (1961) *Advertisements for Myself*, London: Andre Deutsch.

—— (1968) *The Armies of the Night*, London: Weidenfeld and Nicolson.

Mangham, I. L. (1995) 'MacIntyre and the Manager', *Organization* 2 (2): 181–204.

Manhire, B. (1987) 'Breaking the Line: A View of American and New Zealand Poetry', *Islands* 38: 142–54.

Marcus, G. (1975) *Mystery Train: Images of America in Rock 'N Roll Music*, New York: Dutton.

Martin, A. (1993) 'In the Name of Popular Culture', in J. Frow and M. Morris (eds), *Australian Cultural Studies: A Reader*, Sydney: Allen and Unwin, 133–45.

Mason, P. (1990) *Deconstructing America*, London: Routledge.

McHale, B. (1992) *Constructing Postmodernism*, London: Routledge.

McLuhan, M. (1964) *Understanding Media*, New York: New American Library.

McRobbie, A. (1991) 'Settling Accounts with Subcultures', in her *Feminism and Youth Culture*, Basingstoke: Macmillan, 16–34.

—— (1993) 'Shut up and Dance: Youth Culture and Changing Modes of Femininity', *Cultural Studies* 7: 406–26.

Melville, H. (1989) *The Confidence-Man*, Oxford: Oxford University Press.

Mendelsohn, E., M. R. Smith and P. Weingart (1988) 'Introductory Essay, Science and the Military: Setting the Problem', in E. Mendelsohn, M. R. Smith and P. Weingart (eds), *Science, Technology and the Military*, Dordrecht: Kluwer Academic, xi–xxiv.

Merton, R. (1968) *Social Theory and Social Structure*, enlarged edn, New York: Free Press.

Meyer, J. W. and B. Rowan (1977) 'Institutionalized Organizations: Formal Structure as Myth and Ceremony', *American Journal of Sociology* 83: 340–63.

Michaels, E. (1988) 'Bad Aboriginal Art', *Art and Text* 28: 59–73; repr. in J. Frow and M. Morris (eds) (1993) *Australian Cultural Studies: A Reader*, Sydney: Allen and Unwin: 47–65.

—— (1989) 'Postmodernism, Appropriation and Western Desert Acrylics', in S. Cramer (ed.), *Postmodernism: A Consideration of the Appropriation of Aboriginal Imagery*, Brisbane: Institute of Modern Art, 26–34.

Mitts, C.W. (1951) *White Collar*, New York: Oxford University Press.

—— (1963) *Power, Politics and People*, New York: Oxford University Press.

Mitchell, G. (1981) *Truth . . . And Consequences*, New York: Dembner Books.

Miyoshi, M. and H. D. Harootunian (eds) (1989) *Postmodernism and Japan*, Durham, NC: Duke University Press.

—— (1993) *Japan in the World*, Durham: Duke University Press.

Moeran, B. (1990) 'Introduction: Rapt Discourses', in E. Ben-Ari, B. Moeran and J. Valentine (eds), *Unwrapping Japan*, Manchester: Manchester University Press, 1–17.

Morales, R. (1994) *Flexible Production: Restructuring of the International Automobile Industry*, Cambridge: Polity.

181

Morris, M. (1988) *The Pirates Fiancée: Feminism, Reading, Postmodernism*, London and New York: Verso.

—— (1992) 'Afterthoughts on "Australianism"', *Cultural Studies* 6 (3): 468–75.

Mulkay, M. (1972) *The Social Process of Innovation*, London: Macmillan.

Mullins, N. (1980) *Social Networks among Biological Scientists*, New York: Arno Press.

Murray, K. (ed.) (1992) *The Judgement of Paris: Recent French Theory in a Local Context*, Sydney: Allen and Unwin.

Nader, R., P. J. Petkas and K. Blackwell (1972) *Whistle Blowing*, New York: Grossman.

Nagel, T. (1978) 'Ruthlessness in Public Life', in S. Hampshire (ed.) *Public and Private Morality*, Cambridge: Cambridge University Press, 75–91.

Navasky, V. S. (1981) *Naming Names*, New York: Penguin Books.

Nelkin, D. (ed.) (1979) *Controversy: Politics of Technical Decisions*, Beverly Hills, CA and London: Sage.

Noble, D. F. (1977) *America by Design*, New York: Oxford University Press.

Olins, W. (1989) *Corporate Identity*, London: Thames and Hudson.

Orwell, G. (1950) *Shooting an Elephant: and Other Essays*, London: Secker and Warburg.

—— (1957) 'Raffles and Miss Blandish', in B. Rosenberg and D. M. White (eds), *Mass Culture*, New York: Free Press, 154–64.

Paglia, C. (1992) *Sex, Art and American Culture: Essays*, Harmondsworth: Penguin Books.

Parkin, R. and C. Parkin (1974) 'Peter Rabbit and the Grundrisse', *European Journal of Sociology* 15: 181–3.

Patton, P. (1986) *Open Road*, New York: Simon and Schuster.

Pearson, B. (1974) *Fretful Sleepers and Other Essays*, Auckland: Heinemann.

Penman, I. (1986) 'The Plot Chickens', *The Face* February, 70: 76.

Perrow, C. (1972) *Complex Organisations: A Critical Essay*, Glenview: Scott, Foresman.

—— (1984) *Normal Accidents: Living with High Risk Technologies*, New York: Basic Books.

Perry, N. (1979) 'Recovery and Retrieval in Organisational Analysis', *Sociology* 13: 259–73.

—— (1992) 'Putting Theory in its Place: The Social Organization of Organizational Theorizing', in M. Reed and M. Hughes (eds), *Rethinking Organization*, London: Sage: 85–101.

—— (1993) 'Scientific Communication, Innovation Networks and Organization Structures', *Journal of Management Studies* 30: 957–73.

—— (1994) *The Dominion of Signs: Television, Advertising and Other New Zealand Fictions*, Auckland: Auckland University Press.

Peters, C. and T. Branch (1972) *Blowing the Whistle*, New York: Praeger.

Polan, D. (1986) 'Brief Encounters: Mass Culture and the Evacuation of Sense', in T. Modleski (ed.), *Studies in Entertainment: Critical Approaches to Mass Culture*, Bloomington and Indianapolis, IN: Indiana University Press, 167–87.

Poole, M. (1984) 'The Cult of the Generalist – British Television Criticism 1936–1983', *Screen* 25 (2): 41–61.

Poster, M. (1990) *The Mode of Information*, Cambridge: Polity Press.

Postman, N. (1985) *Amusing Ourselves to Death*, New York: Penguin Viking.

Pynchon, T. (1991) *Vineland*, London: Jonathan Cape.

Raban, J. (1990) *Hunting Mr Heartbreak*, London: Picador.

Reich, S. (1990) *The Fruits of Fascism*, Ithaca, NY: Cornell University Press.

Reisman, D. (with R. Denney and N. Glazer) (1950) *The Lonely Crowd: A Study of the Changing American Character*, New Haven, CT: Yale University Press.

Rich, A. (1979) *On Lies, Secrets and Silences*, New York: Norton.

Richter, D. (1974) *Fables End*, Chicago, IL: Chicago University Press.

Ritzer, G. (1991) *The McDonaldization of Society*, London: Sage.

Robertson, R. (1992) *Globalization: Social Theory and Global Culture*, London: Sage.

Roddick, N. (1989) 'Foreword', to V. Ward, K. Lyons and G. Chapple, *The Navigator: A Medieval Odyssey*, London: Faber and Faber, vii–xi.

Rogers, E. and J. Larsen (1984) *Silicon Valley Fever*, New York: Basic Books.

Rohlen, T. P. (1974) *For Harmony and Strength: Japanese White Collar Organization in Anthropological Perspective*, Berkeley, CA: University of California Press.

Root, J. (1986) *Open the Box*, London: Comedia.

Rosen, J. (1993) 'Merchandising Multiculturalism: Benetton and the New Cultural Relativism', *New Art Examiner* November: 18–26.

Rosenberg, H. (1970) *The Tradition of the New*, London: Paladin.

Ross, A. (1989) *No Respect: Intellectuals and Popular Culture*, New York and London: Routledge.

Rothschild, E. (1974) *Paradise Lost: The Decline of the Auto-Industrial Age*, New York: Random House.

Rothschild, J. and T. D. Miethe (1994) 'Whistleblowing as Resistance in Modern Work Organizations: The Politics of Revealing Organizational Deception and Abuse', in J. M. Jermier, D. Knights and W. Nord (eds), *Resistance and Power in Organizations*, London: Routledge, 252–73.

Sachs, W. (1992) *For Love of the Automobile*, Berkeley, Los Angeles, CA and Oxford: University of California Press.

Sacks, H. (1974) 'On the Analysability of Children's Stories', in R. Turner (ed.), *Ethnomethodology*, Harmondsworth: Penguin Books, 216–32.

Said, E. (1981) *The World, the Text and the Critic*, Cambridge, MA: Harvard University Press.

Sato, I. (1991) *Kamikaze Biker: Parody and Anomy in Affluent Japan*, Chicago, IL: University of Chicago Press.

Savigliano, M. E. (1992) 'Tango in Japan and the World Economy of Passion', in J. J. Tobin (ed.), *Re-made in Japan*, New Haven, CT and London: Yale University Press, 235–52.

Scheuring, D. (1989) 'Heavy Duty Denim: "Quality Never Dates"', in A. McRobbie (ed.), *Zoot Suits and Second Hand Dresses*, London: Macmillan, 225–36.

Scimecca, J. (1977) *The Sociological Theory of C. Wright Mills*, Port Washington and London: Kennikat.

Scott, J. (1990) *Domination and the Arts of Resistance: Hidden Transcripts*, New Haven, CT: Yale University Press.

Seabrook, J. (1983) *Unemployment*, London: Granada.

Searle, J. R. (1969) *Speech Acts*, London: Cambridge University Press.

—— (1971) *The Campus War*, Harmondsworth: Penguin Books.

Selby, K. and R. Cowdery (1995) *How to Study Television*, London: Macmillan.

Shortland, M. (1989) 'Skin Deep: Barthes, Lavater and the Legible Body', in M. Gane (ed.), *Ideological Representation and Power in Social Relations: Literary and Social Theory*, London: Routledge, 17–54.

Silverstone, R. (1981) *The Message of Television*, London: Heinemann.

Skinner, Q. (1980) 'Language and Social Change', In L. Michaels and C. Ricks (eds), *The State of the Language*, California: University of California Press, 562–78.

Sloterdijk, P. (1988) *Critique of Cynical Reason*, London and New York: Verso.

Smart, B. (1994) 'Digesting the Modern Diet: Gastro-Porn, Fast Food and Panic Eating', in K. Tester (ed.), *The Flâneur*, London: Routledge.

Smith, D. (1990) *Texts, Facts and Femininity: Exploring the Relations of Ruling*, London: Routledge.

Sontag, S. (1966) 'Notes on Camp', in *Against Interpretation*, New York: Farrar Strauss Giroux, 275–92.

Spivak, G. C. (1987) *In Other Worlds*, New York and London: Methuen.

—— (1990) *The Post Colonial Critic*, London and New York: Routledge.

Stead, C. (1971) *Smith's Dream*, Auckland: Longman Paul.

Stead, P. (1993) *Dennis Potter*, Bridgend: Seren Books.

Steedman, C. (1986) *Landscape for a Good Woman: A Study of Two Lives*, London: Virago.

Steiner, G. (1971) *In Bluebeard's Castle: Some Notes Towards the Re-definition of Culture*, London: Faber and Faber.

Streeck, W. (1989) 'Successful Adjustment to Turbulent Markets', in P. Katzenstein (ed.), *Industry and Politics in West Germany*, Ithaca, NY: Cornell University Press, 113–56.

Stretton, H. (1971) *The Political Sciences*, London: Routledge and Kegan Paul.

Sturrock, J. (1977) *Paper Tigers: The Ideal Fictions of Jorge Luis Borges*, Oxford: Clarendon Press.

Sudjic, D. (1994) *The Architecture of Richard Rogers*, London: Wordsearch.

Sugimoto, Y. (1990) 'A Post-modern Japan?' *Arena* 91: 48–59.

Sutherland, R. S. (1970) *Language and Lewis Carroll*, The Hague and Paris: Mouton.

Taylor, A. (1996) 'Speed! Power! Status! Mercedes and BMW Race Ahead', *Fortune* June 10: 30–8.

Taylor, A. L. (1952) *The White Knight*, Edinburgh: Oliver and Boyd.

Thompson, E. P. (1965) 'The Peculiarities of the English', *Socialist Register*: 311–62.

—— (1968) *The Making of the English Working Class*, Harmondsworth: Penguin.

—— (1971) 'Anthropology and the Discipline of Historical Context', *Midland History* 1 (3): 41–55.

—— (1978) *The Poverty of Theory and Other Essays*, New York: Monthly Review Press.

The Times (1992) 13 April 13.

Travers, A. (1993) 'An Essay on Self and Camp', *Theory, Culture and Society* 10: 127–43.

Trilling, D. (1959) 'The Other Night at Columbia', *Partisan Review* 26: 214–30.

Trilling, L. (1950) *The Liberal Imagination*, New York: Viking.

—— (1978) *Of this Time, Of that Place and Other Stories*, New York: Harcourt Brace Jovanovich.

Turim, M. (1991) 'Cinemas of Modernity and Postmodernity', in I. Hoesterey (ed.), *Zeit-geist in Babel: The Postmodernist Controversy*, Bloomington and Indianapolis, IN: Indiana University Press, 177–89.

Turner, S. P. (1977) 'Complex Organisations as Savage Tribes', *Journal of the Theory of Social Behaviour*, 7: 99–125.

Vandivier, K. (1972) 'Why Should my Conscience Bother Me?' in R.L. Heilbroner (ed.), *In The Name of Profit: Profiles in Corporate Greed*, New York: Doubleday, 3–31.

Walker, J. (1975) *Art Since Pop*, London: Thames and Hudson.

184

Walter, E. V. (1988) *Placeways: A Theory of the Human Environment*, Chapel Hill, NC: University of North Carolina Press.

Ward, V., K. Lyons, G. Chapple (1989) *The Navigator: A Medieval Odyssey*, London: Faber and Faber.

Ward, V. with A. Carter, G. Chapple and L. Nowra (1990) *Edge of the Earth: Stories and Images from the Antipodes*, Auckland: Heinemann Reed.

Wark, M. (1994) *Virtual Geography: Living with Global Media Events*, Bloomington and Indianapolis, IN: Indiana University Press.

Warshow, R. (1962) *The Immediate Experience: Movies, Comics, Theatre and Other Aspects of Popular Culture*, New York: Doubleday.

Weber, M. (1947) *The Theory of Social and Economic Organization*, ed. and intro. T. Parsons, New York: Free Press.

Weick, K. (1976) 'Educational Organisations as Loosely Coupled Systems', *Administrative Science Quarterly*, 21: 1–19.

Weinstein, D. (1979) *Bureaucratic Opposition*, New York: Pergamon Press.

Weinstein, M. A. (1988) 'The Dark Night of the Liberal Spirit and the Dawn of the Savage', *Canadian Journal of Political and Social Theory* 12: 167–79.

Weisband, E. and T. M. Franck (1976) *Resignation in Protest*, Harmondsworth: Penguin Books.

Weiss, L. (1989) 'The Politics of Industrial Organization: A Comparative View'. Paper to APROS conference at ANU, Canberra, Australia.

Wernick, A. (1991) *Promotional Culture*, London: Sage.

Westin, A. F. (1981) *Whistleblowing: Loyalty and Dissent in the Corporation*, New York: McGraw Hill.

White, R. (1983) 'A Backwater Awash: The Australian Experience of Americanisation', *Theory, Culture and Society* 1: 108–22.

White, H. C. (1970) *Chains of Opportunity: System Models of Mobility in Organizations*, Cambridge, MA: Harvard University Press.

Whiting, R. (1989) *You Gotta Have Wa*, New York: Macmillan.

Whitley, R. (1984) *The Intellectual and Social Organisation of the Sciences*, Oxford: Oxford University Press.

—— (1990) 'East Asian Enterprise Structures and the comparative analysis of forms of business organisation', *Organization Studies* 11: 47–74.

—— (1991) 'The Social Construction of Business Systems in East Asia', *Organization Studies* 12: 1–28.

—— (1992) 'The Social Construction of Organizations and Markets: The Comparative Analysis of Business Recipes', in M. Reed and M. Hughes (eds), *Rethinking Organization*, London: Sage, 120–43.

Whyte, W. H. (1956) *The Organisation Man*, New York: Simon and Schuster.

Wilkinson, E. (1990) *Japan versus the West*, Harmondsworth: Penguin Books.

Williams, R. (1973) *The Country and the City*, London: Chatto and Windus.

—— (1974) *Television: Technology and Cultural Form*, London: Fontana.

—— (1977) *Marxism and Literature*, Oxford and New York: Oxford University Press.

—— (1989) *What I Came to Say*, London: Hutchinson.

Williamson, J. (1981) 'How Does Girl Number Twenty Understand Ideology?' *Screen Education* 40: 80–7.

Willis, P. (1977) *Learning to Labour*, Farnborough: Saxon House.

Wilson, B. (ed.) (1970) *Rationality*, Oxford: Basil Blackwell.

Wilson, E. (1957) 'Who Cares Who Killed Roger Ackroyd', in B. Rosenberg and D. M. White (eds), *Mass Culture: the Popular Arts in America*, New York: Free Press, 149–53

Wise, D. (1973) *The Politics of Lying*, New York: Random House.

Wolfe, T. (1968) *The Kandy-Kolored Tangerine-Flake Streamline Baby*, London: Mayflower.

—— (1969) *The Electric Kool-Aid Acid Test*, New York: Bantam.

Wolff, J. (1985) 'The invisible *Flâneuse*: Women in the literature of modernity', *Theory, Culture and Society* 2(3): 37–46.

—— (1991) 'The Global and the Specific', in A. D. King (ed.) *Culture, Globalisation and the World-System*, London: Macmillan, 161–173.

Wolin, R. (1994) *Walter Benjamin: An Aesthetic of Redemption*, Berkeley, Los Angeles, CA and London: University of California Press.

Wolin, S. S. (1961) *Politics and Vision*, London: Allen and Unwin.

Womack, J. P., D. T. Jones and D. Roos (1990) *The Machine that Changed the World*, New York: Rawson Associates.

Woolley, B. (1992) *Virtual Worlds*, Oxford: Blackwell.

Zukin, S. (1991) *Landscapes of Power: From Detroit to Disney World*, Berkeley and Los Angeles, CA: University of California Press.

INDEX

(*Note:* illustrations are shown by bold figures)

absurd, making sense of the 35; *see also* 'taking the piss'
Adams, S. 105
Adorno, T. 4, 20
Adventures of Priscilla, Queen of the Desert 11–12
advertising 36, 38, 42, 46–9, 54–6, 86, **87**, 88, 151–2
Albrow, M. 159
Alice in Wonderland 15–17
allegory 4, 17, 22, 152
Allen, W. 134
Allison, A. 94–5
Amiel, J. 34
Anderson, B. 18, 29, 158
Anderson, R. M. 108, 119
angel of history 4, 13, 168
Animal Farm 48
antipode 16
antipodean camp 6–23 *passim*
Appadurai, A. 72–3
Arendt, H. 107, 122
Armi, C. E. 50
art cars 58–66
artist's grid 60
Asada, A. 85, 100
Aston Martin 51
Aubert, V. 105
Auden, W. H. 33
Audi 54–6
aura 44, 58
Australia 10, 11, 15, 25, 80, 95, 97
auteur 26, 34, 75, 137
authentic replica 79

Ayres, M. 42

'badge culture' 54
Bagehot, W. 116
Bailey, F. 117
Bakhtin, M. 12, 75
Banham, R. 68
Barber, B. 151
Barris, G. 67
Barthes, R. 2, 8, 25, 37–8, 49, 70–2, 75–8, 81–3, 91, 94, 126, 142, 161
Baudelaire, C. 75, 136
Baudrillard, J. 1, 54, 63, 68–9, 74–5, 78–80, 97, 99–100, 134
Bauhaus/Ulm School aesthetic 54, 56, 58
Bauman, Z. 83, 145
Bayley, S. 48, 52, 54
BBC 26, 31, 33
Bell, D. 109
Benetton 2, 36–7, 134; and *Colors* magazine 39
Benjamin, W. 4, 15, 16, 20, 44, 58, 75, 136, 168
Berger, J. *Ways of Seeing* 40
Bergman, I. 25
Berlin 4, 10, 51
Berliner, J. 156
Bickerton, D. 94
Big Mac 153, 155; *see also* hamburger as text
Big Sleep, The 33
Biggart, N. 157
Birmingham Centre for Contemporary Cultural Studies 145
Black, P. 31
Blake, K. 16
Bloom, A. 134–5, 137, 146
Blum, A. 167

BMW 2, 47–68 *passim*
BMW Museum 58
Boas, M. 150
Bochco, S. 34
Bok, S. 101, 107–8
Bonaventure Hotel 68
Borges, J. L. 69, 71, 97–100
Born in the USA 81
Bostonians, The 140
Bourdieu, P. 62, 74–5, 118
Brabeck, M. 102
Brain Dead 14, 18
Branch, T. 102, 119, 123
Brando, Marlon 47
Brannen, M.Y. 70, 83
Brecht, B. 5, 152
bricolage 1, 12, 13, 22, 65, 136
Bridgstock, M. 111
Brimstone and Treacle 26
Brisbane 10, 11, 15
Broad, W. 111
Brookeman, C. 137
Browne, N. 28
Bruck, J. 40–1
Buck-Morss, S. 136
Budapest 160
Burns, T. 109–10, 112–14
Bush, W. 105
Business Week 151

Calder, A. 30
Calder, Alexander 58, **59**, 62
Callon, M. 83, 109
Cambridge 160
Canby, V. 26
Carroll, L. 15–17
Carson, W. G. 105
Carter, A. 95
Castells, M. 72
Certeau, M. de 75
Chain, S. 150
Chandler, R. 32, 140
Channel Four Television 26
Chaplin, Charles 10, 142
Cheers 29
Chicago Hope 29
Clammer, J. 85, 89
Clegg, S. 157, 166
Clement, D. 34
Cleverley, G. 117
Clifford, J. 76
Cobain, Kurt 37

Coca Cola 42
Cohen, S. 103
Collins, J. 134–5
Collins, H. 159
Colls, R. 30
colonial, colonization 12, 14, 17, 64–5
Communist Manifesto 15
Connell, B. 145, 157
Conrad, J. *Heart of Darkness* 32
contracting/consulting system 112
Cook, Captain J. 22
Cook, J. R. 26, 34
corporate system 109–12
Coward, R. 26
Cowdery, R. 29
Crane, D. 111
Creighton, M. 83
Crescimbene, S. 45
Cringeley, R. 51, 113
crisis of representation 18, 80
Crocodile Dundee 11, 12, 18
Crosby, B. 32, 34
Crowley, M. *The Boys in the Band* 5
Crozier, M. 73
cultural cringe 11; *see also* Australia
Cumings, B. 81
Curnow, A. 2
custom cars 66–7; *see also* art cars

Dale, P. N. 76
Dallas 29, 30
Dalton, M. 115
Darnton, R. 75
Davis, N. P. 113
Davis, M. 81
De Mente, B. 83
Dean, M. 106
Dean, James 67
Death Valley 79
Debord, G. 10, 69
Deleuze, G. 126
Della Femina, J. 55
Derrida, J. 18, 73–4, 157–8
desert as metaphor 78
Devons, E. 117
Dickens, C. 75
Dickson, D. 110
Didion, J. 68
differentiation/*différance* couplet 157
Diogenes 5, 20
Disneyland: Los Angeles 6, 42, 69–70,

78–80; Paris (Euro Disney) 45, 73; Tokyo 70, 80, 83, 91
Doc Martens 148–9
Docker, J. 12, 40–1, 147
Dodd, D. 30
Donaldson, L. 154
Done, K. 64, 95–7, **96**
Dormer, P. 51
Dostoevsky, F. 126
Double Indemnity 33
Douglas, M. 148–9
Drury, A. 121
Du Plessis, R. 136
During, S. 14
Durkheim, E. 106
Dyer, R. 6, 12
Dymock, E. 53

Eco, U. 1, 2, 20–1, 41–5, 55, 79, 134
Economist, The 153–5, 157
Edelman, M. 107
Edge of Darkness 26
Edwards, W. 83–4, 91
Ellsberg, D. 101, 118, 123
Encyclopaedia Britannica 98
end of ideology 115
England: as literary invention 30; Queen of 10
ER 27
Esslin, M. 30
Everage, Edna 11
Ewen, S. 126–8, 133–5, 146, 149
Eyerman, R. 68

'Family of Man' photography exhibition 39
Farnsworth, J. 27
Fiedler, L. 139
Field, N. 85, 94
Finkelstein, J. 40
Fiske, J. 12, 95, 135, 149
Fitzgerald, E. 119
flâneur 75; motorised 68; and 'botanising on the texts' 136
Flashdance 33–4
Ford 53
Forest Lawn—Glendale Cemetry 42–3
Foster, H. 166
Foucault, M. 74, 91, 97, 98, 106, 126, 136
Fox, A. 117

France 72, 85; and nuclear tests 69, 73
franchising as a business system 151
Franck, T. M. 104
Frankovits, A. 11
Frears, S. 162
French, P. 33
Friedberg, A. 68
Friedman, D. 164
Friz, M. 52
Fuchs, E. 63
Fuller, G. 26

Galton, R. 34
Galtung, J. 74
gangster film 137
Garfinkel, H. 132
Geertz, C. 73–4, 83, 159, 162
Gekko, Gordon 44, 127
Gellner, E. 76
General Motors 53
Geraghty, C. 28
Germany/Germanness 49–50, 54–8
Getty Museum 42–3
Gilbert, W. S. 26
Ginsberg, A. *Howl* 124
Gitlin, T. 27
Glazer M. P. and P. M. 102, 103, 105
Globe Theatre, London 43
Gluckman, M. 117
Go Trabi Go! 51
Goffman, E. 40, 115
Golden Girls 29
Goldeneye 51
Golding, D. 118
Goldman, R. 38
Goldmann, L. 160
Goodbye Pork Pie 18
Gouldner, A. 115, 119–20
Government Accountability Project 105
Graham, J. 102
Granovetter, M. 156–7
Grapes of Wrath, The 139
Great Dictator, The 10
Greenberg, D. S. 110
Gross, E. 11
Guattari, F. 126

Habermas, J. 5, 77, 109, 112, 117, 120, 157, 167
Hall, S. 143, 162
hamburger, as text 150–8

Hamilton, G. 157
Hampshire, S. 117–18
Hancock 34
Haraway, D. 23
Harootunian, H. D. 71, 98
Harris, M. 150
Harshbarger, D. 118
Hawaii Five O 29
Hawks, H. 33
Hayakawa, K. 16, 18
Heavenly Creatures 13, 14
Hebdige, D. 30, 55, 84, 144, 145–6, 148
Hendry, J. 97
Herbie (*The Love Bug*) 50, 57
Hill Street Blues 27, 33
Hirsch, F. 53
Hirschman, A. O. 53
Hobson, D. 28
Hockney, D. 58
Hoggart, R. 30, 75, 143–4
Holborn, M. 98
Hollywood 27–8, 30, 32–3, 50–1
Honda 86
Hoover, J. Edgar 122
horror comics 139
Horton, J. 108
Hughes, R. 39–40
Hunting of the Snark, The 17–18
Huyssen, A. 5, 133, 141, 147
hybridity 22, 68, 91–5, 97; *see also* oxymoron
hyper-historicity 44

Ibsen H. *An Enemy of the People* 105
Ikegami, Y. 76
In Spring One Plants Alone 22
innovation networks 111–14
institutional blurring 111–14
interaction pollution 40
intertextuality 29
Irby, J. 99
interpretative community 18; *see also* university career systems
'Italianicity' 2, 36, 49; and catholic commercialism 41
Ishiguro, K. 162
Iyer, P. 70, 80–1

Jack the Ripper 34
Jackson, P. 13, 14
Jagger, Mick 134

James, C. 11, 12, 24–5
James, H. 140
Jameson, F. 68, 146–9
Japan 2, 69–100 *passim*, 164; and *bozosoku* (motor cycle gangs) 84, 91; and department stores 83; and *ema* 92, **93** and gift giving 86; and *Nihonjihron* ('Japanese distinctiveness') 76; and OL ('office ladies') 89; and shopping 85–6; and television commercials 86, 89, 91; and weddings 83–4; *see also* Kyoto; Tokyo
'Japlish' 94
Jarvie, I. 117
Jay, M. 157
Jeffrey, I. 39
Jobs, S. 51
Johnson, T. 114
Joyce, J. 14
Jungk, R. 113

Kamenka, E. 159
Kaplan, A. 134, 139
Kennedy Smith, K. 65
Keystone Kops 13
Kimberley, J. R. 154
Kingston, M. H. 162
kitsch 11
Klee, P. (*Angelus Novus*) 4; *see also* angel of history
Klopfenstein, E. 85
Knights, D. 165
Kondo, D. 159, 164–6
Krauss, R. 60
Kristeva, J. 126
Kroker, A. 153
Krygier. M. 159
Kuhn, T. 111, 121
Kumar, K. 109
Kupe 22
Kureishi, H. 162
Kurosawa, A. 91, 94
Kyoto 70, 81

La Frenais, I. 34
LA Law 27
Ladurie, E. 75
Lagerfeld, Karl 67
Lamont, M. 73, 160
Lampert, N. 105
Lange, D. 6, 7, 8

Lange, P. 8, **9**
Lanza, Mario 13
Larsen, J. 51, 113
Larson, M. S. 114
Las Vegas 79
Latour, B. 109–10
Law and Order 27
Lefebrve, H. 77
Lemert, C. 73
Lenanne, K. J. 103, 105
Levitt, T. 150
Lexus 54
Lichtenstein, R. 60, **61**, 63
Life magazine 39
Likely Lads, The 34
Lindberg, G. 44
Lingard, R. 64
Lodge, D. 47–8, 143
Lofgren, O. 68
London Weekend Television 26
Los Angeles 66, 77–8, 81, 138
Louch, A. R. 158
Louvre 60–1
Lukacs, G. 160
Luther, M. 101, 118
lying, politics of 106–8
Lynch, D. 34
Lyotard J-F. 120–1, 166, 168

Maccoby, M. 115
McDonalds 141, 150–8
McEwan, I. 42
McHale, B. 166
MacIntyre, A. 108
McLuhan, M. 24–5
McRobbie, A. 103, 144–6, 148
Macshane, F. 33
Mailer, N. 68, 115
Mainichi Daily News 91, **92**
Malinowski, B. 165
Mangham, I. 108
Manhire, W. 13
Maori 22–3
Map of the Human Heart 22
Marcus, G. 140
Marcus, G. E. 76
Marcuse, H. 79
marginality 8, 17, 73–4, 163–4
Market of Dreams 65
Martin, A. 138
mass culture critique 134
Maurer, W. 61

medieval/modernity encounter 19
Meguro Emperor 'love hotel' 45
Melville, H. 44, 140
Mendelsohn, E. 110
Mendus, S. 108
Mercedes Benz 49–50, 52
Merton, R. 137–8
Meyer, J. W. 116, 118
Miami Vice 27, 33
Michaels, E. 63–5
Mickey Mouse 6, 7
Miethe, T. D. 102
Miller, J. 150
Mills, C. Wright *see* Wright Mills, C.
Mitchell, G. 102
Miyoshi, M. 71, 98
modernity/modernism contrasted 14, 60
Moeran, M. 76, 97
Monument Valley 79
Morales, R. 54, 56
Morris, M. 11, 18
Moscow 154, 156
MTM Enterprises 34
Muldoon, R. (Count Robula) 5–6, 8, 10, 12
Mulkay, M. 111, 113
Munich 52, 63; *see also* BMW
Muriel's Wedding 11
Murray, K. 160
My Beautiful Laundrette 162
myth, mythology 12, 14, 22–3, 37, 46, 137

Nader, R. 102, 119
Nagel, T. 118–19
Navasky, V. S. 122
navigation as metaphor 22, 168
Navigator, The 19–21
Neighbours 17
Nelkin, D. 110
Nelson, M. Jagamara 63–6, **64**
Neuschwanstein (King Ludwig's castle) 45
New York Times, The 26, 101, 105
New Zealand 2, 5, 8, 10, 15, 71, 80
Newton, Helmut 67
Nice Work 47
No Orchids for Miss Blandish 32
Noble, D. 111
North, Oliver 44
Northern Exposure 29
Notre Dame 45
NYPD Blue 29

Olins, W. 50
Ondaatje, M. 162
organization: as ceremony and ritual 117; contingency theory of 153–4, 157; as exploitative expansion of rationality 117; and institutional embeddedness 156–7 (*see also* institutional blurring); and legitimacy 115–16; and secrets 116
Orientalism 71, 80
original fake 44, 79
Orwell, G. 10, 30, 32, 48
Otepka, O. 123
Oxford 16
oxymoron 8, 22, 69, 77, 79, 107; *see also* hybridity
O'Brien, R. 5

pachinko 81–3, **82**
Papson, S. 38
parataxis 35
Paris 63, 73, 160
Parkin, R. and C. 15
Partisan Review 127
Patton, P. 151
Pearson, W. 14
Penman, I. 26
Pentagon Papers, The 101
Perrow, C. 114, 123, 156
Perry, F. T. 83
Perry, N. 38, 116, 136–7, 162
Peters, C. 102, 119, 123
photo-journalism 36, 37–9
photography, as technology of representation 132–3, 146
Piano, The 19
Picket Fences 29
Picture Post magazine 39, 41
pidgin/creole distinction 94
Ploughmans Lunch, The 42; as syndrome 42–4
Polan, D. 5
Pompidou Centre 60, 63
Poole, M. 30
Porridge 34
Porsche 52, 54, 67
positional goods 53
postcolonial 18, 81; *see also* colonial
Poster, M. 30
Postman, N. 24
postmodernism of resistance 5
Potter, D. 26; *see also Singing Detective, The*

Poulain, H. 58
Powell, D. 33
Prisoner's Dilemma 103
purchasing power parity theory 153–5
'put on' 12
Pynchon, T. *Vineland* 138

Queensland 10–11; *see also* Australia

Raban, J. 136
Raging Bull 140
Rauschenberg, R. 63
reading against the grain 72
Reagan, Ronald 8, 44, 147
Rebel Without A Cause 67
Reich, S. 52, 54
Rich, A. 107
Richter, D. 35
Riesman, D. 115
ritualising of controversy 39
Ritzer, G. 150
Robertson, R. 162
Rocky Horror Picture Show, The 5, 6, 8
Robinson, E. G. 140
Roddick, N. 22
Rogers, E . 51, 113
Rohlen, T. P. 165
Root, J. 31
Rosen, J. 36, 38
Rosenberg, H. 115
Ross, A. 137, 141–2
Rothschild, E. 53
Rothschild, J. 102
Rover 56
Rowan, B. 116, 118
Rushdie, S. 162

Sachs, W. 49–50
Sacks, H. 91
Sahl, M. 55
Said, E. 159
San Simeon (Hearst castle) 45
Sato, I. 84
Savigliano, M. E. 100
Scharzenneger, A. 81
Scheuring, D. 149
scientific communication 112–13
Scimecca, J. 47
Scorsese, M. 140–1
Scott, J. 10, 20
Seabrook, J. 144

Searle, J. 119, 122
second order signification 38, 55
secondary deviance 103
Seigel, D. 13
Seigfried and Roy 67
Seinfeld 29
Selby, K. 29
Selznick, P. 115–16
Serpico 105
Shaw, G. B. 25
Shortland, M. 76
Silicon Valley 51, 113
Silkwood 105
Silverstone, R. 25
Simpson, A. 34
Simpsons, The 34
simulacra, simulacrum 1, 45, 68–9, 83
Sinclair, K. 10
Singing Detective, The 25, 30–5
Skinner, Q. 121
Sloterdijk, P. 5, 8, 20
Small World 47
Smart, B. 136, 154, 156–7
Smash Palace 12, 20
Smith, D. 136
sociology of postmodernism, postmodern
    sociology contrast 168
Sontag, S. 6, 12, 21–2
'spectacle' 10, 12, 69
 speech acts 119
Speight, J. 34
Spivak, G. 159, 163–4
Springsteen, B. 80
Stalker, G. M. 112
Stead, P. 26
Stead, K. 14
Steedman, C. 144, 147–8
Steiglitz, W. 119
Steiner, G. 43
Stella, F. 59, **60**, 62
Steptoe and Son 34
Stirling, J. 56
Stoppard, T. *Rozencrantz and
    Guildenstern are Dead* 74
Streeck, W. 56
Streets of San Francisco 29
Stretton, H. 80
Strictly Ballroom 11
structural silence in science 115
structures of feeling 12, 141; *see also*
    Williams, R.
Sturrock, J. 99

Stuttgart Art Gallery 56
Sudjic, D. 63
Sugimoto, Y. 85, 89
Suntory beer **96**, 97
Sutherland, R. S. 16
Sutherland's Law 29
Sydney 2000 Olympics 11

'taking the piss' 172; *see also* antipodean
    camp, Diogenes, J. Scott
Tanaka, Y. *Somehow, Crystal* 85
Tasman, A. 22
Taxi Driver 140
Taylor, A. 63
Taylor, A. L. 16
television: criticism 24–5; discourse 25–8;
    'flow' 29; megatext 28–9, 35; series 28;
    schedule 28; soap operas 28; and
    imagined community 29–30
Thatcherism 42
thaumaturgic underground 41;
    thaumaturgy and technology 46
theoria 158, 167–8
Third Man, The 34
Thompson, E. P. 75, 141, 143–4, 162
Throne of Blood 94
Till Death Us Do Part 34
Times, The (London) 13, 73
Tokyo 45, 63, 77–8, 81
Toscani, O. 36, 38; *see also* Benetton
Trabant 51
Travers, A. 8
Trilling, L. 124–33, 135, 137, 141,
    146–7, 149
truth, regimes of 106–8
Turim, M. 152
Turner, S. P. 117
Twin Peaks 34
Tynan, K. 24–5

university career systems 73–4; and
    pedagogy 136–7, 143–5
US State Department 123
US Internal Security Subcommittee 123
Utu 13, 18

Van Gogh, V. 146
Vandivier case 119; *see also* whistleblowing
Verrett, J. 119
Versailles: Queens Hamlet at 45; Treaty of
    52

Vierzylinder building (BMW headquarters) 56, **57**
Volkswagen 50, 54
Volvo 48

Wade, N. 111
Walker, J. 59
Walter, E. V. 158, 167
Ward, V. 19–21
Warhol, A. 61–3, **62**, 65–6, 146
Wark, M. 2, 51
Warsaw 43
Warshow, R. 137–42, 146, 148–9
Washington Post 105
Waugh, E. 30
Weaver, S. 81
Weber, M. 116–17
Weick, K. 117
Weill, K. *The Threepenny Opera* 152
Weinstein, M. A. 8
Weisband, E. 104
Weiss, L. 164
Wenders, W. 4, 10, 20
Wernick, A. 37, 43
western film 138
Westin, A. F. 102
Wharton, E. *The Age of Innocence* 140
whistleblowing 3, 101–23; as 'inform and dissent' 121–3; as structural signal 103–6

white collar crime 105
White, H. 118
White, R. 14
Whiting, R. 81
Whitley, R. 157, 159, 166
Whyte, W. 115
Wild One, The 47
Wilder, W. 33
Wilkinson, E. 97
Williams, R. 12, 29, 75, 91, 141, 143–4, 160
Williamson, J. 145–6, 148
Willis, P. 144
Willmott, H. 165
Wilson, E. 32–3
Wings of Desire 4, 10
Wired magazine 54
Wirtschaftswunder 52
Wise, D. 107
WKRP Cincinnati 29
Wolfe, T. 66, 147, 149
Wolff, J. 75, 151
Wolin, R. 4
Wolin, S. 115–16
Womack, J. P. 52
Woolley, B. 108
wrapping as metaphor 97
Wright Mills, C. 47–8, 52, 68, 115

Zukin, S. 67, 151